OUTPOST BERLIN

The History of the American Military Forces in Berlin, 1945–1994

Henrik Bering

edition q, inc.
Chicago, Berlin, Tokyo, and Moscow

edition q, inc.
551 N. Kimberly Dr.
Carol Stream, Illinois 60188

Library of Congress Cataloging-In-Publication Data

Bering, Henrik.
    Outpost Berlin: the history of the American military forces in Berlin, 1945–1994/Henrik Bering.
        p.   cm.
    Includes bibliographical references.
    ISBN 1-883695-07-4
    1. Military government–Germany–Berlin. 2. United States–Armed Forces–Germany–Berlin. 3. Reconstruction (1939–1951)–Germany–Berlin.
    4. Berlin (Germany)–Politics and government–1945–1990. 5. United States–Military relations–Germany. 6. Germany–Military relations–United States.
  I. Title.
  DD881.B454 1995
  940.53'144'09431554—dc20   95-11172
                                                     CIP

Printed in the United States of America

CONTENTS

139000

To Helle, my wife.

ACKNOWLEDGMENTS

Special thanks to Col. Robert Sweeney for his early help in locating interviewees, to Sol Gittelman for his help on Nazi education and films, to Arnold Beichman on Roll Back and the Eisenhower era, to Brewster Chamberlain on denazification, and to Hope Harrison on the Ulbricht era.

The "Doughboy" in the main entrance hall to General Lucius D. Clay Headquarters in Berlin. Ten feet tall, this bronze statue, cast in 1946, is a tribute to the American GIs who fought in Europe in World War II. The model for this sculpture by German artist Ernst Kunst was a 19-year-old staff sergeant of the 3rd Infantry Regiment, Thomas Love, who now lives in Oak Hill, West Virginia, and works as a coal truck driver. Love was selected in a division-wide campaign. "You had to have some combat experience, but most of the judging by several generals was on your military bearing and conduct," recalls Love. "The guys in my company thought it was an honor that I had won. But it means a lot more to me now."

INTRODUCTION

For decades, West Berlin was an isolated island, a small enclave of freedom situated deep within communist territory. If you flew in at night, on the approach to Tempelhof Airport, the peculiar symbolism of the city was visible. West Berlin sparkled with light and life, while East Berlin remained enveloped in sullen darkness. It was half a city, frozen in the Cold War.

Brigadier General Frank Howley, one of the early commandants of the Berlin garrison, described the city in his memoirs, *Berlin Command,* as the "tensest, most delicate and most explosive postwar frontier in the world."[1] Whenever the atmosphere among the superpowers worsened, Berlin immediately felt the temperature drop a few degrees. Like nowhere else, world politics and local politics were intertwined; any local conflict had the potential to affect the great capitals of the world.

Today, with Berlin again whole and the East-West conflict mostly a memory in the public mind, there is a tendency to forget how tense the situation once was. But it is not so long ago that Berlin was seen as central to a possible superpower conflict, a nuclear war. *The Berlin Crisis: Prelude to World War III?,* by Deane and David Heller, was published in October 1961, just two months after the Berlin Wall rose to divide the city. "If a good portion of mankind has the possibility of being atomized because of Berlin," the authors wrote, "it behooves each of us at the very least to know the background which has produced the Berlin crisis."[2]

Once the center of evil, Berlin became a symbol of freedom. The mere existence of West Berlin as the showcase of the Free World was a thorn in the side of the Soviet leadership; the inevitable comparisons between the two halves of the city pointed up the failures of the communist system. For Soviet leader Nikita Khrushchev, Berlin was "a bone in the throat of Communism." Alternatively, he threatened that "West Berlin will fall into our hands like a rotten apple." Whatever the metaphorical flavor of the day, the fact that half of Berlin was beyond their control, an outpost of the West, was a constant problem for the Soviets.

The story of Berlin after World War II cannot be told without the U.S. Armed Forces who were stationed there from 1945 to 1994. Events caused the occupation power over a very short period of time to become a protection power, a guarantor of the city's survival and freedom from Soviet dominance. The defense of Berlin has almost mythic dimensions, like the epic of ancient Troy or the great medieval sieges.

Special circumstances created a unique military culture in Berlin. In a city where the smallest mishap could grow into an international incident, a certain kind of soldier was needed—highly disciplined, yet prepared to improvise under pressure. In Berlin, some of America's greatest soldiers first stepped onto the international scene. It was a crucible of character.

These stories are soldiers' stories. Though often told in an understated manner, they tend to be direct and without circumlocutions. Being on the front line necessitates a certain unadorned assessment of reality, where a spade is called a spade, sometimes even a bloody shovel. In short, these are not diplomats' stories.

The Berliners, who withstood every attempt to starve, frighten, and brow-beat them into submission, also tell their stories in this book. Without their fortitude and endurance, the city could not have held.

The defense of Berlin did not take place solely in Berlin, of course. Despite the presence of America's allies, Britain and France, who faithfully played their part, in the final analysis Berlin was defended in Washington. When President John F. Kennedy stated "Ich bin ein Berliner," it was more than rhetorically true.

THE OCCUPATION
OF BERLIN

Nineteen forty-five was not a good time to be German. The policies that had started with Adolf Hitler's power grab in 1933 had ended in cataclysm. Some 40 million civilians and 15 million soldiers had been killed in the war; 20 million of them were Germans. Six million Jews had been exterminated. Adolf Hitler and his mistress Eva Braun had committed suicide April 30 in the Fuehrerbunker along with propaganda minister Joseph Goebbels, his wife, and six children. Germany lay in ruins, its infrastructure smashed to pieces.

For months on end, Berlin, capital of the Third Reich, had been bombed night and day by the Americans and the British. When the city surrendered on May 2 to the Soviets, most of it had been reduced to rubble. Seventy percent of the buildings were either heavily damaged or completely flattened by the bombing and by the final street-to-street fighting. So-called "rubble women" were trying to sort out the debris. Having had a prewar population of 4.3 million, Berlin was now reduced to some 2.8 million.[1]

Men between the ages of 15 and 60 were in short supply; many young boys had perished in the *Volkssturm*, Hitler's last desperate effort to defend the city, as had older men, even those in their sixties and seventies. Their relatives had no idea whether they were dead or being held in Soviet prisoner-of-war camps.

Symbol of victory: Soviet soldier waves the red banner on top of the Reichstag.

Death was everywhere. The dead lay among the ruins, or were buried under a thin layer of dirt where they had fallen. Hospitals were filled with patients suffering from dysentery and typhoid. All bodies that had been buried provisionally had to be reinterred and buried properly to reduce the risk of disease and epidemics. Most were buried in tarpaulins for want of coffins and boxes.

By his order to fight to the bitter end, Hitler had left little for the survivors. The city's bridges had been blown up. There was no electricity, no running water. The water mains were broken, and SS troops had flooded the U-bahn tunnels, drowning those who had sought refuge underground. Their bodies now contaminated the water supply. Add to that broken sewers, which meant that people had to bury their waste in the ruins. Chaos reigned.

Survival meant stealing anything you could lay your hands on; the idea of personal property was inoperational. One *Berlinerin* recalls, "We lived on a residential street, but there was a tiny greengrocer store. It was locked up, the owners had left. The neighborhood decided, this is ridiculous, we are starving and there may be some food left inside. Somebody jammed the door open and we got inside. All we found was *Brausepulver*, powdered soda mix, red, green, and yellow. We were terribly disappointed."

On the walls that were left standing, small pieces of paper announced people seeking to locate missing relatives. A mass migration was about to begin, the likes of which had not been seen in Europe since the Middle Ages. Every day, thousands of refugees came from the East, from East Prussia and Pomerania, from Silesia, from parts east of the Oder-Neisse River now belonging to Poland, and from the Sudetenland, where the Germans were ordered to leave. At the Berlin city limits, signs ordered refugees not to enter. Millions of newcomers expelled from formerly German-occupied areas had to continue their journey westward. Many of them perished from hunger, exhaustion, and disease.

One of the first Americans to lay eyes on Berlin after Germany's surrender in May 1945 was Capt. Jack O. Bennett. At the time, Bennett was chief pilot for American Overseas Airlines (soon to be bought by Pan Am). He was very familiar with Berlin, having studied aircraft engineering in Berlin in the late 1930s on a Rockefeller fellowship. He had flown Hermann Goering's 109 Messerschmidts, and he had enjoyed the company of the city's ladies in the cafes on the Kurfuerstendamm.

"Just by chance, I landed the first plane in Berlin. It was an air-transport command airplane on contract to my airline. The airplane was an American DC-4 Skymaster. It had an American flag painted on the tail, but it was not a military airplane. I landed in Tempelhof about three o'clock in the afternoon in early May."

What Bennett saw from the air bore little resemblance to the Berlin he had known: miles and miles of devastation, a city where the center had been totally destroyed, dark silhouettes of bombed-out buildings rising against the horizon. Only a few landmarks, such as the Brandenburger Tor, remained standing.

Incongruously, just before landing, he caught a glimpse of a woman giving birth on top of a rubbish heap.

"As I taxied in, the Russians lobbed mortar shells over my head. Jimmy Forestal, Secretary of the Navy, was on board. He came running up to the cockpit and wondered what the hell was going on."

"As we pulled into the airport terminal, one of the most magnificent airport terminals in the world, the Russians were busy shooting all the windows out with artillery." Pointing their submachine guns at the open cabin door, the Russian guards told Bennett that the passengers could get off, but not Bennett himself or his crew. Not prepared to entrust the servicing of his airplane to others, Bennett refused to obey the order and shoved the machine pistol aside. The Russians backed down, and the crew and pilot got off and gassed up the airplane.

Bennett then asked the Russians why they were shooting the windows out of the terminal. The Russians would not tell him, but a couple American officers offered an explanation. "The Russians know that the Americans are going to move into this sector. They are blowing up Tempelhof Airport so the Americans won't have an easy time of it."

At the time, Bennett knew nothing about sectors. All he knew was that his reception had been downright unfriendly. "General Patton had wanted to continue all the way to Moscow. That day, I did too," he recalls. This early encounter proved an omen of things to come. Bennett and his crew spent the night in the Tempelhof Flughafen officers club, which until a few nights earlier had been held by SS troops. One officer joked that the beds were still warm from its departed SS occupants. Bennett and crew flew out the next day.

▍ THE DIVISION OF BERLIN ▍

The sectors the American officers referred to in their conversation with Bennett were part of the postwar settlement for Germany. The London Protocols worked out between the United States, Britain, and the Soviet

Union on September 12, 1944, spelled out the future division of Germany into three occupation zones. At the very last moment, liberated France had been allowed to take its place among the victors of World War II, through the persistent efforts of French leader Charles De Gaulle. The Soviets agreed to give France a role in Germany only if the French zone was carved out of those of Britain and the United States, which it subsequently was.

Similarly, the capital of Berlin, which was deep within the Soviet-controlled zone, was divided into three sectors, later four, and given a special status under joint administration by the four victorious powers. It was to be a special area belonging to no one zone. According to the agreement between the allied victors, Berlin would "be occupied by forces of each of the Four Powers. An inter-allied governing authority (the Kommandatura), consisting of the four commandants, appointed by their respective Commanders in Chief, will be established to direct jointly its administration." Each of the commandants would serve in rotation as chief commandant.

By agreement, Berlin was to be taken by the Russians, while the Americans concentrated on the last pockets of resistance south of Munich, where the Germans were expected (wrongly, it turned out) to make a final stand in the mountainous terrain. At this point, the Americans did not attach particular importance to the capital of the defeated Reich.

"Berlin itself is no longer a particularly important objective. Its usefulness to the Germans has been largely destroyed, and even their government is prepared to move to another area," so General Eisenhower informed Army Chief of Staff General George C. Marshall on March 30, 1945. Marshall concurred. "The battle of Germany is at a point where it is up to the field commanders to judge the measures which should be taken. To deliberately turn away from the exploitation of the enemy's weakness does not appear sound."

Some have since blamed Eisenhower for that decision, arguing that he could have easily taken Berlin since he had three bridgeheads across the Elbe at the time. Eisenhower's decision was made purely on military

Germany in 1937 (solid border) and sliced up after defeat in 1945 (dotted lines). The Federal Republic of Germany emerged from the American, British, and French zones (Tri-Zone), and the Soviet zone was transformed into the German Democratic Republic. Territories under Polish and Soviet administration are now regular parts of these countries.

grounds to avoid further casualties. In fact, it cost the Russians three-hundred thousand dead to take the sixty-seven kilometers from Frankfurt on the Oder to Berlin. The American decision was based on the view that Berlin was no longer an important military object. What it ignored was the city's political significance.

Blaming Eisenhower is unfair, however. In the United States, generals do not make political decisions. The ultimate responsibility must rest with President Franklin D. Roosevelt. Just before Roosevelt's death on April 12, Winston Churchill, who was keenly aware of Berlin's symbolic importance, had tried to persuade the American president to get British and American troops to participate in the attack on Berlin, but Roosevelt had rejected the idea on the grounds that it showed lack of trust in America's ally, the Soviets.

The formal arrangement for Berlin between the victors looked simple enough. Berlin consists of twenty districts. The northeastern part of Berlin would be the Russian sector, consisting of the districts of Pankow, Prenzlauer Berg, Mitte, Weissensee, Friedrichshain, Lichtenberg, Treptow, and Koepenick. To the west was the British sector, consisting of the districts of Tiergarten, Charlottenburg, Spandau, and Wilmersdorf. The French sector, consisting of Reinickendorf and Wedding, would later be carved out of the British sector. To the south, the districts of Zehlendorf, Steglitz, Schoeneberg, Kreuzberg, Tempelhof, and Neukoelln composed the American sector.[2]

But taking actual possession of the American, French, and British sectors proved to be a more difficult matter. On June 17, a reconnaissance advance team of about 500 men and 150 vehicles, led by then Colonel Frank Howley, started out for Berlin from Halle. Their purpose was to hire workmen to repair buildings and prepare the arrival of the 1st Airborne Army paratroops and 2nd Armored Division, known among friends as Hell on Wheels. At the bridge over the Elbe at Dessau, Howley's column was stopped. The Soviet officer in charge informed Howley that, according to his orders, only 37 officers, 175 men, and 50 vehicles could cross.[3]

After hours of wrangling with the Russian officers, Howley gave in and was allowed to proceed, but soon found his column delayed again under a variety of excuses, among them that the city had not yet been cleared of land mines. Along the way, Howley's men saw impressive steely-jawed Cossacks posted at regular intervals; they were obviously there to put on a show. What they also saw were disheveled troops, many of them from the other side of the Urals, driving Asian-type horse wagons looking like boats that were piled high with loot. Soon the real reason for the Soviet delaying tactics became clear; they were busy stripping the city and its environs of anything of value.

The advance party got as far as Babelsberg, but they were forced to turn back to Halle, doubting that they would ever set foot in Berlin. Howley and his next-in-command Colonel John Maginnis did manage a short trip to the city, claiming that they had to meet a plane at Tempelhof Airport. They took advantage of the fact that their Soviet chauffeur had no map, whereas they did, and got a good look at the city.

It was not until the U.S. Army threatened not to evacuate Saxony and Thuringia, which according to the London Agreement were to be part of the Soviet zone, that the Russians agreed to let the Allies move into their sectors.

Finally, on July 1, the Americans made their entry into the city. "A disagreeable summer rain was pelting down when we finally straggled into Berlin in the late afternoon," writes Howley in *Berlin Command*. "The Russians had not allowed us to look over our sector before coming in, although that had been the agreement and none of us knew exactly where to go once we arrived."

"Had we been able to follow our original plan, my preliminary reconnaissance party would have been there followed by the housekeepers, and our army—as always—would have moved in quietly on an organized basis. As it was, hundreds of officers and men milled around, looking for places to stay in the ruins, and most of them, in class A uniforms, would end up sleeping on the muddy ground in the rain."[4] Maginnis described it in his diary as "without doubt the most depressing entry ever of a victorious power into the capital of a defeated nation."[5]

Howley's own military government detachment was better prepared for what awaited them. They were in full field equipment and struck up camp in the Grunewald forest. By 10:00 P.M., he notes with satisfaction, a hot meal had been served, and everybody was tucked in for the night.

The main forces followed on July 2 and 3. U.S. troops almost had to fight their way into Berlin. Lt. Col. Louis W. Correll, from Spokane, Washington, who was thirty-four at the time, commanded the 17th Armored

The Old Glory (left) was raised on July 1, 1945, over Colonel Howley's first headquarters encampment in the Grunewald forest (below).

Engineer Battalion of the 2nd Armored Division. "We were at the Elbe River," he recalls. "We had been waiting for our move into Berlin. We were supposed to have a parade in Berlin on the Fourth of July. The Russians were doing everything they could to keep us out. They actually tore up part of the bridge across the Elbe that we were going to get our heavy armor across. They started tearing the decking off, using the excuse that it would not hold our tanks. We had to sneak across another bridge that was in Russian territory at night." The whole division moved into Berlin at night and found Russian troops in the area they were supposed to occupy. "We had to roust the Russians out of there," he says. "They weren't even expecting us."

As the first U.S. military commandant of Berlin, Major General Floyd L. Parks held an occupation ceremony in the Adolf Hitler Kaserne in Berlin on the Fourth of July. The Russians, however, were not prepared to let the Americans settle in just yet. After the parade, which was attended by General Omar Bradley, they were informed by Marshal Georgi K. Zhukov, head of all the Soviet forces in Germany, that they could not take over the American sector before the planned Allied Kommandatura was set up, and no one knew when that would be.[6]

This did not sound promising, so General Parks decided to take the Soviets by surprise and move into his quarters early the next morning, presenting them with a *fait accompli*. The Soviets usually didn't start their day before noon, and when they arrived for work the next day, they found the Americans installed. For a few days, the uncertainty of the situation meant that the Germans in the American sector had to obey two masters who often gave contradictory orders, a state of affairs that lasted until the Russians finally withdrew to their own sector on July 12. Among the first acts of the Americans was to get rid of the huge portraits of Stalin and his generals. The billboard wood was needed for fuel, according to the official explanation.

What the Americans found bore little resemblance to the enemy they had been fighting. "When we came in, we expected that somebody would be shooting at us from every corner," recalls Sergeant Simon Marmor with the 1st Allied Airborne. "We came from the *autobahn*. It was a beautiful sunny day. Instead of shooting at us, they threw flowers at us."

"On Argentinische Allee in the suburb of Zehlendorf, I noticed some dead horses in the street. The stench was awful." The horses were not there for long, though. "The locals cut big pieces of meat off the carcasses. They were glad to get something to eat."

U.S. headquarters were established in what had been a district headquarters for the German Luftwaffe on Kronprinzenallee, later Clayallee, in the leafy suburb of Dahlem. The building had sustained only light damage during the bombings, and by the end of 1945, it was fully operational as the headquarters of the U.S. Commandant of Berlin and of military government for Germany.[7]

Before anyone could move into the headquarters, the place needed a good scrubbing and a good deal of repairs. Marmor was one of the group who had been selected for the job of preparing the facilities for the occupation forces. An Austrian Jew, he had emigrated to the United States, and he came back to Europe as part of a hospital unit stationed in Britain, which catered to the B-17 Flying Fortresses and the B-24 Liberators in Bury St. Edmunds. In Berlin, he found one big clean-up job awaiting him.

"I was given the job of cleaning out the compound. The Russians had just left a few days before. A lot of the Russians did not know where the toilet was. The place was demolished. They had been cooking their meals on the parquet floors," says Marmor.

Finding one's way in Berlin was a challenge because rubble and ruins look much the same everywhere. Private First Class Stanley Hoglund was twenty at the time and part of the 296th Combat Engineer Battalion, which was attached to the 2nd Armored for a while. He had been through the whole grand tour of the war, from Omaha Beach, through Paris to Sedan, Bastogne, and Malmédy. In Berlin his talents were much in demand, for Private Hoglund's specialty was sign painting. The city had lost definition. Often, recalls Hoglund, "You could not pick out a landmark and recognize your surroundings. These were mostly signs for buildings to help people find their way around."

The Americans found lodgings for their officers in the area around the Onkel Toms Huette subway, close to the headquarters. It was an area of mixed villas and apartment buildings, surrounded by a wire fence put up by the Americans. Officers were assigned four to a house. The troops in the headquarters regiment were housed in the apartment buildings with whatever furniture was left there, two or three to an apartment.

William A. Knowlton was a young combat officer who had been transferred to the headquarters regiment in Berlin to take over the transportation battalion. "We were sometimes accused of having taken the big houses in order to live high on the hog," says Knowlton. "But the reason we did that was that the big houses had belonged largely to people who were rather well known within the Hitler administration, and therefore nobody was living in them. Whereas the little houses had three or four families jammed in them, from *Fluechtlinge*, refugees and all these other people coming in. Therefore you displaced many fewer people when you took over a bigger house than when you took over a smaller one."

The former red-brick barracks of the Royal Prussian Guards, which during World War II housed the ordinance school, was likewise occupied and renamed Roosevelt Barracks after General Theodore Roosevelt, Jr., who had been awarded the Medal of Honor posthumously in 1944.[8]

There were two other troops quarters. One was Andrews Barracks, which had been the army academy during the years of the Kaiser and had become the barracks for Hitler's personal guard, the SS Leibstandarte.[9] This was named after General Frank Maxwell Andrews, the man in charge of the military build-up in Britain. General Andrews had perished in an air accident over Iceland.

The other was McNair Barracks, named after the man responsible for the training of U.S. ground troops after the American entry into the war, Lieutenant General Leslie J. McNair, who had been killed in France. McNair Barracks was located in the former AEG Telefunken factory, one of Germany's leading electronics factories where research was done on Hitler's much-vaunted miracle weapons. Each barracks housed one battalion.[10]

Captain Frank A. Camm belonged to the engineer battalion with the 78th Infantry Division. As an engineer, he was primarily interested in getting the troops quarters of the regiments and the field artillery in good shape for the winter. At least there was no need to open the window for fresh air; the bombing had knocked out all the windows and put holes in the roofs.

In time-honored fashion, Camm and his men had to scrounge for materials.

> *One of the big things we needed was gypsum, which is used to repair plaster and walls. The Russians had access to all gypsum that was in Berlin. They would not take marks from us because they had the printing machine, they did not need marks. They could print all the German marks they wanted. In anticipation of the winter in Berlin, we had picked up a lot of sheet metal and light metal products and brought them in railroad cars into Berlin, so we could make light metal guard houses and close our jeeps with metal tops. We had some extra. I managed to swap several car loads of sheet metal with the Russians for gypsum.*

Nor was housing the only problem. Lots of other items had to be procured. The Allied Kommandatura was located in Kaiserwerther Strasse, deep in the American sector in a building that had belonged to an insurance company.[11]

"Allied" meant that flags were needed of the occupying nations, and flags require flagpoles. Camm's men were asked to put up four flagpoles. "No sweat. We went out in the woods and cut four pine trees, and stuck them up. In the morning they had their flagpoles. That was the nature of our work as rough combat engineers. We were not very polished in what we did, but we sure could get things done."

The permanent occupation forces, which relieved the first occupation forces of the 2nd Armored Division, were the 82nd Airborne Division and the 78th Infantry Division. What they found when they arrived in late July was a city trying to dig out from under monumental destruction. Theodore Mohr came with the 82nd Airborne with the lead convoy. He was a technician fifth grade, or what is sometimes called "a corporal without testicles," chuckles Mohr. He was the chauffeur for the division's signal officer.

Ullstein

*Army Chief of Staff General George C. Marshall
inspects troops of the 2nd Armored Division, feared as
"Hell on Wheels," lined up on the AVUS autobahn,
July 21, 1945.*

"I saw many women, most of them older women, who were standing next to rubble piles chopping mortar from bricks, with their bare hands," says Mohr. "They did not have gloves or any protection. In many cases the hands were bloody or they were callused to a terrible degree. These women worked on and on and passed the bricks from one worker to the next. They placed them in a very orderly fashion where they could be used for the construction of new buildings." One estimate held that it would take sixteen years to get rid of the rubble at a rate of ten fifty-car train loads a day.

Others recall the inexorable smell of fire and bodies rotting in the ruins. Frank Banta arrived in August, working for the military government in the textbook- and film-censorship section. Later he became a civilian educational specialist.

> *The smell is absolutely unforgettable. There is no way to give a picture of the city; you can show pictures of ruined streets, you can show pictures from above, from planes, showing the city was chaos, but you cannot convey the impression of walking or riding or bicycling through street after street after street of ruins. For years after that, when I went back to Berlin, if I was there on a hot summer's day and walked past a pile of ruins, I was instantly back in 1945.*

At the time, Melvin Lasky was a young first lieutenant in the 7th Army Historical Division, a so-called combat historian, equipped with a camera, a typewriter, and a jeep, based in Heidelberg. The idea was to get talented writers to give a personal description of what they saw. They had access to all the material in the battalions and company records and would conduct interviews with the combatants. "We were supposed to help write the history of the war, like little Tolstoys running around writing *War and Peace*," he says.

A budding Tolstoy would want to see vanquished Berlin, of course. That's what the war had been all about. So, he and his driver piled into their jeep and took off into the unknown. To get to Berlin, they improvised their way through the Soviet zone, staying mostly on the byways. At one point, they had to get on the autobahn, which was international, but controlled by the Soviets with a sentry placed every one hundred yards. The sentries would snap to a smart salute every time an allied jeep went by on the motorway. Before long, Lasky's right arm was stiff from saluting.

They got to Berlin without running into trouble. "We took three streets to the left, turned to the right two streets; we did twenty-one turns without finding a single livable tenement," he recalls. "And yet people lived there. One could tell from little wisps of white smoke coming from the ruins. People were living in holes as if they were furry little animals. They were too frightened or too weak to come out."

U.S. Army Military History Institute

Ruins, rubble, and a truck-load of soldiers who are
happy that the war is over.

Throughout the war, Lasky had specialized in examining Gestapo headquarters, of which he knew the exact location from refugee friends. He had visited the Gestapo headquarters in Kaiserslautern, in Frankfurt, and in Heidelberg. He now wanted to see the Fuehrerbunker under the Reichs Chancellery in Wilhelmstrasse, the very epicenter of evil. "It was rather an emotional thing: This was the monument to Destruction." At that time, the papers were still lying around on the floor.

At one point during the trip, Lasky's luck seemed to run out: Crossing a bridge in the Soviet sector, he was hailed by a Russian sentry and ordered to stop. This was not an authorized trip. They were just war tourists, and Lasky had no orders, which meant they could be taken as spies. Which made Lasky fall back on one of the first laws of survival in

Berlin: When in trouble with the Russians, step on the gas, turn left—since bullets don't go around corners—and get the hell out of there. Lasky chuckles as he imagines the Russian reporting the incident: Crazy Amerikansky, in a Jeepsky, named Lasky. This was not the last time the name Lasky would figure in a Soviet report.

▮ THE SOVIET HEAD START ▮

When the U.S. troops arrived, the Soviets had already been there for two months. In this instance, Joseph Goebbels' propaganda proved prescient. He used to remind the Germans how the Soviets were sharpening the steel caps on their teeth the better to bite the women of Berlin, and he painted, in painful detail, a picture of how the Russians would treat the capital if it should fall into their hands. The Russian fighting troops that took Berlin were not sophisticated troops, many of them coming from the other side of the Urals. If an old pistol or a portrait of Adolf Hitler was found in a house, the entire row risked being razed. At the same time, huge billboard portraits of Stalin proclaimed the Soviet dictator to be the "German people's best friend."

Berlin residents were required to fly huge Soviet flags of welcome. On closer inspection, some of the flags that have survived reveal themselves to be old Nazi flags with the swastika in the middle removed and the hammer and sickle sewed on with yellow cloth.

Berliners who lived through this period have horrible stories to tell. Aloys Wehr, who would play a role in establishing good relations between Americans and Germans in the postwar period, was a student who lived in Berlin with his parents and his sister. He knew some Russian since his grandparents had had Russian forced laborers working on their farm, near the Polish border. That knowledge may have saved him and his family during the last days of fighting in Berlin.

A young Russian officer and five men had manned a cannon in front of the Wehrs' apartment building in the Tempelhof district. During a lull in the fighting, the officer and his men asked if they could freshen themselves. Wehr offered to take them up to his parents' first floor apartment. The Wehrs, like all Berliners, saved all the water they could in old cups and cans, and in the bathtub which contained the family's supply of drinking water for the next week. Since it was essential to keep the Russians out of the bathroom, Wehr took them to the kitchen and gave them a few bottles of water.

Afterwards, the soldiers sat down in the living room where Wehr's mother brought them tea and they made polite conversation. The Russian lieutenant proceeded to check the apartment for ammunition or hidden weapons. Wehr's schoolbooks were in the kitchen in a cupboard, including the obligatory fat volume of Hitler's autobiography *Mein Kampf*.

The atmosphere abruptly changed. "So, you are Nazi," exclaimed the lieutenant. Some quick explanation in Russian was clearly called for. "You told me you were a student in Russia," Wehr improvised. "I can see you in Russia have to buy and read books of the communist ideology. I'm a student in Nazi Germany, and I am forced to have these books and read them. I'll tear out the title page with the large photo of Adolf Hitler, and you will take a pencil and express your feelings." This explanation seemed to mollify the Russian. In big Cyrillic letters, he wrote across the picture: "Hitler, murderer of nations will be brought to a deserved justice. He cannot escape from a just punishment" and signed his name and the date. Lieutenant Nicolai Semjonov. May 26, 1945.

After this tense encounter, the two went back to the living room where the Russian noticed the piano and asked to hear Johann Sebastian Bach's "Ave Maria." More soldiers gathered beneath the window of the apartment to listen to the music.

If this remarkably civilized outcome had created hopes in the German family, these hopes were quickly shattered. There was a knock on the door, a neighbor. The neighbors had heard that there was a Russian officer in the apartment, and they were desperate for someone to intervene in the next building where women and girls were being systematically raped and molested. "I cannot do anything about it," the Russian lieutenant stated. "I have no command over other soldiers. Your mother and your sister are only safe as long as I am in your apartment."

"You cannot imagine how shocking this moment was for my family and for me," says Wehr. "I will never forget what I heard during those nights and I still have nightmares about it, of women screaming and crying."

Helga Mellmann, who was thirteen at the time, has similar recollections. Her family lived in an apartment house that contained a police station on the first floor and was therefore designated to be blown up by the Russians. Her father was the chimney sweep and the only man in the house. He had to walk with the Russians through every room and touch everything so that they could be sure that the house was not booby trapped.

> *All the women in the house stayed at our place. How they thought my father could protect them, I do not know. One Russian came who had been sent by a woman from the next house who had advised him to go there, there are more women. We were just sitting there, petrified. My father spent an hour talking him out of it. This time, we were lucky. The Russian apologized and went away. On the way, he tried to take the telephone, but couldn't rip it out.*

One day, recalls Mellmann, the Russians arrived with three cows around 8:00 A.M. "We pick up sausage at nine o'clock tonight. If not, we will shoot you all," the Russians told them. "And they meant it. They were very serious. We had no electricity. They got their sausage in time. Have you ever tried to put three cows through a meat grinder by hand?"

The women of Berlin tried their best to make themselves unattractive, which under the conditions was not hard to do. They bundled up like old women and smeared flour and dirt in their hair. Some shaved their heads and dressed up in boy's clothes. This did not necessarily spare them. During the two months that the Russians were alone in Berlin, the Russians raped an estimated ninety thousand women and girls, and these were only the women who sought medical help. Many were attacked by a platoon of seven or eight. Venereal disease became widespread. When the gas was restored in the city, a rash of suicides broke out. In one case, a father tried to kill his daughter who had been raped. He only managed to cut her optic nerve.

As one U.S. intelligence officer was to remark later, if the Russians should ever appear about to win the propaganda battle, all the West needed to do was to set up a radio broadcasting station that would broadcast the two words "Frau komm" twenty-four hours a day. That would immediately lessen the appeal of anything coming out of Russia.

When the looting and raping was brought up in conversation with Russian officers, the reaction was mostly a shrug and a statement that this was small potatoes compared to what the Nazis had done to their country.

There were also moments that would have been pure comedy but for the underlying threat. A standard Russian phrase was *"uri, uri,"* "your watches, your watches." This was not a request, it was an order. You would see Russians strutting around with wristwatches up to their elbows, proud as peacocks. Bicycles were another object of great desire for the Russians. Fantastic scenes of Russians on bicycles were common. They were apparently a novelty in the Soviet Union. The Russian soldiers would drive, fall off, try again, and laugh their heads off.

Aloys Wehr had a very old bicycle. One day when the fighting had died down in southern Berlin, his mother asked him to ride his bike to his aunt's house in a neighboring district. His grandmother was staying there, and the family was trying to find out whether they were all still alive. Evidence of fierce fighting was everywhere, damaged tanks and German deserters hanged from street lamps.

When Wehr came to one of the broad avenues in Neukoelln, about one hundred yards ahead of him, he saw a Russian soldier trying to ride a new bicycle. "We Berlin boys liked to boast even under hardships, and so when I approached him, I took my hands off the handlebars," says Wehr.

No sooner did the Russian see that than he pulled his pistol and told Wehr to stop. "Of course I had to stop. He had the gun. He said, 'Your bike is much better than mine, I cannot ride on mine at all, and you can ride on yours even with your hands off the handlebar. You take my bike and I take yours.' I had to give him my old bike, and for many years I had a good bike."

One anecdote about Russian behavior seems to have entered the

Berliner collective consciousness and is told again and again with great gusto:

There is a loud knock on the door. A furious Russian enters, gesticulating wildly with his machine gun. "Where is my fruit?" "What fruit, tovarish?" asks the Berliner innocently. "The fruit I was just washing upstairs," the Russian screams and heads straight for the bathroom and points accusingly at the toilet. "I wash here, pull string and suddenly fruit is gone. Give me back my fruit," he roars and shakes the Berliner. The story is generally told with a variety of embellishments. Sometimes it involves dusty apples or plums. One especially elaborate version has the Russian washing canned cherries!

During the time from May to June, 1945, when the Russians were still in sole command in Berlin, they managed to strip 85 percent of the city's remaining industrial capacity for transfer to the Soviet Union. This included refrigeration plants, factory machines, the American Singer sewing plant, generator equipment, lathes, and precision machine tools. Much of it could not possibly be of any use later, having been ruined in the process by rough handling. Equipment had been pried loose from the floor with crowbars and was left rusting on railroad cars waiting to be shipped to Moscow. The Russians also stripped some Berlin telephone exchanges, all the way down to the floor boards.

Equally important was the fact that the Russians took the livestock. They rounded up all cattle in Berlin, a total of about seven thousand cows, leaving it to the western Allies to figure out how to feed the city's infants without milk.[12]

▍CELEBRATING VICTORY ▍

Having finally settled in, the victorious Allies were ready to hold their victory parade on Unter den Linden in September, the occasion being the August 14 surrender of Japan. Frank Howley gives a particularly vivid description in his autobiography.

Clutching baby and bear—a family searching for water and food in the Berlin wasteland.

"

[Marshal Georgi Zhukov] was there in all his glory. He wore robin's egg blue trousers, with yellow stripes, topped off with a dark green blouse and a bright red sash. Across his chest, and almost down below his hips, hung so many decorations that a special brass plate had to be worn to house this immense collection, giving the impression of being riveted to the Russian's chest.

The decorations included the highest in the Soviet Union, as well as many from the Allies. Zhukov is a big man, with a big, broad chest, but there was no room left. In an emergency, he had hung one decoration, a gold saucer affair, on his right hip.

General Eisenhower sent the spectacular George S. Patton to represent him at the celebration—but in another way. He was dressed in a simple battle jacket, with a few ribbons, but his gleaming boots and polished helmet outshone all of Zhukov's medals. As far as I can remember, nobody else at the parade attracted the slightest attention.

The Russians had arranged their customary surprise. Each nation paraded its best troops. The 82nd Airborne with their white gloves through their shoulder straps, parachute silk scarves and polished guns slung over their backs, looked very dressy, not at all like the sky devils of Normandy. The French scout cars performed the neat trick of turning turrets in salute; the British marched along, taking it all in the day's work.

As for vehicles, the western powers were content to parade with light armored cars and other comparatively light equipment. There the Russians had us. With a dreadful clanking of steel, one hundred giant, new Stalin tanks rumbled into view and rolled down the historic street past the reviewing stand. All Unter den Linden was dwarfed. As they passed in review, the shiny muzzles of their guns pointed up to the sky.[13]

■ AMERICANS AND BERLINERS ■

Fresh from having taken the "Hit out of Hitler and the Muscle out of Lini," as a popular tune put it at the time, the American troops were a sharp contrast to the Russians. U.S. soldiers were clean and well disciplined, with spiffy uniforms, their vehicles were well-maintained, and they were loaded with bubble gum and cigarettes. Not that the Berliners should expect much. In the beginning, U.S. troops were under strict orders not to "fraternize" with the civilian population.

Back on May 16, 1945, Gen. Lucius D. Clay, at his first staff conference as Deputy Military Governor and Commanding General of the U.S. Group Control Council, had emphasized what kind of government he had in mind for the Germans. The emphasis was on punishment.

I would like to make it perfectly clear that the government we propose to set up in Germany is going to be a military government, and the Germans are going to know it is a military government.

We have time enough later to consider the long range treatment of Germany and the regeneration of the German people. Our first objective is to smash whatever remaining power Germany may have with which to develop a future of war. War criminals will pay for their crimes with their lives and their sweat and blood. That is the first objective of military government in Germany.[14]

At the time, there had been a few instances of American officers who had been too friendly towards the imprisoned *Reichsmarschall* Hermann Goering, giving him a cordial Man of History treatment. When the news hit the papers in the States, it had caused an uproar.

Initially, U.S. troops viewed the Germans as Nazis and Krauts. There were to be no dealings with them whatsoever. "Not only I, but all of us were full of hate," says Simon Marmor. "So when we saw how people looked and how they were doing out there, we felt it was just punishment. After all, these were the mothers of the Nazis and a lot of them were Nazis themselves. As far as I was concerned everybody was a Nazi." The Americans got a certain satisfaction from watching the fashionable ladies of Dahlem down on their knees with buckets and brooms.

But the mood changed very quickly. It did not take long to see that the women, old men, and young boys who were left in Berlin were not much of an enemy. They were just miserable and hungry. The U.S. troops were under orders not to throw food into the garbage because the Germans might pick it up. Anything discarded had to be doused with gasoline. Few soldiers obeyed the order.

And for purely practical reasons, some degree of cooperation had to be established with the defeated nation. American troops were eager to get home. If they were to run Germany all by themselves, that would be a distant prospect.

"We put a lot of the civilians to work for us," recalls Stanley Hoglund, the sign painter. "We did not blame the civilian population so much. We blamed the SS. We had run into their atrocities all the way from Normandy so we had no great love for them. And then when we saw some of the concentration camps that intensified our dislike." Hoglund took part in the liberation of Buchenwald.

Now Hoglund had to work with Germans. One of them was Karl, or "Charlie," as he was quickly called, who had been a machine gunner on the Russian front. "His feet had frozen, and he had lost all his toes. He had to have a wooden block in his shoes to keep him steady when he walked." The other was an older man, sixty-five or so, who had been a tool designer. "He was very precise in his painting. He would really make the letters stand out." He had his wife and daughter to take care of who lived in a heavily damaged building.

It was an awkward situation for both parties. "They viewed us as conquerors, not as friends," says Hoglund. The older man in particular found the situation hard. "I think he felt somewhat chagrined they were reduced to working for occupation troops." Because of the fraternization ban, the U.S. soldiers were not supposed to talk to the Germans. As they had to work alongside each other, this proved impractical. At times, especially at mealtimes, the Germans would open up. They still talked about the big parades in Berlin, but realized the situation Hitler had gotten them into.

Lunch could be an especially trying time for the Americans, recalls Hoglund. "The worst thing was when we had to eat. Since it was summertime, we ate outside much of the time. It was difficult to eat our lunch when you had people looking at you with hungry eyes. So we shared our food a lot of time with people."

Simon Marmor who in the meantime had become personnel officer, and who eventually ended up with some thirty thousand people in his employ, slowly saw his attitudes change when he started working with the Berliners. "Everybody had a different story. I found out they were like people anywhere else."

Every morning, three hundred to four hundred people lined up outside in front of the Telefunken factory, now McNair Barracks, looking for work. Marmor would be barraged with requests from officers wanting secretaries, waitresses, and cleaning women. Of course, the colonels who wanted secretaries all wanted blond, blue-eyed, beautiful girls. In one case, Marmor went out and picked a woman who was forty years old and asked her if she could type and speak English. Having reassured himself that this was the case, he offered her a job. Promptly, he had one irate colonel on the horn, telling him in no uncertain terms that this was not what he wanted. Marmor coolly pointed out that the personnel office could not help him with what he really wanted. "You asked for a secretary. You have a secretary." As could be expected, the colonel immediately filed a complaint against Marmor.

From the start, it fell on personnel officers like Marmor to sort out the Nazis. According to Military Government Directive No. 24, any member of the Nazi Party was automatically excluded from positions of power of major income and responsibility and was permitted to do only menial work. Marmor would go through the passport-sized *Arbeitsbuch*, which contained every working German's employment record, looking at every job change and how much money the individual had made. As part of the denazification program, prospective job seekers also had to fill out *Frageboegen*, questionnaires that sought to determine in what activities they had been engaged during the war. If cleared, they were put back into the emerging civilian infrastructure.

If sorting out the Germans was complicated, keeping Americans and Germans from each other turned out to be just as hard. Frank Camm did his heroic best to follow the nonfraternization order, immediately informing his own battalion that no shenanigans would be tolerated. "The first two or three months we were there, we were fighting a continuing battle. Our officers would inspect the barracks at odd hours, every day, even in the middle of the night, rooting out these women, many of whom had figured that this was a nice warm place to live. We just did not allow civilians into our barracks area at all, men or women."

Camm got a very vivid illustration of this problem one morning, when he decided to watch the troops at reveille. "I got up about ten minutes before reveille and stood outside to see how it went. Ten minutes before reveille, the barracks all opened up and hundreds of women came running out. Ten minutes later, out came the soldiers and in regular formation. So I learned that they had women living in the barracks with the men. That was against the rules, very strictly."

As battalion commander, Camm set up a club where beer was served to keep the men in American clubs rather than out with the Germans. That worked for a while until Camm was informed that serving beer was against the rules. "When that happened," says Camm, "we had to stop serving beer, the men stopped going to the clubs, and we had increasing problems with them going out with the Germans."

An example of the first uncertain contacts between GIs and Germans was Aloys Wehr's experience one evening in August 1945. Wehr was on his way home, having escorted a friend's sister home from dancing school at 11:00 P.M. It was pitch dark, there were no street lamps, but he knew the way by heart. Suddenly, he heard steps behind him, making his heart beat faster. There was nobody in the streets at this hour. As Wehr hurried up, so did the steps. Somebody slapped him on the back, then there was loud laughter, and a voice said in broken German, *"Du schreck?* Are you afraid?" "Of course I am afraid," Wehr replied. "But from your accent, I recognize that you are American. We'd better converse in English." So, the soldier walked him home.

When they reached his apartment house, Wehr invited the soldier inside and offered to wake his mother so she could make coffee for them. As he opened the front door of the house and switched on the light in the stairwell, he realized he had been talking to a black soldier. Wehr had never seen a black person in Nazi Germany.

Having been pulled out of bed, Mrs. Wehr made coffee. "The poor American took a sip from the coffee, and from his face I recognized he thought we were going to poison him. At that time, we couldn't afford the black-market prices for coffee. What we used as coffee was roasted and ground grain, which was supposed to taste like coffee." Reassured that the Germans were drinking the stuff, the American swallowed hard and politely did the same. When he left, he said, "I'm so homesick. May I come again?"

From that night on, Corporal Jerry Salters from Spartanburg, South Carolina, came most nights after duty, meeting also Wehr's friends and his sister's friends. By the end of September, Salters suggested a party. He would take care of crackers, nuts, almonds, and Coca-Cola. His only condition was that he would like to invite one of the officers. Blacks and whites had separate units, but the officers in the black units were white.

"The whites do not treat us very well except for one lieutenant," Salters said. When the Wehr family readily agreed, Salters allowed that there was one small problem. "The lieutenant is nice to us, but he hates the Germans."

Despite his misgivings about the Germans, the lieutenant came along. "The lieutenant was three or four years older than I was," says Wehr. "He did not speak a word of German. My parents did not understand English, but they sat together round the big stove in the living room. The lieutenant had brought a bottle of bourbon. I still remember the brand: Three Feathers. After a short time they were in a very vivid discussion, round the stove."

From that night, the lieutenant, too, began coming after work. Technically, of course, this kind of contact was illegal. In case the MPs should notice the jeep outside, Wehr was instructed to tell them that his mother was doing their washing. The corporal and the lieutenant introduced the Wehr family to more soldiers. Over the years, their apartment became a gathering place and a home away from home for numerous Americans stationed in Berlin.

American soldiers are American soldiers. By August, battlefield troops had been replaced by fresh troops from stateside. They started plying the German frauleins with nylons and chocolate bars, and the children of Berlin got their first taste of American bubble gum. Some were so happy they swallowed it whole. And the newly arrived soldier was not prone to believe that his pretty girlfriend's family could have been Nazis, whether that had been the case or not. In the long run, the nonfraternization rule was simply unenforceable. In a letter to Secretary of War Henry L. Stimson in August, Clay bowed to the inevitable and announced that the fraternization ban had been lifted.

▌ RESTORING ESSENTIAL CITY SERVICES ▌

What was needed in Berlin was no longer fighting men, but people who could get a city up and running again and do it on the double. The U.S. military government team in Berlin consisted of public sanitation engi-

Magnum Photos

After defeat and devastation, life blossoms in the ruins. Four survivors and a precious possession.

neers, professional policemen, municipal experts, and public accountants. As Frank Howley writes in *Berlin Command*, "They were the type needed to revive a city, not by cracking the whip and shouting, but by a few quiet, firm words of expert advice. This probably was the greatest military government unit that ever existed."[15]

The dimensions of their mission were overwhelming: To impose order on chaos, to rebuild the essentials of the city's infrastructure. Damage assessments were made and fast. It was clear that the city center had been more affected than the suburbs as regarded water mains, gas lines, and electricity lines. Policies were set by the Allied Kommandatura, instructions given to the German civilian authorities, and the supervision done by the Allied Public Works groups. No unauthorized orders of confiscation could be given by individual officers, which brought an end to the arbitrariness that had ruled Berlin since its fall.

One of the first jobs was to get the trains and buses running again so that U.S. soldiers could get around the city. In charge of the transportation battalion, William Knowlton sought to restore the Berlin bus company. "We used double decker buses, which we painted olive drab to carry the Allied soldiers round Berlin," recalls Knowlton. "The U-Bahn turned out to be useless because it had been flooded by Hitler. And the S-Bahn could not go around because it ran through the Russian Zone, and also, there were breaks in the line." The buses that were there were only for use by allied soldiers.

Shortage of personnel soon forced Knowlton to begin hiring German civilians. Interestingly enough, the 3rd Panzer Division had its own alumni network, and they put out the word that an American was looking for drivers. The great attraction was not the pay, but the hot meal at noon. Pretty soon, a large number of Knowlton's drivers came from the 3rd Panzer Division. The officers and the sergeants were American, but everybody else was German. "If I had gone out in the morning and said, *'Dritte Panzer Division, Achtung! Still gestanden,'* everybody would have popped to."

Berlin's bridges were in bad shape. In 1939, Berlin had 167 road bridges. Of these, 118 had been destroyed or severely damaged in the fighting. This problem affected all sections of the city's public works services. Because of shortages of materials, only the most important bridges were repaired. The U.S. Army Corps of Engineers went into action and repaired some of the bridges that had been assigned to the German city government because the civilian workmen simply were not in shape to keep up the hard work; they lacked everything from food to shoes to clothing.

Getting the mail delivered again turned out to be another problem. The *Reichspost,* which had been tightly controlled by the Nazis, had to be denazified, which meant that Berlin suddenly had the oldest postal workers in the world. Soon a limited postal service was re-established in Berlin. All mail going through the Soviet sector was subject to censorship, which was a time-consuming affair. To get around the cumbersome system, enterprising Berliners tried to establish a private courier service, using bicycle messengers. After Soviet protests, this was quickly *verboten*.

Berlin's telephone facilities had been stripped bare by the Russians, right down to the linoleum. Before the war, Berlin had counted some 600,000 private telephones. When the Americans came in, there were barely 4,000 left. "If the Germans wanted telephone service, they should not have started the war," came the laconic answer from one Russian officer. Through the help of the Signal Corps, Berlin had 6,000 phones by September, more than half in the American sector. Some measure of local service was established, but the Russians were holding up long distance service between Berlin and the western zones of Germany, which accordingly did not link up until February 1946.[16] By May 1946, there were 6,511 telephones in the American sector, or 0.72 telephone per 100 citizens. The minimum requirement was determined to be five telephones per 100 people.[17]

The bowels of Berlin, its complicated sewer system, were in bad condition, especially at points where sewer lines had been carried across water courses by bridge, as in the case with the bridges over the Teltow and Landwehr canals. These sewers were now spewing forth untreated sewage in the amount of 200,000 cubic meters a day. They had to be repaired before winter set in. Draining commenced of the S-Bahn tunnel at Anhalter station, which had become flooded when SS troops blew up the Landwehr Canal in the war's final phase.[18]

Berlin's water mains had to be restored. By August, the water was drinkable. As a precaution, the Allies ordered three times the normal amount of chloride in the water.[19] Coal, gas, and electricity were strictly rationed. Military needs came first, followed by the needs of hospitals, the food industry, transport, stores, shops, and finally civilians. There was just enough gas for a family to cook one hot meal a day. An army of civilian inspectors and meter readers was sent out to see that people complied with the rules.

Making sure that the city was fed was of crucial importance for the military government. If the most basic creature comforts, food, shelter, and heat, could not be ensured, the cooperation of the population was unlikely. Workers could not work. Riots could break out. In Berlin, the food situation was made worse by the refusal of the Soviets to supply the western sectors. In fact, the Soviets insisted that the Americans provide a greater share of the food supplies, despite the fact that the Americans had just turned over the fertile regions of Thuringia and Saxony to the Russians. These represented the hinterland, which would supply Berlin under normal circumstances.

The difference between the five different ration classes could mean the difference between life and starvation. The highest ration was 2,500 calories, which would go to people doing heavy work and to intellectuals, while ration 5 was not really enough to survive on: Initially, it was 1,250 calories, which was later improved to 1,500 calories. This consisted of 300 grams of bread, 7 grams of fat, and 20 grams of meat.[20] At least it held steady in the American sector. In the British and the French sectors, the calorie count went as low as 1,000 and sometimes even lower. Popularly referred to as the "Hunger card," ration 5 was for housewives, the unemployed, and former party members. Many Berliners who had to survive on this meager fare were single women with children whose husbands were either killed or in prison. Berliners were not alone, however, in facing rations. The rest of Europe was feeling the pinch, too, as a result of a worldwide food shortage.

Understandably, German soldiers on their return were forbidden to wear Wehrmacht uniforms, the outward symbol of Nazism. Unfortunately, those uniforms were often the only pieces of clothing returning soldiers owned, and there was an acute shortage of material with which to make new clothes. The Russians were about as sympathetic as they were to the shortage of telephones. "No clothes," Howley quotes one of them as saying in the style of Marie Antoinette. "Well, let them wear underclothes." The solution was to give returning soldiers two weeks to have their uniforms dyed and all insignia removed.[21]

Survival during this period for the Berliners meant using one's wits at all times. Recalls Inge Niemeyer:

> *My mother had no income since my parents were divorced. My mother started a small business of sewing, knitting and braiding, employing several of her friends and acquaintances. They would also make sandals of the cord from Venetian blinds and slippers of old pieces of carpet. Each piece would be entered in the work book. Often my mother would inflate the figures, so that the holder of the book would get a higher ration grade, say a grade 3 rather than a grade 5. The difference was literally the difference between starvation and survival.*

When the tax collectors started operating again, Mrs. Niemeyer had to change the figures back so that the holder would not be hit by the tax man. If she got caught, she said, she had done nothing to be ashamed of. "You had to survive. This was the rule of the time."

The household consisted of Niemeyer, her brother, her mother, and her aunt, who were the ones who were originally registered there; additionally, there were her grandmother, her grandmother's sister, and her two children, who came as refugees from Pomerania, and two family friends from the bombed-out Berlin Mitte—ten persons altogether, who were crammed into a small house in Zehlendorf. Electricity was strictly rationed. To get a little extra heat, a brother broke the seal on the electric meter and turned it back. "We were terrified that the meter reader would come unannounced and notice that the meter was running the wrong way," she says.

As soon as the trains were running again, Berliners packed whatever they owned of value that had escaped the attention of the Russians—china, crystal vases—and jumped on a train to the countryside to barter for food with the farmers, who kept their produce and would only barter.

The Berliner city folk bitterly remarked that the farmers could milk their cows by the light of crystal chandeliers if they so pleased.

These foraging expeditions were not risk free. People hung from the steps, stood on the buffers, and sat on the roofs of the trains, and, occasionally, when the train stopped at a station, Russian soldiers would go through the train, looking for young men as cheap labor. Many disappeared and never came back. The girls who sat at the top of the train car would shift their position and dangle their legs over the side, hiding the young men who were lying down flat behind them. "There was no week or day without some horrifying experience," says Niemeyer. "And this just to get something to eat."

In Berlin, every available plot of land was used to grow food. Tennis courts were turned into vegetable fields. The *Tiergarten*, Berlin's great park area, where the Berliners used to stroll in the shade, had had its trees razed in the bombing; it was soon turned into small garden plots. Any unclaimed spot along the street was a potential kitchen garden.

Though death from starvation was not widespread, hunger was ever-present. Children and old women would reach through fences for nettles growing on the other side. Somehow, nettles were said not to sting when made into salad. Or they could be boiled like spinach. When the acacias were in bloom, the children would eat them by the handful.

Despite the order to destroy any leftovers, the kitchens of the Americans were an important source of food. Families stood in line waiting to pick up whatever the Americans discarded. "Sometimes we found newspapers and other things swimming in it," says Niemeyer. "The first time we saw it we wanted to throw up, but when you are that hungry, you just fish the newspaper out and eat it anyway."

▌ PUBLIC HEALTH ▌

Malnourished and living in desperate, unsanitary conditions, Berlin's population was ripe for epidemics. Infections, tuberculosis, enteritis, and typhoid fever were rampant. In the period July 1 to December 31, 1945, 13,041 cases of typhoid fever were recorded.

When pediatrician Ruth Mattheis returned to Berlin after the war, the shortage of doctors was acute, which allowed her to pick and choose where she worked. In October 1945, she started work in the Zinnowwald Hospital near Zehlendorf in the children's wing. In addition to the epidemics, there was a great number of children who had been brought back from hospitals in Czechoslovakia suffering from bone tuberculosis. Many had entirely lost connection with their families.

At the peak of the German war effort in 1943, hospital beds had numbered thirty-eight thousand in Berlin. By 1945, that was down to ninety-three hundred. And the hospitals were running out of narcotics and anesthetics. Emergency wards were set up in temporary quarters. Over a six-month period, the number of hospital beds was boosted to forty-one thousand.[22] Thirty tons of medical supplies were delivered from U.S. Army stocks, and an additional one hundred tons of supplies were bought from civilian firms.

A wide-ranging campaign of immunizations was started. By May 1946, 84 percent of the population in the U.S. sector had received their shots. Main concerns in the early months were the constant stream of refugees from the East. Many were louse infested and brought disease with them. Officially, of course, the refugees were not supposed to enter the city, but this was impossible to control completely. At refugee centers, it was mandatory for newcomers to be dusted with DDT by means of spray guns. Stagnant pools, breeding grounds for mosquitoes, were sprayed with DDT from the air.[23]

Conditions were further worsened by the fact that 1945 was a terrible year for flies in Berlin. Another traditional disease carrier, the rodent, was less significant. A visiting British specialist in the field of pest control found the number of rats in the city to be remarkably low. His theory was that the rats did not find enough food.

At that time, the American-German women's clubs took a very active part in trying to improve conditions for the Berliners. Mattheis became good friends with the wife of an adviser to General Clay, who was a very useful contact. "First we asked for general things, clothing, shoes, toys. Sweets came by themselves. But I also needed special nutrition for babies, so Mrs. McKibbin, that was the name of the family, took me to the

PX and very generously bought this kind of food until we learned that this was not permitted because it was made for the American babies and not for ours."

Also in short supply was plaster of Paris for the children with bone tuberculosis. "I mentioned to our generous ladies that we lacked plaster of Paris. They brought a big box with plaster of Paris. So I had to explain why I needed cotton in addition to it."

Though best known as a disease that attacks the lungs, tuberculosis can attack almost any organ. Bone tuberculosis requires patients to stay in bed for a very long period. Some children developed this disease at the age of three and were able to stand and walk again only by age twelve or thirteen. They remained in casts for years and years. At that time, antibiotics had just made their emergence.

The fact that Mattheis was a doctor helped save her family. "Both my parents, who at that time were pensioners, got category five which was very, very low. Working as a physician in the hospital, I would have gotten category two, but as I also had tuberculosis patients, I got a category one ration to boost my immune system. The combination of one category one and two category fives was tolerable. In addition, you could donate blood to get extra. In this way, I kept the family going quite nicely, but unfortunately I contracted tuberculosis."

If that first winter was tough, the real shock hit the following winter, 1946–47, which was one of the coldest in memory. In many cases, old people died in their beds and were carried out stiff as cord wood.

▮ THE BLACK MARKET ▮

In a situation as desperate as this, a black market will inevitably spring into existence. Despite U.S. attempts to keep inflation down with price controls, rent control, and wage freezes, it was a losing battle. Inflation led to hoarding and a distrust of currency and banks. The black-market areas of Berlin were the Tiergarten and Potsdamer Platz, which had been Berlin's transport nerve center. Wolfgang Kohler was well placed to observe these goings on. Still a schoolboy in Dresden during the final days of the Third Reich, he was sent westward by his father, towards the advancing American troops, to avoid being taken for the *Volkssturm*, Hitler's last-ditch defense effort, consisting of young boys and old men. He now worked as a translator for the MP battalion, which had promptly renamed him "Jack."

"There was very little to eat for civilians and the black market was flourishing," says Kohler. "One pack of American cigarettes at that time was worth 2,000 Reichsmarks. You could pick up a beautiful set of Meissen china for a carton of cigarettes. I knew a fellow, a civilian photographer for the air corps, who came to Berlin and then stayed as a civilian photographer. He paid for a beautiful villa with one case of cigarettes, that is, 50 cartons. The villa is still owned by his widow."

The wheeling and dealing was intense. Recalls Teddy Mohr, "A sergeant in our company asked me one day if I knew how to get rid of some wrist watches. What he had was a Red Cross toilet bag. He had emptied the razor and the shaving cream out and had put in thirty-five small World War II watches that had been written off as battle loss. He had put those in a bag evidently planning to take them home after the war."

Mohr took the bag to Alexanderplatz where he met a Soviet captain whose spoken English sounded amazingly as though he was straight out of Brooklyn, which was almost true. "I looked at him and said, 'Captain what are you doing in that uniform?' 'My mother and father emigrated to the United States before Stalin came to power, and then in 1933, when the United States recognized the Soviet Union, my father and mother decided to go back to the Soviet Union. I went to high school in Brooklyn.' He was drafted into the Soviet army."

"Are you interested in buying wrist watches?" Mohr asked and stated his price, three thousand marks apiece, the going price. "I'll meet you here in three hours," the Russian from Brooklyn promised.

Three hours later, the Russian came back with an attaché case. The two went around the corner Columbiahaus on Alexanderplatz, and the Russian opened the case, which was full of 1,000 mark bank notes. "Captain," Mohr protested. "The printing plates the U.S. Treasury provided to the Soviet army to print occupation marks did not include 1,000 mark plates. Those 1,000 marks greened with green ink I do not believe are valid occupation marks. I do not want anything but occupation marks." As he rubbed his finger across the bill, the ink came right off. The money was counterfeit.

So, the Russian promised to come back at four, and Mohr agreed to give him one more chance. At four o'clock, the Russian showed up again, accompanied by a giant Soviet soldier in a huge greatcoat, the type normally worn in the middle of the Russian winter. The captain opened the suitcase, and this time it was filled with occupation marks. He counted out the 35 times 3,000 marks, put them in a bag, and gave them to Mohr, who gave him the bag with the 35 watches. The Russian ordered the soldier to open his coat, which revealed a lining hung all over with watches. "The captain said 'OK.' 'OK by me,' I said. I never saw him again."

The U.S. military government chose to turn a blind eye to certain aspects of the black market, the exchange of cigarettes and food, for among other things, antiques and cameras, explains J. Fergus Belanger, an economic adviser to General Clay, whose task it was to break up the economic cartels, the concentrations of economic power that had made Germany such an efficient war machine. This official tolerance was not to encourage black-market activities, but to discourage eruptions of mass violence rooted in hunger. The black market provided sort of an emergency valve.

Among the MPs themselves, there was also a certain disinclination to go after American troops engaging in black-market trading. "There were several cases of military personnel who committed suicide after black market involvement had been disclosed," notes Belanger. Often, a warning mysteriously would reach the soldiers of an impending MP raid. The large amounts of money sent back by U.S. soldiers were officially classified as gambling proceeds.

The economic situation in Berlin was made worse by the fact that shortly after V-E day, the Soviets had asked the United States to deliver the plates on which the new Reichsmarks were to be printed so that they might print their own. Unfortunately, no agreement had been reached as to how many marks the Soviets could print. When the Americans were

The Bettmann Archive

A German camera for American cigarettes—a typical black-market transaction.

printing occupation money, they tried to print only as much as could be backed by gold or hard currency. The reserves were taken away to the United States for safekeeping.

The Russians, however, had no such qualms and were printing marks with abandon. "The Russians would come across with huge bundles of 100 mark notes, one pocket full of Makhorka, the coarse tobacco they wrapped in newspaper and smoked, while the other was cramful of marks," says Kohler. Finance experts at the time estimated that the Russians must have printed some 10 billion marks. This in effect gave the Soviets the means to make large purchases for nothing, and it debased the currency in every zone since all the bills looked alike.

Between the gigantic clean-up effort, the friction between the occupying powers, and the lack of economic control, the effort to govern Berlin was foundering. Long-term planning was urgently called for.

THE FUTURE OF A CITY AND A COUNTRY

What to do with Berlin, indeed what to do with Germany now that the war was won, lay at the heart of the conundrum facing the Truman administration. In the long run, it was not tenable to have a population subsisting on minimum rations and black-market goods. What had happened after World War I when the defeated, impoverished, and humiliated Germany fell under the spell of the Nazi Party remained a powerful warning of what not to do.

In December 1945, a government report warned President Truman of the consequences of delay and suggested that it was time to decide "how far we are going in destroying the industrial structure in Germany." The military potential of the country remained a cause of great concern in Washington. What the officers in the field observed, however, was economic chaos leading to instability. They saw a Germany weary with war and in greater need of rehabilitation than restrictions.

"The most obvious characteristic about German industry in the U.S. zone is that it is all but dead," was how one American military economist expressed it at the time. The same applied in spades to Berlin, which had sustained the war's heaviest bombing.

But exactly what kind of peace and what kind of future did the Allies foresee? That question was, of course, debated before the end of the war in Europe. One American vision of postwar Germany was contained in the so-called Morgenthau Plan, named after Franklin D. Roosevelt's secretary of the treasury, Henry Morgenthau, Jr. According to the Morgenthau Plan, the Germans, once defeated, would never rise again as a military power, or any other kind of power for that matter, but would devote themselves to agriculture and cattle raising and the general wearing of *Lederhosen*. They would not be permitted to rebuild their industries.

In fact, all heavy industry would be stripped away, dismantled, and given to the nations that had been the victims of Adolf Hitler's aggression as restitution. German mines would be flooded. The Saar area with its rich deposits of coal would be given to the French. The Ruhr Valley, the country's industrial heart, would be turned into an international zone. The plan was to leave Germany "so weakened and controlled that it cannot in the foreseeable future become an industrial area."[1] (When details of the Morgenthau Plan leaked, it was immediately picked up by the Nazi propaganda chief Joseph Goebbels and used to much effect to stiffen the German resolve to fight to the bitter end. Jack Kohler recalls that his school in Dresden devoted an entire day to describe the evils awaiting Germany from the Morgenthau Plan.)

Initially, President Roosevelt did not object to the Morgenthau Plan, and proponents of a harsh settlement generally had the upper hand in the debate until mid-1946, while the passions aroused by the war and by Nazi brutality were yet fresh in the memory.

But different visions of Germany's future emerged even a few months after the end of the war in Europe. They stressed Germany's reintegration into the world of civilized nations rather than revenge. On September 6, 1945, the *London Times* ran an editorial: "The crucial and inescapable fact is that an industrially productive Germany is essential to the material prosperity of most of Europe. If Germany is to be converted into a primitive and third rate industrial nation, it is the population of Europe who will foot the bill."[2]

At about the same time, the British magazine *The Economist* pointed out the danger of "converting Germany into an idle, starving slum" and wrote that it was not hard

. . . to demonstrate the utter lunacy of the Allies' policy towards Germany. It must be becoming apparent to the simplest intelligence that to compress 50 to 60 million into a territory roughly the size of Britain and then totally disindustrialize it can only lead to the collapse and the disaster we are already witnessing. The more it impoverishes the Germans, the more surely unregenerate it makes them, the more necessary it makes the complete destruction of Germany as a means to a defense.[3]

Winston Churchill argued strongly that to reduce Germany to impoverishment would be counterproductive. Much of the responsibility for World War II could be ascribed to the hard peace imposed on the Germans after World War I in the Treaty of Versailles. Huge war reparations had caused the economic collapse, poverty, and public discontent in Germany that made it possible for Adolf Hitler to come into power. It created the myth that Germany had been stabbed in the back, the *Dolchstosslegende*.

Churchill, whom nobody could accuse of being soft on Nazism, saw that a void would develop in the middle of Europe if Germany were to vanish. There was a need for a democratic and self-sufficient Germany to block the road for Soviet ambitions, which were becoming more ominous by the day. (Not surprisingly, the Soviets found the Morgenthau Plan much to their liking.) Gradually, not least because of Soviet actions in Eastern Europe, the Churchillian view prevailed. In the United States, Churchill's view was shared by Secretary of State Cordell Hull and Secretary of War Henry L. Stimson. Towards the end of the war, President Roosevelt's own attitude towards the Morgenthau Plan had cooled considerably.

Most importantly, the reservations about the Morgenthau Plan were shared by Harry Truman. In his memoirs, *Year of Decision,* Truman writes, "I was deeply concerned that the peace to be written should not carry within it the kind of self-defeating provisions that would enable another Hitler to rise to power. . . . My aim was a unified Germany with a centralized government in Berlin." When Henry Morgenthau asked to be part of the American delegation of the Potsdam conference, Truman turned down his request and accepted Morgenthau's resignation.[4]

Harry Truman had had a chance to observe firsthand the conditions in the fallen capital of Berlin. On his trip to the Potsdam conference, the last big wartime meeting between the United States, Britain, and Russia, held July 17 to August 2, 1945, on the former country estate of the Hohenzollern just outside Berlin, he traveled by car and what he saw only confirmed his views of what had to be done. Truman was himself a veteran of World War I, and he had seen plenty of carnage, but he had never seen such destruction.

Truman later wrote about seeing "the long never-ending procession of old men, women and children wandering aimlessly along the autobahn, and the country roads carrying, pushing or pulling what was left of their belongings. In the two hour drive, I saw evidence of a great world tragedy, and I was thankful that the United States had been spared the unbelievable devastation of this war."[5]

An attempt to reach a conclusion about Germany was made with the Potsdam Agreement, which was signed in August 1945 by Clement Attlee (who replaced Winston Churchill as a result of the British elections during the conference), Harry Truman, and Joseph Stalin. Unfortunately, by combining some of the punitive flavor of the Morgenthau Plan and elements of Harry Truman's much more benevolent vision for Germany, the Potsdam Agreement turned out to be a not very satisfactory document.

The good news from the Potsdam Agreement was, as far as the Germans were concerned, that there was no provision for the dismantling of Germany as a country. Whether the question was industry, transportation, banking, or agriculture, Germany was to be treated as one. The same would go for the country's political structure. In due course, Germany was to take its place among the free and peaceful peoples of the world, "given the opportunity to prepare for the eventual reconstruction of their life on a democratic and peaceful basis."[6]

But the Potsdam Agreement was also concerned with punitive measures, some of which ran counter to the reconstruction of the country. It stated that German militarism and Nazism should be destroyed, German industry would never again be used for war purposes, and German war criminals would be tried in court. Reparations were to be paid to countries that had been the victims of Nazi aggression. It also placed a ceiling on German living standards, which it decreed should be the lowest of the neighboring countries.

Meanwhile, the Soviets reserved for themselves the right to remove anything they liked from their own zone. To this they added a wish list from other parts of Germany. After the level of industrial production that would enable Germany to subsist (but not become a military threat) was decided, the excess would be available for reparations, and of that Russia would claim 25 percent.[7]

The guidelines given to the four military governors gave them considerable room for maneuver and leeway in the interpretation of the Potsdam Agreement, which meant that the worst consequences of the plans to dismantle the factories could be averted. The so-called "disease and unrest" rule in the U.S. guidelines gave the military governor the right to handle every contingency according to his best judgment, from starvation to industrial production, so long as his actions were taken to prevent "disease and unrest" among the German population.[8] From the men in the field, however, complaints were constant about the unworkability and the contradictions in their directives. A new policy needed to be thought out, and in contrast to the Potsdam Agreement, it had to be one that took as its point of departure the situation on the ground.

In early 1946, doubts about the wisdom of the announced policies began to show, especially among the American personnel on the ground. If Germany was ever to get on its feet again, it had to be self-sufficient. How would that be possible if a lot of its industries were taken away in reparations? How could there be industrial production if most of the coal in the Ruhr went to other countries? The American taxpayer could not be expected to foot the relief bill forever, to the tune of some $2 billion a year in economic relief.[9] The idea of de-industrializing a nation of 55 to 60 million people on a much-reduced territory was seen as unwise.

Nor was the prospect of an eastern Germany that continuously soaked up economic assistance for the exclusive benefit of the Soviet Union appealing to U.S. military officials. And of progress towards treating Ger-

B. I. Sanders/AP/Wide World Photos

Corporal Edwin Sundquist from Salt Lake City—after the nonfraternization order was lifted— enjoys the experience that not every German is an enemy.

many as one unit and formulating a joint policy for all zones, there was none. In May 1946, the United States announced a halt to reparations from the U.S. zone.

The levels permitted for industrial production had simply been set too low to be practical in the long run. A report produced for the U.S. government in June 1946 states that the plan permitted just 1.7 pairs of shoes per capita per year for all of Germany.[10] Despite the agreement that Germany was to be treated as a unity, in actual fact, the boundaries in particular had the effect of restricting trade between the occupied zones. Travel restrictions, different rules and regulations, made normal trade almost impossible.

Add to this the highly arbitrary distribution of raw materials in Germany. The American zone was particularly vulnerable on this point because while it had plenty of light manufacturing industry, it had few of the raw materials needed.

Complicating life in Berlin were the increasingly strained relations with the Soviets. Meetings in the Allied Kommandatura were turning into marathon arguments. On points of procedure and on policy, the Russians, much to the initial puzzlement of the Americans, behaved as though Americans and Russians were not allies but enemies. It quickly became clear that the U.S. and the Russian outlook for the postwar world differed radically.

"We went to Berlin in 1945, thinking only of the Russians as big, jolly, balalaika-playing fellows, who drank prodigious quantities of vodka and liked to wrestle in the drawing room," writes General Frank Howley in *Berlin Command*. Initially, Americans made every effort to accommodate their wartime ally. Continues Howley, "We were going to get along with the Russians and we were quite willing to start off on their terms. . . . The policy we were to follow in Berlin for many months [involved] doing almost anything to win over the Russians, to allay their suspicions and convince them we were their friends."[11]

"It was a rather slow process," recalls Teddy Mohr.

I think all of us who were here did not want to believe it. We were aware of the lend-lease policy and programs of the U.S. government at the beginning of the war. Everything the Soviets drove, whether it was a truck or a jeep, was manufactured in Detroit.

All of us wanted to believe that the Soviets were not such a bad bunch of people. The fact that the Soviets had pillaged and raped and ravaged the city somehow seemed to be poetic justice for some of the things we knew that the German army, particularly the SS troops, had done in Russia and Poland.

Egon Bahr, a Berliner who later was to become a prominent politician, vividly recalls the manifestations of that attitude among the Americans. "I met the first American in June 1945. I came out from the city hall, and three Americans in uniform came up to me, with a 'war correspondent' stripe on their shoulder. The first question they asked me was 'Have you witnessed that the Russians have violated women?' When I said 'yes' they turned around, and I heard one of them say '*auch ein Nazi*' (another Nazi)." Only after a while did it become clear to the Americans that there might be some truth to what the Berliners were telling them.

There were a lot of early incidents between the Americans and the Russians, mainly because the Russians would continue to return to the

American sector to loot. Says Jack Kohler, who witnessed it all at close quarters with the MPs, "You would see a couple of Russian soldiers walking along, and suddenly start pulling the bicycle out from under some woman. You'd see Russians moving through the American sector, carrying mattresses on their backs." In one case, where the woman protested against having her bicycle pulled away under her, a Russian officer drew his pistol and killed her on the spot.

The confrontations between Russians and Americans over these incidents could get very violent. The Wannsee district is a collection of beautiful villas, most of which had been requisitioned by the American army; by the fall of 1945, it served as officers quarters. One day, while the officers were gone and the only people there were the house maids and servants, a group of Russian soldiers arrived and started looting the villas. The German staff got word to the Americans, who sent some of their people, and before long there were six dead Russians on the sidewalk. The U.S. commander, General Gavin, got hold of the Soviet commander, who sent over a Russian truck to pick up the bodies. No fuss was raised over it from the Russian side.

After a while, the Russians realized that they had to maintain better discipline or their army would be undermined. The NKVD (Soviet intelligence) troops were charged with maintaining order and were assigned to U.S. military police to keep their own people under control when they came to the western sector.

"These guys were brutal," says Kohler.

 Our station was in a German bank. As a lock up, they used the vault in the basement of the bank. To get down to the vault you had to go down a metal staircase. Night after night, they would pick up Russian officers, up to the rank of colonel and drunk as hell. If they did not want to walk down the stairs, they just kicked them. They would then pick them up and throw them into the vault. Some stayed for three days.

The bleak atmosphere is well captured in an episode told by Kohler from the winter of 1945–46.

It was the end of February, it was carnival time. The city was all dark and I was going back to our station in Neukoelln when I heard music and people laughing. There was a ballroom full of masked people in costumes, celebrating Fasching. *They had ersatz schnapps, which tasted like gasoline. I'm sure they had had nothing to eat all day.*

I saw this girl who looked pretty good. She was wearing a mask. I chatted her up, but she wouldn't take her mask off. 'You'll have to wait till midnight. That's when we can take the masks off,' she said. I decided to hang around. A few minutes later, I hear somebody screaming on the dance floor, 'Russe! Russe!' And suddenly the whole dance floor was cleared. And there was a guy standing in the middle of the dance floor, drunk with a gun in his hand.

I ran down the stairs and called the station. The NKVD people and our guys arrived. They told him to drop the gun, which he refused. He was so drunk he could hardly hold the gun straight. Finally, one of the Russians walked over to him and in characteristic fashion hit him over the head with his machine gun, dragged him over to the stairs and threw him down the stairs. Everybody applauded. Of course, we had to take him back to the station, so I missed the midnight unmasking. So I'll never know what the hell this girl looked like.

THE COMPETITION FOR THE GERMAN MIND

Beyond the necessities of life, the military government also had to address the mind of the population. On the most profound level the challenge was to rid German society of Nazi ideology, and, as the Americans saw it, to pave the way for a postwar democratic state. That meant publishing newspapers, setting up a radio station, reforming education, and restarting the city's cultural and political life. The Americans gave Berlin a city constitution and held city elections.

However, every step of this endeavor was complicated by the relationship with the Russians. As pointed out by Will Tremper, now a well-known Berlin journalist and filmmaker who at the age of 17 started as a police reporter with the *Tagesspiegel*, "When the Russians took over in Berlin the first of May 1945, they organized the local government, the mayor and the chief of police. So when the Americans and the British came, everything was under Russian control in all Berlin."

In February 1945, psychological units had been prepared for the cultural and social side of the American occupation government. The creator of the psychological warfare branch of military intelligence was the legendary and flamboyant Major Hans Habe, who ran Camp Sharpe near Gettysburg, Pennsylvania. His units included writers and authors who were to be in charge of restructuring cultural institutions, from theater, film, and music to newspapers and radio. Habe's first big project was to publish an American newspaper for occupied Germany called *Die Neue Zeitung*.[12]

Henry Alter was a young intelligence officer in the psychological warfare unit. He had been a student of the theater in Austria, but being half Jewish, he had managed to emigrate to the United States. He had been drafted in the fall of 1943, and while initially trained in field artillery, he had transferred to military intelligence in early 1944. He had received training in the interrogation of prisoners of war and then attended Camp Sharpe. One of his first assignments in Germany was reconnaissance in Munich, a center of the German film industry, where among other things he had interrogated the actor Emil Jannings, who had been a mainstay in German propaganda films. Alter was then sent to Berlin to the District Information Services Control Command for Berlin. His official title was Film, Theater, and Music Officer.

When Alter arrived in Berlin in July, he found that the Soviets had wasted no time. They had already established a *Kammer der Kunstschaffenden*, an art center at Schlueter Strasse 45, off Kurfuerstendamm under the authority of the Stadtkommandant Nikolai Bersarin, with people in every field—film, theater, music, and cabaret. At the time, the personnel was mixed, communists and noncommunists. The Soviets clearly had a cultural policy from the very start. The policy was not just to make sure that the Germans were entertained; the purpose was *die Seelen der Deutschen zu erobern*, to conquer the souls of the Germans.

The *Kabaret der Komiker* on the Kurfuerstendamm's south side had already been reopened, the audience being mainly Russian officers and a smattering of British and American officers. They were putting on a very successful evening of skits and entertainment. But the centerpiece of the evening was a song sung by Brigitte Mira called "Berlin kommt wieder," "Berlin Will Come Back," which at the time was a big morale booster for the Berliners. "It was an impressive demonstration of the spirit that existed in this utter misery," says Alter.

Just how seriously the Russians took the cultural aspect of the occupation was evident from the fact that they opened the opera almost right away in the Admirals Palast, one of the few theater buildings with a stage that had not been destroyed. Extra rations were given to the singers; trucks were made available to move costumes and scenery. "We saw *Rigoletto* there two or three weeks after we arrived," says Alter, "and that was by no means the opening performance of the opera. The opera was already running. And people had to go to the theater at four, because by eight, they had to be home. It was an amazing, slightly unreal world that we got into."

Because the Russians had gotten off to a head start in Berlin, it was of the utmost urgency that the Americans caught up as quickly as possible. The policy that came out of Washington was still very punitive with an emphasis on denazification at all costs. However, the officers on the ground found that more flexibility was often needed to compensate for the Russian head start. "We would have been stamped as the barbarians vis à vis the 'culture friendly' Soviets," says Alter. "The initial policy had to undergo some modification. Denazification remained central, but at the same time, the need was soon perceived to encourage the rebuilding of cultural activities in our sector."

"We eliminated two members of the Berliner Philharmonic," says

Alter. "I am sure there were more that could have been eliminated, but by that time we already knew that this orchestra was a gem and a cultural asset of the very first order." There were a few hurdles to getting the orchestra going. Alter had to rescue the orchestra's instruments, which were stored in the Titania Palast movie house, from the attentions of the troop entertainment branch, which had cast its covetous eyes on them. Then the first conductor licensed by the Americans, Leo Borchard, was accidentally shot by an MP and somebody else had to be found. The license was given to the Romanian conductor Sergiu Celibidache.

During Alter's five months in the entertainment unit, only one theater license was given out by the Americans to a German; the recipient was Karl-Heinz Martin for the Hebbel Theater. In conformance with the American policy that the works of authors who had been blacklisted by the Nazis should be the first to be heard in Berlin, the opening night was *The Three Penny Opera* by Bertolt Brecht and Kurt Weill, an occasion that very nearly turned nasty. Midway through the play, the villain, *Mackie Messer*, Mack the Knife, challenges society: *Zuerst das Fressen, dann die Moral* ("First fill our bellies and then talk to us about morality").

"When that line was sung, the audience, who I am sure were hungry and lived in the corners of destroyed buildings, nearly rioted," says Alter. "People were shouting, stamping, clapping, getting up from their seats, but fortunately not out of them. It was a touch and go situation whether the curtain would have to come down." The curtain did stay up, and the play stayed on the repertoire. The line that caused all the uproar was not changed, but sung in a more restrained way in subsequent performances.

Normally, however, the theater and other entertainment provided a respite from a very grim reality for the Berliners. To a remarkable extent, the Berliners also proved capable of poking fun at their own situation. James Gilroy Annan, now Lord Annan, was at the time an advisor in the political division of the British military government. He recalls a cabaret in which the actors would sit in two rows, pretending to be going out to the countryside by train to scrounge for food. Imitating the sound of the train, they muttered the words *Kartoffeln, Kartoffeln, Kartoffeln* ("potatoes,

potatoes, potatoes") in unison. Signifying that the train had entered a tunnel, they suddenly jumped up and shrieked "POLIZEI! POLIZEI!" at the top of their lungs. And then, out of the tunnel again back to *Kartoffeln, Kartoffeln.* Somehow, this seemed to sum up the atmosphere in Berlin.

The film industry, too, had to be revived. Nazi propaganda minister Joseph Goebbels saw film as the most important art form, and the German film industry had been totally controlled by his ministry, churning out a mixture of blatant Nazi propaganda films and escapist fare. In fact, the Nazis were still making movies as the Allies were closing in in 1945. Goebbels was convinced that the war could be turned around and the Russians defeated with great patriotic movies. The movie *Kolberg* thus celebrated the beleaguered citizens of Kolberg who in 1806–07 formed a civilian militia in their stand against Napoleon. To produce the movie, Goebbels pulled 187,000 soldiers off the front and dressed them in period costumes.[13]

Because of Goebbel's legacy, the western powers were extremely careful when it came to showing films for a German audience. "In the movies, we had a very ascetic policy," says Alter. The guidelines specifically stated that movies were not to entertain the Germans, only to supply them with information. The four licensed movie theaters in the American sector at first played only documentaries, and there were mandatory showings of Auschwitz footage. Later, only carefully selected American movies, like *The Good Earth*, Charles Chaplin's *The Gold Rush*, *Rembrandt* with Charles Laughton, and *I Married a Witch* with Veronica Lake were shown, and the few German movies that made it to the screen were made by artists deemed politically sound. During the winter, it was decided to relax the policy some to take the mind of the German population off the hardships.

Cultural activities in the U.S. occupied zone of Germany, including the American sector of Berlin, were to take place only with a license from the military government. To take charge on the German side of film distribution, which had been his field before the Nazis, Alter picked Rudolf Goldschmidt, who had spent five years in hiding in Berlin, a so-called submarine. "His political background was that he was an obvious victim who had crawled out of the basements where he had lived for the past four or five years."

Overall, says Alter, "The difference between the Eastern sector and the Western sectors was that we and the British did not believe there was such a thing as a state definition of culture. The Soviets most certainly did."

❙ THE PRESSES RUN AGAIN ❙

Of the western Allies in Berlin, the British came out with the first newspaper, *The Berliner*, which was actually more of an information sheet than a newspaper. The first real American newspaper was *Die Allgemeine Zeitung*, the first issue of which came out on August 7, 1945.

The news that day was pretty big. Says Peter Wyden, who had arrived in Berlin in mid-July as a sergeant in the information division, "We had the bombing of Hiroshima as our opening gun, so to speak." Next week the front page story was President Truman's announcement of the surrender of Japan on August 14. World War II was over.

"You have to understand that all this was done in a hell of a hurry, under considerable time pressure and considerable manpower pressure," says Wyden.

Nobody was sleeping very much. There was not too much time to fool around with niceties. We got ourselves a terrible little cold-water apartment in Tempelhof because it was near the Ullstein publishing house and lived there throughout the winter, without any heat, like the Germans. We simply could not spare the time to run out to Zehlendorf where it was comfortable and where the rest of our people were.

Wyden was the city editor of the paper, and he had quite a time impressing American practices on the German reporters. The first task was to try to get them to distinguish between fact and opinion. The second, to keep things short. The simple business of catching the reader quickly with a summary first paragraph, to grab his attention—that was not known among the Germans. Says Wyden, "That was fairly much of a chronic problem, and in some German newspapers it still is."

Egon Bahr was hired by *Die Allgemeine Zeitung* at the age of twenty-three. It was his first real job. Recalls Wyden affectionately, "I sent him off to cover some manhole explosion, a very minor thing that did not turn out to be anything at all. He came back very conscientiously and wrote this immense article. I threw it back at him, and said to him in German *War and Peace* we do not need."

"Peter was my master. I learned from him to put, if possible, in the first sentence who, what, when, where, how much," remembers Bahr. "It was very instructive." Bahr also recalls that when Wyden was scheduled to go back to the States, Wyden said good-bye to the staff and left the room. Then his head reappeared in the doorway and he said to Bahr, "Behind this door, you will find some shoes for you." And off he went. "This was a pair of American army shoes, brown and unforgettable. Without those shoes I would never have been able to survive. I had these shoes for seven years. I loved them."

Die Allgemeine Zeitung operated only until November 11, 1945, when its role was taken over by *Der Tagesspiegel*, an independent German newspaper that was given a license by the Americans. Initially, *Der Tagesspiegel* was dedicated to establishing genuine contact between the Soviet Union and the western democracies. That all changed with the forced merger in the Soviet sector between the Social Democratic Party and the Communist Party to form the *Sozialistische Einheits Partei*, SED, the Socialist Unity Party. This followed massive demonstrations in the spring of 1946 as well as the rejection of the merger by the Social Democrats in the western sectors. The event became one of the first serious clashes between the occupying powers, and *Der Tagesspiegel* soon became the main organ for anti-Soviet feelings.

Over the airwaves, the competition between East and West became intense, too. When the western Allies arrived in Berlin, they found that the Red Army was solidly in control of Radio Berlin, as they were of much of everything else. Radio Berlin was the city's main radio station, located in Masurenallee in the British sector. That it clearly lay outside their own sector obviously did not overly worry the Russians.[14] (In fact, they didn't leave until 1952.)

Radio Berlin broadcast daily glowing reports of rapid reconstruction in Soviet-occupied territories, while maximizing reports of discontent in the western parts of Germany. The Russians also made much out of distinguishing between the Nazi leadership and the general population, which again was calculated to go down well with their German audience.

The western powers proposed a joint sharing of the station among the occupation powers. Unfortunately, the Soviet idea of sharing consisted of offering the western powers one hour a day of radio time combined. While still pressing the Russians on the subject, the Americans first tried to break the Russian radio monopoly with so-called *Drahtfunk* or "wired wireless," which started operation on February 7, 1946.[15] Instead of using the ether as the vehicle of transmission, the programs were sent over the telephone wires, and the result, supposedly, could be received by an ordinary radio set.

Juergen Graf signed up with the American radio very early, so early that, at the time, he was the only reporter. As a young man he had first been hired by the Russians, but was quickly detected by the Americans and persuaded to switch sides. He does not make much of his decision to join the Americans. "This was not a political decision. A boy of eighteen does not think that much. The cigarettes tasted better, the whisky was better than vodka, the uniforms were cleaner, and the cars were more tempting. This is the truth."

One aim was to try to dispel the mental isolation of the German listener, who had been subjected to twelve years of Nazi brainwash. Questions of collective guilt were debated, of guilt and innocence, of what it had meant to be a member of the Nazi Party. What was sought was a "reorientation," to encourage democratic habits of thought, respect for the opinions of others, while retaining an ability to form one's own. What was discouraged was an unquestioning acceptance of everything coming from above, especially if issued by someone in a uniform.

The *Drahtfunk* covered the Nuremberg trial of Nazi war criminals and debated what should be done about the small fry, those who joined the Party out of opportunism or social pressure. It was debated what "just following orders" meant and what the consequences would be of an order disobeyed. "We did a lot on the Nuremberg trials. I was only a visitor because I was a young boy of eighteen," says Graf. "An older man, a former teacher did the coverage of the first big Nuremberg trials. We did not have a line from Nuremberg to Berlin, but we had military planes flying every day, in and out, so we got the tapes from him. That was our first real big current events report."

The idea was also that the radio would expose the Berliners to world literature, and to important figures of other countries. In its promotion of pluralism, it would engage in political debate with representatives from all parties, in keeping with General Eisenhower's directive to the military government that "you will assure that your military government does not become committed to any political group."

It would debate questions such as the Soviet maneuver of the merger of the Social Democratic Party and the Communist Party, giving the democratic arguments against and the communist arguments for, leaving it to the listeners to form their own opinions. The station was still careful not to criticize the Soviets directly, as they were still seen as allies of America.

The works of composers who had been banned by the Nazis, such as Mendelssohn, Offenbach, Mahler, and Hindemith were played. The *Goetterdaemmerung* music of Wagner, music for supermen to dream by, and the hare-brained operettas of Franz Lehar, also appropriated by the Nazi regime, were out.[16] In the beginning, the station had all of seven phonograph records and had to borrow from private citizens. Not everybody was thrilled by this newfangled American import. One older listener complained that the American station forced him to choose between democracy and Bing Crosby, or communism and Tchaikovsky.

Programs like "Books We Were Forbidden to Read" continued to introduce authors who had been banned, such as Thomas Mann, Stefan Zweig, and Arthur Koestler.

It soon became clear, however, that the *Drahtfunk* was no match for the powerful Soviet sender. The weakness of the *Drahtfunk* system was, in a nutshell, that the reception was awful. During the bombing of Berlin, too much water had seeped into the subterranean cables. During the first weeks of operation, the station received a total of eight letters, all complaints. One irate listener complained that the reception was so scratchy that she permitted her husband to play the radio only when she was out.

I still have a cartoon which the most famous cartoonist at that time, Hans Gossart, made of a little man sweating. You saw all the wires in the studio, and the sweating man was me. Behind me was a technician. The technician was saying, 'Don't get excited, Mr. Graf,' nobody can listen to you anyway.' Everybody wondered, especially employees like me, that this enormously rich country, America, started a radio station that way.

When it was concluded that *Drahtfunk* was simply not up to the task, and when all efforts to talk the Soviets into sharing Radio Berlin had failed, the Americans finally launched "Radio in the American Sector," on September 5, 1946, which instantly became known by its acronym RIAS.[17] It was first located in Winterfeldstrasse and was later moved to Kufsteinerstrasse in June 1948.

As the aggressiveness of the Russians grew, the aim of educating the Berliners in the ways of democracy was broadened, though there was still no criticism of the Russian ally as such. The radio covered the Berlin elections on October 20, 1946, laying out in detail the choices before the electorate.

The station promoted the Marshall Plan, which the Soviets were presenting as an American attempt to colonize Europe. But promoting American-style democracy presented its problems. "Symbols which are deeply meaningful to us through long usage, such as the 'Bill of Rights,' 'Lincoln's Gettysburg Address,' the term 'mugwump,' 'the Civil War,' and the 'Founding Fathers' are so unfamiliar to the average German radio audience as to be meaningless," a report of the military government concluded. "Since the broadcast is only fifteen minutes long, it is felt that more familiar symbols could be found that would not require explanation." Rather than transferring American concepts, it was more reward-ing to build on European traditions.[18]

Generally, that was the experience of the U.S. military team. Ideas that came from the outside, specifically from the Americans, did not take well. Ideas that came from the Germans, on the other hand, and were sup-ported by the Allies, were successful. The same was the case when it came to newspapers, which were written by Americans in the beginning, but were soon turned over to Germans. After all, Germany in many ways had been one of the most highly cultured countries in the world. It had a splendid tradition of science and literature, philosophy and music, classi-cism and Christianity. What it emphatically did not have was a splendid tradition of government.

Getting Berlin's education system running again was another major endeavor. Very often the students came from families with one parent, the father having been killed in the war or in a prison camp. Under such circumstances, when social and familial authority has broken down, juve-nile delinquency becomes a major concern.

An army report showed that 25 percent of Berlin's schools were totally destroyed and another 25 percent unusable.[19] Half were considered repairable. The total school-age population of Berlin was 300,000. The new school to which Helga Mellman was assigned was temporarily housed in a former concentration camp. The building was crawling with lice. "During the lessons, we would sit with a safety pin and whoever picked up the most lice won the game. We finally got our school back. We had to clean it up. You wouldn't believe the dirt in there. I have never seen anything like it." Again, it was the problem with the Soviets and the toilets.

The condition of many of the children was not promising. Food was in short supply, and the kids had so little stamina that they fell asleep dur-ing class. "The school rooms were frigid in the wintertime. There was no heat for them. I have a picture some place of a school room with the chil-dren, I think both boys and girls in the picture, but it is difficult to tell as they are all wrapped up in overcoats, mufflers and gloves sitting at their desk," recalls Frank Banta, the U.S. education specialist with the mili-tary government. Minds were concentrated on surviving, on obtaining food and heat. The all-important donations of CARE packages from the United States, which helped German families through the worst times, did not start arriving until the summer of 1946.*

As many children as possible in the last two years of the war had been sent out of Berlin, and younger children might come through horrendous experiences unscathed. Comments Ruth Mattheis, the pediatrician, "In the air-raid shelters, I saw babies sleeping quietly in the laps of their mothers." However, in older children the psychological scars could be severe. Having seen her neighborhood go up in flames, one girl for instance could not light a match from fear. Like other children, they played what they had lived through. They would play "rape," "here come the Russians," and during the blockade they played "airlift." "We did not hinder it because we thought it was a certain method to get it out of their system," says Mattheis.

Frank Banta remembers the attitudes of German students in summer school. "They were avid for contact with the outside world. They had been cut off from everything that had been going on, except what they could get clandestinely. They had not met foreigners, non-Germans, except perhaps as slave laborers. They were extremely hopeful, they felt that something bad was over and that there was a new beginning."

Because the education system was another of the primary control mechanisms of the totalitarian state, the teaching profession had a high proportion of Nazi Party members. An estimated 50 percent of Berlin's teachers had been members of the Party and were therefore unfit for teaching.[20] Instead, young and untrained teachers were used to fill the

---

*For the children of Berlin and for their families, one of the few rays of light in 1946 was the CARE packages, which began arriving from the United States in August 1946. CARE (Cooperative for American Relief in Europe), founded as a private, nonprofit initiative, was targeted at all the war-ravaged European countries. However, Germany soon became the main recipient of these donations. What Marshall aid later did for the German economy as a whole, the CARE packages did for the individual family.

A packet containing food and clothing cost ten dollars to put together and weighed 13 kilograms. *Berlinerin* Barbara Klein still remembers when the parcel arrived and a piece of chocolate was put on a plate to be carefully shared among the children. "It was almost a religious experience," says Klein. In the period 1946–52, one million CARE packages were distributed.

vacuum. After a day of classes, in the evenings, the new teachers would attend seminars.

Aloys Wehr was one of these new teachers at the age of nineteen. "After the battle of Berlin, young people of my age who had not been members of the Nazi Party, but had a proper education, were urged to become assistant teachers in the schools. This is how I became a young teacher, first at a Tempelhof elementary school, a girls' school."

New schoolteachers were carefully screened. Trained as a navigator, Gert Radde had served in the German navy on a minesweeper in the Kieler Kanal and in Rotterdam harbor. He had also been engaged in laying mines along the British coast. Towards the end of the war, when most of the German fleet had been destroyed, he had been transferred to the marine infantry where he had surrendered to the Americans. Later he worked for the British, again on a minesweeper, and in 1946, he was permitted to go home and join his family in Berlin.

By then he was twenty-two years old and joined the newly founded *Paedagogische Hochschule.* Before being admitted, however, he was grilled by two of the school's teachers who carefully explored his thoughts and beliefs. The educators clearly wanted a clean break with the past. At the Hochschule, Radde experienced a new atmosphere where the students were asked for their opinions, a new feeling for somebody who had grown up in a totalitarian state.

Under the Nazi regime, German children had been conditioned to accept death, the supreme sacrifice. Radde and his fellow teachers wanted a school that could prepare them for life. "We wanted a new kind of school, one that aimed at promoting a democratic mind set."

Needless to say, an entire generation of school books had to be tossed out. The Nazi content varied from subject to subject, but almost every book was dedicated to *Der Fuehrer.* Biology and anthropology, history and archeology were highly influenced by Nazi ideology, constantly referring to Germany's Aryan heritage. In physical education and art, the glorification of the human body was ever present, which of course meant the Nordic body.

Books of German literature had received special treatment by the Nazis. Jewish writers like Franz Kafka or Heinrich Heine disappeared

Private Werner Nathan holds the sacred Torah, which had been hidden during the Nazi terror, in the first celebration of the Jewish New Year Rosh Hashanah after the war in a make-shift Berlin synagogue, summer 1945.

completely. Suddenly the author of *Lorelei* was listed as unknown. In music, Jewish composers like Felix Mendelssohn disappeared completely.

The Nazis had a certain knack with picture books, which showed the Germans occupying all the parts of Europe they claimed to be historically theirs, particularly in the East. Geography books everywhere mentioned Poland as a German colony. One was called *Was weisst du vom deutschen Ostland?* (*What do you know about the German East?*). They were all written in Fraktur, the old German writing that looks so impressive, as if it were carved in stone.

Even in mathematics, notes General Clay in his memoirs, the Nazis could sneak in their propaganda; little Hansi would learn to count bullets and bombs, rather than apples and oranges. Or students would be asked to calculate how many soldiers to a column if they march in threes and the column is nine deep. These efforts were of course continued after school with the *Jungvolk* and the Hitler youth, conditioning them for the military.

Providing substitute school books represented a terrific logistical problem because there was a shortage of absolutely every material. Paper was extremely expensive, and there was little available. And it takes time to write a book and to publish it, even when the materials are available.

The U.S. military government had some of the old textbooks from the Weimar Republic reprinted, but the Soviets objected, arguing that there still were militaristic passages. Perhaps they had a point: A fifth-grade reader contained passages like Frederick the Great's stirring address to his troops before the battle of Leythen, "Let us beat the enemy, or let us be buried by his batteries." One calculus book for seventh graders used the economic and territorial losses of the Treaty of Versailles as examples.

Some schoolbooks were imported from Switzerland, and teachers had to improvise. Mimeographed copies of new books were passed around. Says Banta, "I do not think one can say that German education was back on track before the late forties, early fifties."

Equally important were the youth initiatives arranged by the army in the American sector. In April 1946, General Joseph T. McNarney ordered that, throughout the American occupied zone and in Berlin, mature officers be assigned to look into youth problems. "If we fail in this, we are simply making trouble for ourselves." By mid-June when the first meeting of youth advisers was held in Munich, the military government of Germany had approved twenty-five hundred youth groups with three-hundred thousand members.[21] Says Wehr, "As my American friends knew that I was a teacher, they asked me if I could help them organize the Tempelhof GYA program (German Youth Activities) to be a counselor for young Germans. The GYA was a very good program. The boys and girls came by the thousands."

In the beginning, it was mainly a sports program. American soldiers would come to the sports arenas and gyms to teach American sports like basketball. In Nazi Germany, sports clubs had tended to promote military training for young people. The kinds of sports banned after the war were those considered to have a martial application: boxing, mountain-climbing, yachting, rowing, jujitsu, weight lifting, field athletics, skiing, and cycling. Sports that were approved were: volleyball, basketball, hockey, rugby, soccer, skating, tennis, bowling, and fishing, as well as elementary calisthenics.[22]

When the list was published, it aroused some critical comment and some hilarity in the United States. If rugby is not a warlike sport, what is? After all, the Battle of Waterloo was said to have been won on the playing fields of Eton. Among others, *Time* magazine commented that the sports not abolished tended to be the ones that were most popular in America and Britain.

According to Tracy Strong, who had been with the 7th Army and now was a master sergeant, because of the precedent set by the Hitler Youth, uniforms were out, which led to a debate over precisely what constituted a uniform. Does the same color shirt and pants make a uniform? Pins recognizing a person as a member of the Catholic or Protestant youth organization were deemed acceptable. But there were other difficulties. All types of firearms were of course strictly banned in Germany. Recalls Strong, "One of their problems was how do you start a race if you can't have a starting gun? We told them just to take two boards and clap them together. It sounds kind of ridiculous now."

Particular emphasis was placed on the fact the groups would have democratically elected leaders. Among the major youth groups in Berlin were the church groups, Protestant and Catholic, the Social Democratic group called *Die Falken*, and the *Freie Deutsche Jugend* (FDJ), which was the Communist youth group. At its head was an intense and very determined young fellow whom the Russians had brought with them from Moscow, one Erich Honecker, who later was to become East Germany's leader. "We were trying to be very neutral supporting all youth groups," says Strong. "We had a small grant and we asked the leaders of the groups to come in and meet us in the office and let us know what they were going to use the money for, for camping, education or whatever."

True to form, the FDJ immediately tried to take over the others. A single youth organization would be so much more convenient, Honecker and his friends argued, but the FDJ did not get very far with these plans. Honecker had to confine his activities to the eastern zone.

There were also discussion groups and musical groups. One day, Aloys Wehr was approached by the chaplain of the black U.S. military unit, with which Wehr had made contact. The chaplain had heard about his musical talents. "So many German children learn English in school. Can't you organize a choir that can sing American spirituals?" Sure, Wehr said. There was only one small problem. "Chaplain, what is a spiritual?"

Having had this explained to him, Wehr set about organizing a choir and within a few days he had a group of thirty German boys and girls, ages ten to eighteen. They met late in the afternoons in the soldiers club to study spirituals. "After four weeks, I told the chaplain we were ready. On a Sunday morning at 10:30 we were picked up by an American military truck from the GYA club and taken to the barracks. You cannot imagine my feelings. I had never been a choir director, and I was not sure if the rhythm I had studied with the children was correct."

He needn't have worried. The choir was a big hit, and many of the congregation were touched by the emaciated appearance of the young singers. Afterwards the children were treated to oranges, bananas, and candy and then taken to the mess hall and given a hot meal. Shortly after, Wehr was approached by another Protestant minister who asked if Wehr could make a choir for whites. The Catholics, no doubt wondering why they should be left out, asked him to sing for them also.

The winter of 1945–46 was rather mild, so plans for closing the schools were abandoned. The Russians still found ways to play little games. They would give the schools in their own sector almost their complete coal rations while cutting those of schools in the western sectors. They had six educational officers, whereas the United States had only one, Major Philip Shafer. It was not until a year after the Americans moved into Berlin that Shafer was allowed to get a bigger staff.

▮ DENAZIFICATION ▮

One of the most vexing tasks facing the military government and one that was never entirely resolved was the process of denazification. "The question of who is a Nazi is often a dark riddle," a 3rd Army report put it more

Interrogation of the "the blonde poison," Stella Goldschlag-Kuebler, by German police investigator Jean Blomé. Kuebler, a Jewish Nazi agent and collaborator who hunted down hidden Jews in wartime Berlin, giving them up to the Gestapo, was handed over to the Soviets and spent ten years in a camp. She was convicted in two later trials by German courts but was not jailed—both sentences were remitted because of the time already served. Chief of detectives Jean Blomé was later unmasked as an ardent Nazi, Johannes Blom, himself.

U.S. Army Signal Corps

than a month after Germany's surrender. "The question of what is a Nazi is also not easy to answer."

The initial idea was to get rid of the entire top layer of German leadership. According to Joint Chiefs of Staff directive 1067, which provided the guidelines for U.S. military rule in Germany, members of the Nazi Party who had been more than nominal participants, all active supporters of Nazism or militarism, and all other persons hostile to Allied purposes would be removed and excluded from public life and from positions of importance in quasi public and private enterprises. In September 1945,

Military Government Law No. 8 was added, which explicitly stated that former Nazis could not hold important positions in business.[23]

That decision, which would affect every level of society beyond that of common laborer, ran into a lot of German opposition. There were some 12 million Germans who had been members of the Nazi Party, according to the party's central registry, which was discovered in Munich in a pile of wastepaper waiting to be pulped. The problem was that if you made a clean sweep, based solely on membership, as had been first envisioned by Allied policy makers, there would not be enough competent men to run the country for a generation. Again, this was in strong conflict with the aim of getting the American boys home from the war.

The always impetuous George Patton could be relied on to put his boot in his mouth, as he certainly did on the question of denazification. He did not like the prospect of having to rely on inexperienced civilians. On August 11, 1945, he wrote to General Eisenhower that denazification was going too fast. "It is no more possible for a man to be a civil servant in Germany and not have paid lip service to Nazism than it is for a man to be postmaster in America and not have paid lip service to the Democratic Party or Republican Party when it is in power."[24] This promptly earned him a rebuke from Eisenhower for seemingly not having understood what the war had been all about. Patton later repeated himself by asking a financial investigator "if he did not think it is silly to try to get rid of the most intelligent people in Germany."

A U.S. military government report states, "The denazification program has rendered the available German personnel unable to assume immediately the burdens of production activity and industrial statistical reporting. We have reached the stage where we must determine much more specifically what we are going to do about minor hirelings of the Nazi party and its satellite agencies."

In one sense, intellectuals could be judged harsher than others because they ought to have realized the consequences of the ideas they endorsed, more so, say, than the greengrocer who might have been making a bit of money on the side through his Nazi membership, trucking in vegetables to their gatherings.

The problem with the weeding-out process was that the junior officers like Henry Alter to whom the task was entrusted knew full well that a lot of people would have been smart enough never to have been members of the party. But that did not mean they had not held positions of great influence. Conversely, it was also possible to have been a party member for reasons of opportunism and yet have been relatively harmless. That would not exonerate party members, but it does suggest the complexity of the task.

Not only were distinctions not clear-cut, but there was considerable disagreement among Americans how best to proceed with this process. *Die Neue Zeitung* was torpedoed by Hans Habe's superiors because he wanted a more forward-looking editorial line than the Eisenhower policies permitted, as Habe recounts in his memoir *Im Jahre Null*.[25] Habe thought that the only way to deal with the Germans, now that the war was over, was to treat them like human beings of some intelligence. His superiors thought that any officer arguing this way was trying to protect somebody for personal reasons.

This is not to suggest that by sticking to the rules, in the vast majority of cases, Alter and his colleagues were not right. "Initially, we had to go by the book, and by going by the book we were probably right in 75 percent of the cases," says Alter.[26]

The administration of the denazification program was turned over in part to the Germans in October, under allied supervision of course. German judges heard the cases in the *Spruchkammer*, and instead of dividing people up into Nazis and non-Nazis, five different gradations were made. Among the points taken into account was *when* people had joined the party. The opinion of the official military government was that the earlier people had joined, the worse they were. The first one million members who had signed up before 1933 were considered the hard core.

More leniency was accorded people who had joined after May 1937. That was when public employees were required to join the party. If they had refused, they would have been out of a job. And exceptions were made; people in crucial professions, like doctors and dentists, were given temporary permits. Railroad workers, who had high membership rates in the party, simply could not easily be dispensed with.[27] Those who could produce certificates stating that they had taken part in the resistance were cleared. Before long, a major traffic developed in the so-called *Persilscheine*, the "snow white certificates," named after the popular detergent.[28]

Later, when the Cold War began to dominate western policies, the American and the British side started to compromise on denazification. By 1948–49, a person who was needed for his ability could be so important that the Americans overlooked things in his personal history, which under military government law would have disqualified him. Industrialists with names like Thyssen and Krupp, who were originally treated as war criminals, were so badly needed that they were eventually again permitted to become part of the establishment.

The Russian interpretation of the denazification process turned out to be even more elastic than that of the Americans. When it suited their purposes, an ex-Nazi SS general could become a colonel in the local police force. On the other hand, if it suited their ideological concerns, they would have a big trial and shoot the guy. Will Tremper recalls that one of his first scoops as a journalist was the discovery of a major figure of the Third Reich installed as head of police by the Russians.

I wanted to talk to the head of police. They would not allow me to talk with him since I came from the Tagesspiegel. *Then I found out—this was the first crisis between East and West in the local government—that the chief of police, Paul Herbert Markgraf, whom the Russians had brought along with them, was a Ritterkreuztraeger (a recipient of the Nazi Knight's Cross).[29] He was first put in prison by the Russians and then became a member of the Russian-run national committee for a free Germany. The official policy was anti-militarism and here they had a militarist par excellence at the head.*

When Tremper put that in the newspaper, all hell broke loose.

As a freshly baked democrat, I went to his office in the East Sector to ask for Markgraf's comment about my article. He did not show up. Who showed up instead was the Russian commander of the military police and two other guys who arrested me. My editor at the Tagesspiegel *immediately called the office of Col. Howley and told Howley's press officer what happened to his police reporter.*

Howley immediately arrested two SED functionaries in Schoeneberg in the American sector. The same evening at ten o'clock I was exchanged with these two SED functionaries at the center of Potsdamerplatz.

"The competition resulting from the opposing ideological systems would increasingly dominate the thoughts of all the participants," writes Brewster Chamberlain, Director of the United States Holocaust Research Institute. "And, eventually the confrontation replaced the notion of controlling the Germans."

▐ THE FIRST ELECTIONS ▐

It soon became clear that, despite a Soviet official commitment to a multiparty system, what was emerging in the Soviet sector was a political regime and an economic order in the Soviet mold. These efforts were headed by Walter Ulbricht, a German Communist who had spent the war in Moscow.

One of the Soviet occupation's first actions was to suggest a fusion of the Communist Party and the Social Democrats into the Socialist Unity Party, the SED, the better to present a united front against all manner of fascist recidivists, activists of the Vatican, and plotting Nazis. Party officials were threatened with the loss of jobs if they opposed the merger. The Soviet methods were less than subtle. People started disappearing off the street, never to be seen again—prominent journalists, judges, local opinion-makers, and Social Democrats.

Initially, U.S. officers had been reluctant to get involved in city politics, especially to be seen as opposed to their wartime Russian ally. However, it was becoming clear that without U.S. support, the forces of democracy in Berlin would be steamrollered by the tactics of the East German Communists. The Social Democrats fought the merger tooth and nail, and appealed to the western occupation forces for help.

Despite a massive Communist propaganda effort, the opponents of the merger efforts won overwhelmingly, with 82.5 percent of the city's Social Democrats opposing the move in a referendum of SPD members held on March 31, 1946. The Social Democrats in the eastern sector never got to vote on the question, since for some reason "technical difficulties" got in the way.

On October 20, 1946, 90 percent of Berlin's eligible voters cast their ballot in the first free election in thirteen years. The Social Democrats (SPD) came out big winners with 48.9 percent. Next came the Christian Democrats (CDU) with 21.5 percent, and last the SED with 20 percent. The first mayor elected by the city assembly of Berlin was Otto Ostrowski (SPD), who resigned a few months later following a vote of no confidence from his own party. His elected successor was Ernst Reuter (SPD), who was, however, vetoed by the Soviets; his place was taken for a time by deputy governing mayor Frau Louise Schroeder (SPD). This was not just an election about local matters; it was a choice between two different

Berlin's legendary mayor, Ernst Reuter.

systems of government, between western democracy and eastern totalitarianism.

The SED defeat came in spite of a determined campaign by the Soviets to influence the outcome by methods such as canceling Social Democratic political meetings in East Berlin five minutes before they were supposed to start (making the SPD look disorganized), giving food and notebooks to schoolchildren courtesy of the SED, favoring the inhabitants in the Soviet sector in the distribution of imported coal and vegetables. Intimidation, too, was used, threatening people's jobs. Nevertheless, the Berliners had stated clearly where their sympathies lay.

The American on the front line in Berlin for four years was Director of Berlin Military Government, Colonel Frank Howley. He turned out to be a formidable adversary for the Soviets. Having arrived with the first American troops in June 1945, he provided continuity through eight U.S. military commandants and rose to become brigadier general and commandant number nine on December 1, 1947. Like Patton, he was an old cavalry man and he did not like the striped-pants people in the State Department. According to Karl Mautner of the 82nd Airborne Division, who was liaison officer between the American military government and the mayor's office, "I am one of the few who will defend him up and down. Because I liked the guy. He could indeed be very unpleasant. He was a real Irishman with a temper."

Howley's own strong right-wing leanings were no secret, but he knew nonetheless that the people to work with were the Social Democrats in Berlin, and he did not listen to those staff members who advised him not to trust socialists.

"He was a good public relations man who had the right *Schnauze* (the fast reply) at the right moment, which the Berliners loved and the press, too," says Mautner. While Clay would often insist on honoring U.S. agreements with the Allies to the East scrupulously, he still found good use for Howley and his hot temper. "Clay used Howley like a fiddler. He turned him loose. If things went too far, he just whistled him back. Howley was a good man in the right spot at the right time."

Or as Howley himself comments in *Berlin Command* about his Soviet counterpart Major General A. G. Kotikov, commandant of the Russian sector: "My four years in Berlin gave me gray hairs, but I have the satisfaction that I gave him stomach ulcers. That, at least, makes us even."[30]

▮ THE ONSET OF THE COLD WAR ▮

Relations between the wartime Allies continued to decline. In January 1947, the British and American zones were merged to become what was known as the Bizone. The Americans were adamant in stressing that this was a purely economic move, not a political move.

Back on February 9, 1946, Joseph Stalin made a speech in Moscow in which he emphasized the incompatibility between the communist and capitalist systems and the inevitability of war between them. He called for the Soviet people to prepare for the showdown. Soon after, Winston Churchill made his famous speech in Fulton, Missouri, where he warned against the "Iron Curtain" that was descending throughout Europe, dividing it into two hostile camps.

Still, until October 1947, the Americans continued their policy of preserving a veneer of unity between the Allies in Berlin. Disagreements, it was held, should not take place before the Germans. That position proved increasingly untenable.

In the spring of 1947, Melvin Lasky returned to Berlin as a foreign correspondent for a string of small newspapers and literary magazines. In a series of articles in the *New Leader*, an American leftist (but anticommunist) weekly, Lasky had attacked military government for being too complacent about the Communist attempts to gain a foothold in Berlin's trade unions and political parties.

Lasky was also arguing that the Americans were not doing enough for the people who were resisting Communist pressures. When, for instance, the Social Democratic leader Kurt Schumacher flew into Berlin, there was nobody to pick him up at Tempelhof Airport. Schumacher was crippled, having lost an arm in World War I, and could not walk as a conse-

U.S. Army Military History Institute

Generals in command: Lucius D. Clay (l) and Frank L. Howley.

U.S. Army Military History Institute

Number 1 in Berlin: General Howley, with his beloved Horch.

General Howley's favorite adversary, Soviet General A. G. Kotikov, ready for battle in the Allied Kommandatura. Of him Howley said, "My four years in Berlin gave me gray hairs, but I have the satisfaction that I gave him stomach ulcers."

quence of having been held in a concentration camp by the Nazis (his leg was amputated in 1948). In fact, Lasky, who at the time had no connection with the military government, took it upon himself to get his Buick out on the tarmac and get Schumacher safely to his destination.

"It was ridiculous. The Communists dominated SED, had all the money in the world and all the facilities, while we left our friends, anybody who would be resisting the Russians, in the lurch."

At one of General Clay's official press conferences, after yet another series of Soviet provocations, Lasky asked the general, head on, if he was now prepared to talk back when the Soviets accused the Americans of being imperialists, oppressing the Germans. To which the General answered, "Yes." The following day, the headlines ran in the German

Brigadier General Frank L. Howley resigned, disgruntled, from his Berlin post on August 1, 1949. He fired a parting shot against the politicians in Washington: "I am not a member of the State Department's team," which was taking over gradually the occupation of Germany from the military. Major General Maxwell D. Taylor, Chief of Staff of the European Command (r), who succeeded Howley as Military Commander in the divided city, is briefed by the Cold War veteran.

papers that Clay had finally decided to take off the *Glacehandschuhe*, the kid gloves, and from now on would be addressing Soviet attacks directly.

From now on, the United States would respond immediately to Soviet propaganda, "attacking Communism in every form wherever it existed," in the words of General Clay, who issued the order on October 25, 1947.[31] As a result, operation "Back Talk" was launched, and American radio

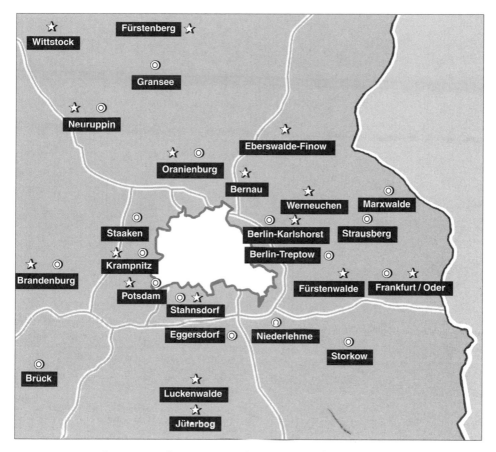

Communist forces surrounding the city of Berlin.
(Stars: Soviet forces; Circles: East German forces)

broadcasts took aim at Soviet lies, exposing Communist tactics and purposes. Listener mail, much of it from the Soviet sector, was kept under lock and key for the protection of the letter writers. By January 1948, RIAS had become the most listened-to station in Berlin.

Lasky was subsequently invited by Clay to become a cultural adviser to the U.S. military government. He was twenty-six at the time and became editor of the magazine *Der Monat*. Lasky was given a free hand to create the kind of magazine he thought was needed without any censorship or interference, though it is fair to say that some of Clay's advisers at headquarters had grave misgivings about what Lasky was trying to do.

The aim of the magazine was to create a broad democratic alliance embracing the left of center and the right of center; the left of center would include the noncommunist and anticommunist left, and the right would be the nonfascist and antifascist right. The idea was that they would have more in common, believing in a pluralistic society, than in engaging in capitalist-socialist recriminations.

In the magazine's pages, Social Democrats like Ernst Reuter and a young Willy Brandt would appear, the latter a protégé of Reuter's. During the Nazi era, Ernst Reuter had twice been sentenced to a concentration camp, and twice sentenced to death, but his life had been saved through the efforts of charitable organizations in the United States and Britain that put pressure on the Nazi government. Instead, he had been permitted to leave Germany and go into exile. He spent the war in Turkey, trying to assist Germans, many of them Jews, who were fleeing Hitler.

Brandt, too, had had to flee Germany. He went to Norway, where he had fought the German occupation troops with the Norwegian underground. The conservative point of view would be represented by philosophers like Wilhelm Roepke and Friedrich von Hayek, the eminent Austrian monetarist economist and political philosopher, who in his 1944 book, *The Road to Serfdom*, argued that centralized planning would eventually lead to the end of the liberal capitalist state.

In retaliation for his outspoken criticism, Lasky was immediately singled out by the Soviet propaganda machine. After a speech at the East Berlin Writers Congress in October 1947, where Lasky commented on the similarities of the Nazi police state and the new Communist police state developing in East Germany, the chief cultural officer to the Soviet occupation force, Major Dymschytz, suggested that he should be immediately arrested while Colonel Tulpanov, the chief political adviser, recommended that he be "burned in oil."

In Berlin, the Russians were busy spreading the rumor that the western forces were about to leave the city. This had an unsettling effect on Berliners, who saw themselves as lost if the Soviets took over. To further this impression, high-ranking Soviet officers would have their drivers drive them around the areas where western officers were billeted, as if checking out their own future lodgings and mentally making notes of what the kitchen drapes would look like, where the samovars would stand, and picking out the perfect spot for the picture of comrade Stalin.

The Americans had no plans of leaving, however. In Washington, the question of Germany's and Europe's future was being intensely debated. American policy makers soon realized that an impoverished Europe beset by hunger and discontent would easily fall to communism. The piecemeal loans and emergency donations that had been given so far were not going to do the trick.

Worried about the deteriorating situation in Greece and Turkey, where local Communists were making political headway strongly supported by Moscow, the Truman government launched its policy of containment, designed to keep Soviet expansionist dreams at bay. In asking for financial and military assistance for Greece and Turkey, Truman expressed the following principle, a doctrine which was to bear his name: "I believe that it must be the policy of the United States to support free peoples who are resisting attempted subjugation by armed minorities or by outside pressures." But Turkey and Greece were not the only countries that were vulnerable to Soviet destabilization. France and Italy both had large and well-organized Communist parties.

The grand design for the revitalization of Europe conceived by the Truman administration was the European Recovery Program, which Truman insisted on naming the Marshall Plan, after his Secretary of State, General George C. Marshall. It was a wide-ranging plan for the rebuilding of Europe, and the invitation to accept American aid included the Communist bloc. Marshall stated in his speech to Harvard graduates in June 1947, "Our policy is directed not against any country or doctrine, but against hunger, poverty, desperation and chaos. Its purpose should be the revival of a working economy in the world so as to permit the emergence of political and social conditions in which free institutions can exist."

Harry Truman compared the situation to that of the South in the American Civil War and wanted to spare Europe the suffering felt there. "You can't be vindictive after a war. You have to be generous. You have to help people get back on their feet."[32] For the first time in history, a victorious nation offered to help restore its former enemies as well as allies. At a time when the United States was recovering economically from its wartime efforts, the over $10 billion that the plan cost (Truman had asked Congress for $17 billion) was an extraordinary gesture.

East European nations like Poland and Czechoslovakia certainly thought they could have used some of the money to rebuild, but were told by Moscow to fall back into line. The plan, according to the Soviet view, was just another new way of spreading American imperialism. "The intention of the Marshall Plan is to rob independent European countries of their self-reliance and place them under American control," an angry Molotov harrumphed in Paris.

THE AIRLIFT

It was the currency reform of June 20, 1948, that marked the breaking point in relations between the occupying powers. In accordance with the Potsdam Agreement, which stated that all of Germany should be treated as one unit, the Americans had been willing to extend the badly needed reform of the Reichsmark to the whole country. Nobody had faith in the currency anymore. According to the official exchange rate, the Reichsmark was worth 40 cents, but its real value was only about one third of a cent. No amount of price control could save this situation; people were simply not willing to sell their goods for money and kept them for barter.

The barter system, which gave the ordinary German a way to survive, was a terrible drain on society and stood in the way of the rebuilding necessary for Germany to feed, clothe, and house itself in the long run. When the currency is not trusted, neither the farmer's potatoes nor factory-made goods move anywhere, except in exchange for something equally tangible. As a contemporary military report put it, "The hoarding of goods in towns, counties and states, and exchange by barter is a throwback to the middle ages; indeed this medieval method of trade in an overpopulated Germany is likely to result in famine, disease and death, rivaling any records of medieval times."[1] Constant rumors of an imminent currency reform were in the air. There was no incentive to work since wages would be worthless.

The problem was that the Russians would agree to a currency reform only if they retained the exclusive rights to print the new bills in their printing plant in Leipzig. As far as the western powers were concerned, that was out of the question because the Russians then would control the new mark, and they had already helped sink the old currency by their indiscriminate printing of paper money.

Instead, on the evening of Friday, June 18, after the shops had closed, the Americans announced a new currency in the western zones that was to take effect on Sunday; the Reichsmark was devalued to one tenth of its former value and became the new Deutschmark, the foundation of Germany's postwar *Wirtschaftswunder*. On the question of currency reform, General Clay again showed his greatness. At a last meeting, taking place five days before the currency reform, Ludwig Erhard—then joint economics minister of the British and American zones and later Federal economics minister and chancellor, father of the German economic miracle—pleaded with General Clay to make the exchange rate of 10 marks to each 100 Reichsmarks a little less harsh for groups such as the war cripples and the war widows. General Clay gently answered: "I realize that you as a democratic German politician could never push this harsh currency reform through. Be glad that you can hide behind the broad back of the military government. If we once start making exceptions, we will water the whole thing down and then it will not be effective."

"This was brilliantly proved by the economic miracle," says Robert H. Lochner, who at the time was a translator for General Clay. (Generally speaking, though, Erhard was not a man to prevaricate on questions of economic principle. It was on his insistence that the price controls left over from the Nazi era were lifted on July 7, 1948.)

Berlin was not immediately affected since the Americans had promised not to extend the reform to the occupied city. On June 23, however, the Russians struck back with *their* new currency, the East mark, intended also for West Berlin's territory.[2] And that, in turn, caused the

Americans to make the Deutschmark the official currency in the western sectors of Berlin. The Deutschmark bills shipped to Berlin were stamped with Berlin's escutcheon, which features a bear, and the letter B—therefore declared *Baeren-Mark* by the relieved Berliners. For some days, supreme confusion reigned. Russians furiously insisted that the western Allies had forfeited their right to be in Berlin and threatened to arrest anyone found in possession of the new Deutschmark.

Since April, access to Berlin from the western zones of Germany had become more and more difficult, hampered by new Russian formalities and unaccountable "technical" problems. Now the screw was given another turn; the Russians tightened their grip on all land access routes to and from Berlin, roads and railways, under the guise of "technical difficulties" and "urgently needed construction work." Barge traffic on the Elbe, too, was stopped. Over the next few days, these technical problems became "more serious than originally assumed," and, regrettably, they were compounded by "malfunctions" of a power station that was crucial for Berlin's power needs.[3]

A terse U.S. communiqué states what happened: "A U.S. military freight train was stopped at Marienborn at approximately 0500, 21 June. Train was not allowed to proceed to Berlin due to refusal of train commander to permit Soviets to open cars for inspection. At approximately 5 P.M. 22 June, Soviets took over train under threat of arms, attached it to a Soviet locomotive and sent it back to Helmstedt—all this under strong protests of our train commander."

At the same time, the Soviets announced that power stations in the Soviet sector would stop supplying electricity to the western part of the city; they accounted for more than a third of the city's power supply. In addition, the blockade stopped coal deliveries for the power plants in the western parts. On the night of June 23–24, the blockade became total. The idea was to starve western Berlin's two million citizens into submission, totally dependent as they were on food and energy from the outside.

According to William Stearman, a U.S. diplomat intimately familiar with all the intricacies of Berlin's status, access was always the key problem in Berlin. "The reason is that we really never got rights of access spelled out in Berlin, unlike in Vienna," he says. At the end of World War II, Vienna was exactly in the same situation as Berlin, also a hundred miles behind the Iron Curtain, inside the Soviet zone. The difference was that, in the case of Vienna, all American rights of access had been spelled out in infinite detail with nothing left to interpretation. General Alfred M. Gruenther, who negotiated the access for Vienna, figured correctly that what you don't have in writing, you don't have. "If you look at the access agreements for Vienna, you will be amazed at the detail," says Stearman. "We never had any problems with access to Vienna."

Several theories have been advanced about why a similar thoroughness was not applied to the case of Berlin. Some U.S. senior diplomats held that access was self-evident and that it would upset the easily upsettable Russians to ask for anything so crass as a written guarantee. President Truman did in fact write Stalin to get the rights of free access to Berlin on paper, a letter Stalin simply ignored. The assumption was that by their presence in Berlin, the western Allies would also have complete access to the city.

According to another theory, spelling out the details of the access routes could paradoxically limit access as the Russians might insist on observing the letter of the agreement, and the western Allies wanted unrestricted access. The only agreement on access in existence was on access through the air, which was concluded in 1945. "The Soviets were very legalistic in that respect when it suited them and they caught us," says Stearman.

In the view of historian W. Philip Davidson, the Soviet aim with the blockade of Berlin was to put the western Allies in a double bind. The Soviets wanted "to prevent economic recovery and the formation of a West German government, or failing this, to incorporate the population and resources of West Berlin into East Germany." Thus the Americans would be forced to choose between West Berlin and West Germany. Either way, the Americans would lose.

General Clay would have none of it, and he adamantly rejected any thought of giving up Berlin. "If Berlin falls, Western Germany will be

The Bettmann Archive

*Berliner "Steppke" watch a descending cargo plane
atop a hill of rubble near Tempelhof Airport.*

next. If we intend to defend Europe against Communism, we should not budge. We can take humiliation and pressure short of war in Berlin without losing face. If we withdraw, we endanger our European position."[4]

In 1948, General Clay was almost alone among American leaders in believing that it could be done. It was not just the State Department that was prepared to give up on Berlin—the Defense Department was, too. General Omar Bradley, Chairman of the Joint Chiefs, and Secretary of State Marshall both looked at the situation in traditional military terms and saw that Berlin was indefensible. They were arguing for a withdrawal, according to historian Jean Edward Smith, the biographer of Clay. Clay acted on the conviction that the Russians were not prepared to go to war.

But it was not a promising position to defend, with a combined allied troop strength in Berlin of sixty-five hundred men. Frank Howley writes in *Berlin Command*, "Militarily, we did not stand a chance. The Russians could have moved into the areas and liquidated us before you could say 'Politburo.' We had only two battalions of troops, which would have been powerless against the Soviet panzer divisions." After World War II, the United States had quickly demobilized and was psychologically and politically unprepared for a new conflict. By June 1948, total U.S. Army strength in Europe was only ninety-three thousand and the reinforcement prospects grim.

To make up for this weak position on the ground, President Truman ordered sixty U.S. B-29s to Britain, which arrived on July 17. Thirty more arrived in August. The B-29 was capable of carrying the nuclear bomb, and the United States was still the only nuclear power in the world. The planes that arrived in Britain were not fitted to carry the bomb, but this, of course, the Soviets were not to know. By merely dispatching the bombers, the Truman administration sent a warning to the Soviets.[5]

What was not perhaps realized in Washington in 1948 was how badly the Soviet Union had been hurt in the war. Soviet statistics on casualties stated the number to be between 6 and 8 million, but it became known after the fall of the Soviet Union that the total count was probably closer to 28 million. Nor was the extent of the destruction of the Soviet Union known. The last thing Stalin wanted was a war with anybody, though he was perfectly prepared to push his luck through bullying and intimidation if it could result in concessions from the western powers.

Clay's first recommendation was to send an armored column through to Berlin, daring the Soviets to interfere with it. In fact, notes William Stearman, there was a precedent for this kind of solution. Just prior to the Berlin blockade, the Soviets had demanded from the British that their troops carry identification cards with photographs, which apparently the British did not have, or did not want to produce, since the London agreement stipulated free access through all sectors of Berlin for the four occupation powers. As the British refused, the Soviets denied them access.

In response, the British filled a convoy of trucks with armed troops in battle dress and drove them up to the Soviet checkpoint where they were denied passage. The officer in charge of the column got out of his truck and gave an order to fix bayonets. Down the line, the clicking of bayonets being fixed could be heard. Then, the officer walked up to the barrier across the road, flipped open the rail, and the convoy went through. That was the last the British ever heard of that particular problem. Had the Americans tried a similar tactic, it is possible that the blockade could have been broken with land forces.

But the idea of breaking the blockade was nixed by Washington as too risky. The fear was that an attempt by American troops to force their way over land could easily result in a shooting war. And there were logistical problems, such as bridges that could be blown in front of an American advance. The Soviets could simply take out the bridge over the Elbe at Magdeburg, immobilizing an American force without firing a shot.

Instead, Clay came up with the idea that the city could be supplied from the air. In April, after Soviet provocations had become more persistent, U.S. forces had already been supplied by air for a short period with some two hundred tons of goods.

First known as the "LeMay Coal and Feed Delivery Service," after the commander of the United States Air Force in Europe, Lieutenant General Curtis E. LeMay, the Berlin airlift got off the ground on June 26. The operation was later given the code name "Operation Vittles."[6]

By the agreement of 1945, three air corridors had been set aside that connected the western occupation zones with Berlin: "Aircraft of the occupying powers might at any time make use of three corridors, of a width of twenty English miles each, which branch out from Berlin in a westerly direction, one towards Hamburg, one towards Bueckeburg and the third towards Frankfurt."

This is not to say that Clay had no misgivings about the airlift, according to Robert Lochner; feeding a city out of the air had simply never been tried before, and Clay particularly worried about carrying Berlin through the dark, cold winter months. Ernst Reuter helped reassure Clay. The two had developed a relationship of great trust. Reuter had become the personification of resistance to communism as he had been to Nazism a decade earlier.

Clay pointed out the enormous hardships this would mean to the Berliners. Reuter looked at him and said quietly, "You worry about the airlift. I will take care of the Berliners." That was enough for Clay. He confided to Lochner, "Only then did I recommend the airlift to Washington."

The experience of sitting 104 miles behind enemy lines was less than pleasant for the American troops, who could not even send their dependents out of the city since such a move could trigger panic among the Berlin population. A conscious decision was made that American soldiers and their families would share the hardships of the Berliners. In effect, these families were hostages in Berlin. Everybody had to sit tight.

At first, the airlift was seen as a stop-gap measure, a device that would gain the western Allies time at the negotiating table. In August, negotiators reached what they thought to be an agreement with the Soviets in Moscow. In reality, it was a compromise that would have severely weakened the allied position in Berlin. The Soviets would lift the blockade, Joseph Stalin promised, if the western Allies would accept the East mark as the common currency for all Berlin. The western negotiators said yes, provided the British, the French, and the Americans would share control of the currency. To this Stalin gave his oral assent. The agreement would certainly have undermined the confidence of the Berliners in the staying power of the western Allies, and fortunately it never went anywhere. When the final directive for the extension of the East mark arrived in Berlin from Moscow, it contained nothing about the common control of the currency, and without that Clay refused to sign.[7]

The logistics of the airlift were awesome. In fact, on paper the job looked impossible. How could 920,000 German families, almost 3 million people be fed? According to the original estimates, in order to survive, the city would need 2,000 tons of coal and 1,439 tons of food per day from June through October. For December, the total volume needed would be some 4,500 tons.[8] The planners thought a total of 2,000 tons would be their upper limit.

One of the first pilots to get a call was Jack Bennett, who was then with American Overseas Airline, which later became Pan Am. Bennett was sitting in his office in Frankfurt on June 26, 1948. It was about six o'clock in the evening when the telephone rang. A voice came on the line from Rhein-Main Air Base.

'Captain, can you fly coal to Berlin?'

My feet came off the desk and I said, 'Look, we are running a passenger airline, not a freight airline. I can't put coal in a passenger airplane. The coal dust will ruin the seats.'

The persistent voice at the other end said, 'How about putting the coal in sacks?'

'It is not going to work. The coal dust will still ruin the seats.'

'How about potatoes?'

'I can't do that. My New York headquarters will just raise hell if I fly freight.'

But the voice persisted, and finally Bennett relented under pressure. "I will do it under protest, but only under protest," Bennett said, wondering why the air force didn't use its own planes. The reason was, it turned out, that the base had all of two Skymasters. The rest had been dispersed after the war and were now all over the world. Bennett was asked to report by eight o'clock, and soon found his plane loaded with potatoes.

The operation would demand huge quantities of cargo planes. The standard C-47, the so-called "Goonie Bird," with a capacity of three tons of cargo was too small for this purpose. Only the big Douglas Skymaster C-54, with its ten-ton cargo capacity, would do. Unfortunately, at the beginning of the blockade, the 60th and 61st Troop Carrier groups from Headquarters U.S. Air Force Europe had only 102 C-47s and two of the newer C-54s due to the sharp cutbacks on U.S. military expenditures following the end of the war.[9]

So, an order went out to the far corners of the earth that all available C-54s were needed in Germany to participate in the rescue of Berlin. The planes started arriving from air bases as far away as Guam, Hawaii, and Panama, bringing the number to 225 C-54s in a few weeks. Among the first reinforcements for the transport squadrons in Germany were crews from Hawaii, who normally only flew in blue skies.

"It was a cowboy operation when I got there in July," recalls Gail S. Halvorsen. "It was a joke if you could take off after your buddy and get back to Rhein-Main before he did. It did not matter how you did it, just so you beat him." Halvorsen was a young lieutenant from Utah who was in Mobile, Alabama, flying transport aircraft to South America when he heard about the blockade of Berlin. He immediately volunteered to go to Germany, arriving in Frankfurt on July 8, 1948.

In the beginning, when the shortage of crews and aircraft was acute, pilots would fly three round trips in a 24-hour period from Rhein-Main air base. This took about seventeen hours, counting ground time, wind, and traffic delays. "We'd land at Tempelhof, stand by the airplane and the second the last sack of flour or potatoes was off the airplane, we'd get the engines started and head back for more," says Halvorsen. "We could not even go into the airport terminal. We used to go there in the beginning for

View of Tempelhof airfield.

A mobile snack station at Tempelhof.

refreshments and have some hot chocolate, but General Tunner prohibited that and set up portable snack bars on wheels to come by each aircraft."

Everything that was needed to keep the city running was flown in those machines. The average C-54 payload was twenty thousand pounds, usually consisting of coke or industrial coal sewn in burlap sacks, or food. At first, the Air Force had experimented with dropping the coal sacks from low-flying aircraft to save landing in Berlin, but that idea didn't work too well. All you get when dropping coal from an aircraft is a lot of coal dust.

But everything else was powdered—powdered milk, powdered eggs, powdered potatoes, powdered mushrooms. A famous cartoon from the time shows a stork flying from the West into Berlin. The stork has a diaper in its beak. No baby, though. Instead the diaper sports the label "Powdered Baby."

Of the airfields, only Tempelhof in the American sector and Gatow in the British sector were usable. The original runway at Tempelhof Airport had been extended, and two extra runways had to be built. But this was not sufficient. A third airport was clearly needed. The most suitable strip of land was found in the French sector close to the Tegel forest. Work was started immediately.

The early spirit of the airlift is captured in one of Jack Kohler's experiences, when he was a member of a counterintelligence unit. One of his cases was in West Berlin. Because Kohler's partner in the intelligence unit had been shot down repeatedly during the war, he refused to fly. Of course, there was only one way to get to Berlin, and that was on a C-54. So Kohler got to take the trip on a C-54 loaded with coal in duffel bags.

"We left from Fassberg air base in the British zone," he recalls. "There were four or five other guys sitting on these coal sacks, hanging on for dear life." The pilot and the co-pilot were from Hawaii. The pilot was an older man, comparatively speaking. At the age of around forty, he was "Pops" to everybody else, who were in their twenties.

Suddenly, they heard an incredible noise beneath the plane, and just as everybody was wondering what the hell was going on, the pilot pulled up and came back. "I think we just hit the red light on the top of Schoeneberg City Hall," Pops cheerfully informed his shaken passengers. "We've got a little problem, I don't think we got the wheels out. Don't worry, we'll just do a belly landing. I just talked to the tower. It's nice and soft, it has been raining, there is a lot of mud. So we'll just slide down there. All right, just hang on to those coal sacks. Don't worry about a thing."

The plane approached the airport again. Suddenly, the ground was there. The plane started rolling along and eventually came to a halt. Naturally, the passengers wondered what had happened to the undercarriage. "Well," said the pilot, "I saw that nice runway, and the fire engines out there, and I thought, maybe I'd take a chance, maybe the wheels are out and maybe the instruments are just fucked up." Which was indeed the case.

Kohler's co-passengers had all been in civilian clothes, so he didn't know what they were going to Berlin for. They hadn't said much during the trip, but on hearing Pops' account, they suddenly all came to life. "The guys who were sitting on top of the coal sacks started ranting and raving at the pilot. I thought they were going to kill him." It turned out they were aeronautical engineers from Patterson Air Force Base coming out to establish the ground control system. "Don't you realize that the goddam airplane was full of coal dust and if the wheels hadn't held, in one spark we would have gone up like the atom bomb," they yelled. "Gee, I never thought of that," answered Pops.

About a month into the airlift, Major General William H. Tunner arrived, and with him the airlift took on a more organized aspect. During the war, Tunner ran an airlift over the Hump, the Himalayas, that is, from India to China. He was the most experienced man in the United States as far as the transportation of cargo from point A to point B was concerned.

Securing "hot cargo": coal in burlap sacks.

U.S. Army

Tunner took over from Curtis LeMay as commander of the Combined Air-lift Task Force.

On one of his first trips, Tunner had the unpleasant experience of see-ing his airplanes stacking up in bad weather. Instead of being a minute apart, they were only thirty seconds apart. He immediately decreed that, from now on, if the airplanes got too close, and a pilot missed his first approach to Berlin, instead of making a second landing attempt, he would fly back to his base through the middle air corridor. "This was really smart," says Bennett. "Otherwise we would have had a lot of crack ups. But it really hurt to fly a full load back to Frankfurt."

One problem was the number of different types of aircraft in the opera-tion. The British did their bit in the airlift, which they appropriately named "Operation Plane Fare," but their planes were not standardized to the degree the American planes were. The Brits flew in a motley array of aircraft, Dakotas (as the British called the C-47), Lancaster bombers, and York bombers that were not built to carry coal. As a consequence, they had a hellish time arranging schedules. One very useful British contribu-tion was the flying boats, the Sunderlands, which were the only planes treated with sufficient anticorrosion protection to allow them to trans-port salt. They were landed on one of Berlin's many lakes. In the begin-ning, the French had no planes since they were all in Indochina.

As Tunner saw it, flying an airlift required precision work. The planes had to land like clockwork to get maximum usage out of them. The effort had to function like a mass production line. There was to be no mixing up of airplane types. A C-47 flies 160 miles an hour and a C-54 flies 200 miles an hour. Either you fly one or you fly the other. To avoid bunching up, the planes had to fly in rigid flight patterns through the three corridors.

What Tunner wanted was total predictability. As he writes in his auto-biography, *Over the Hump*, "This steady rhythm, constant as the jungle drums, became the trademark of the Berlin Airlift, or any airlift I have operated." And he continues, "I don't have much of a natural sense of rhythm, incidentally. I'm certainly no Fred Astaire, and a drumstick to me is something that grows on a chicken. But when it comes to airlifts, I want rhythm." According to Tunner's idea of an airlift, "There is no

U.S. Army

A British Sunderland is unloaded on Tegeler See.

frenzy, no flap, just the inexorable process of getting the job done. In a successful airlift, you don't see planes parked all over the place. They're either in the air, on loading or unloading ramps, or being worked on."

In the Berlin Airlift, Tunner found an ideal rhythm of landings at three-minute intervals at each airport. That's 480 landings a day, and of course an equal number of takeoffs. He wrote, "The real excitement of running a successful airlift comes from seeing a dozen lines climbing steadily on a dozen charts—tonnage delivered, utilization of aircraft, and so on—and the lines representing accidents and injuries going sharply down."[10]

Needless to say, the Soviets did their best to harass the airlift pilots. Soviet fighter planes would scramble and buzz their planes. One British plane crash was caused by a Soviet fighter plane that came too close to a passenger jet, killing all thirty-four on board. Meanwhile Soviet ground crews would conduct anti-aircraft exercises right next to the air corridors with shells exploding right and left. They would also try to interfere with radar by dropping aluminum strips and jamming the voice frequencies.

Bennett found himself selected for special treatment.

 *It was a beautiful summer evening, one of these evenings where you can lean back and put your little finger on the control wheel. We could see the airport runway right ahead. The radar was talking to us and everything was fine. Suddenly a blinding light hit us in the eyes. The light came from a powerful search light on a tower in the east. All you could do is drop your eyes down and look at the instruments. Sooner or later you would get below where they can hurt you.*

The kind of pressure under which the pilots operated had to find an outlet somehow. Predictably, there was a certain amount of rivalry among the pilots. One sore point was over pay, because the civilian pilots made much more than the army pilots. "I had a pilot come in once saying they wanted corridor pay," says Bennett. "I said, 'Listen, don't you do this. You guys are making maybe ten times as much as a military airlift pilot. *Time* magazine would take us apart if we do this. So just shut up.' Every six months, the chief pilot checked the pilots out, and I sent him home shortly after. He was no good anyway."

The airlift also produced its own banter, which helped pass the long hours, with its own particular mixture of jokes and rhymes. In those days, Bennett explains, there were rules against making jokes on the air. A joke could cost you a $15,000 fine from the Federal Communication Commission. But during the airlift, Tunner let the pilots say what they wanted and never subdued the wisecracking. He knew the kind of pressure they were operating under, and he knew that the monotony of the routine could be deadly. One Englishman, whose identification letters were TB, would break into a lugubrious cough when asked to identify himself. A Texan used to play his mouth organ. Cracks about the Russians would be couched in Dick Tracy slang so that only an American or a Brit would catch the joke.

▌ THE CANDY BOMBER ▌

Despite his tight schedule, Lieutenant Gail S. Halvorsen from Utah decided to embark on his own little adventure, which ended up turning into a pretty big story. As a pilot, he never did get to see much of the city or the people he was supplying day after day. "All we'd see from the air was the terrible devastation. We wondered how that many people could live in that rubble. We could recognize the Brandenburger Tor and the Reichstag, but that was about all." Like most of the other pilots, Halvorsen believed that the blockade would be of limited duration, so he was anxious to see some of Berlin before it was all over. One day, he decided to skip sleep and go back to Berlin to check the place out. He grabbed his camera and jumped on a friend's plane; there was a jeep waiting for him at Tempelhof.

Halvorsen wanted to get a snapshot of the difficult landing approach to Tempelhof. As he was taking his photos along the inside of the barbed wire, some thirty kids appeared on the other side of the fence. Some of them started to talk to Halvorsen in brand-new school English, asking what he was doing.

From his trips to South America, Halvorsen was used to being followed around by crowds of kids. In fact, the pilot routinely carried gum and chocolate as means of escape. But something about these kids was different from the ones he had seen before. "These kids hadn't had any gum or candy for months. They had barely enough to eat. While they were at the fence, not one asked for gum and candy. They were too proud to beg."

Halvorsen reached into his pocket and found only two sticks of gum.

He broke them in two and passed the four pieces through the barbed wire, waiting for a fight to break out. But it didn't happen. The kids who got the half stick carefully tore off the wrapper and the tinfoil, and passed it out so the others could smell it. Their eyes opened wide. "I couldn't believe my eyes. These kids would smell it and remember what it was like to have gum."

For 30 cents, Halvorsen figured he could give each kid a full stick of gum—and they could keep the wrapper. Only, he did not know just when he would see them again. About that time an airplane flew straight over his head and landed on the runway behind him. He got an idea. "Look, if you kids promise to share, I'll come back here tomorrow and drop some of that gum and chocolate out of my airplane right in this open space between the barbed wire and the apartment buildings." "Jawohl," came the cry from the children.

Just as he was starting back for his jeep, a small girl piped up. How were the children to know which was Halvorsen's plane? A good question since every few minutes an airplane landed at Tempelhof. Halvorsen thought for a moment. "Tomorrow when you see a big C-54 wiggle its wings back and forth, that's the one."

When he got back to Frankfurt, Halvorsen bought as much candy from the base exchange as his ration would allow. He told his two crew members he needed their rations also. They were suspicious at first, but then assented. "We loaded it up, and it was a double handful. It smelled so good I just could not wait to get back to Berlin." One small problem remained, however. What would happen if one of the kids was hit on the head by a piece of candy traveling at 110 miles an hour? It just might make the wrong impression. So to each package, Halvorsen carefully attached a small parachute made of a handkerchief. The plan was to drop them when coming in to land at Tempelhof using the flare chute. On the flight deck of the C-54, behind the pilot seat is a flare chute, like a stove pipe that comes out of the flight deck for emergency flares.

The first time Halvorsen and his crew were over Berlin, it was still dark. Next time, it was morning and clear. And there were thirty kids waiting. Halvorsen saw the kids in a flash, wiggled the wings of his plane, and shoved the candy out of the chute. "We couldn't tell whether we had managed to drop it before the airport's barbed wire fence. After unloading, we taxied out along the fence to take off and looked down, and there were three handkerchiefs waving through the barbed wire."

As each week's ration became available, Halvorsen's crew made their drops. The crew was sworn to secrecy so as not to get into trouble with their superiors. Meanwhile, on the ground, the children came back every day looking for more, and the crowds got bigger. On one trip, there was a blanket of fog over most of Western Europe, and Halvorsen's crew doubted they would be able to make the return flight. When Halvorsen ran into base operations at Tempelhof to find if he could land in Frankfurt because of the bad weather, he found a huge stack of mail on the table reaching almost to the ceiling. It was addressed to "Uncle Wiggly-Wings" and to the "*Schokolade Flieger,*" the "Chocolate Bomber."

For two weeks, the crew did not make any drops for fear of arousing attention from their superiors, but they still saved candy. They planned to do just one more drop. Having completed the drop, they came back to Frankfurt, where an officer was waiting for them, ordering Halvorsen to see his colonel. Halvorsen was chewed out for fifteen minutes.

"What have you been up to?" the colonel demanded. "I have been flying like mad," came the innocent answer. The colonel pulled out a copy of the *Frankfurter Zeitung* and threw it on the table in front of him. There was a photo of an aircraft with parachutes coming out of it. "You almost hit a German newspaperman in the head with a candy bar, and he has got the story all over the world. The general heard about it and called me, and I knew nothing. I looked stupid and now I'll never get promoted. Why didn't you tell me?" "I did not think you'd approve," Halvorsen replied. But the general thought it was a great idea and Halvorsen was ordered to keep going. Appropriately, the press dubbed Halvorsen's enterprise "Little Vittles," and the idea immediately caught on with the other pilots. Because of Halvorsen's idea, U.S. pilots earned the nickname, "The Raisin Bombers." On each run, the sky filled with little parachutes for Berlin's children.

Bennett's civilian pilots wanted to drop candy for the kids, too, but

UPI/Bettmann

The candy bomber, Lt. Gail S. Halvorsen from Utah, rigs his home-made parachutes with the parcels full of candy, gum, and chocolate.

there was no way he could allow them to do it. "We were flying under United States federal aviation rules. If we opened that cockpit window and threw out as much as a cough drop, it was a $15,000 fine."

When the story hit the United States, people started sending candy and handkerchiefs to Halvorsen at Rhein-Main. Some of the handkerchiefs were black-laced and perfumed because the news releases had pointed out that Halvorsen was a bachelor. Some candy shipped to Halvorsen from the United States came into the port of Bremerhaven where it was loaded into box cars for shipment to Rhein-Main. Sentries had to be posted to guard the precious cargo, which would be worth a fortune on the black market.

AP/Wide World Photos

Eagerly awaited by Berlin children, Lt. Gail Halvorsen's Skymaster approaches Tempelhof Airport.

Two German secretaries were assigned to handle all the letters from the children of Berlin, but the best letters were given to the pilots. One little girl, Mercedes, wrote that the cargo planes upset her white chickens, but she did not mind as long as she would get a candy parachute. She asked Halvorsen to hit her chicken coop and provided directions where to make the drop. After some unsuccessful saturation bombing, he had still not hit her home. Instead, they sent a packet by mail in Berlin.

Mercedes Wild still keeps Halvorsen's letter. She was that little girl of seven, and she still lives in the same house, where her mother's chicken coop was in the yard. "I got the idea to write a letter because the planes were so close that I could see the pilots, and I thought they could see the

Bob Hope and Irving Berlin perform "Operation Vittles," a song by Berlin, in Berlin. The title refers to the "sweet bombing of Berlin" by U.S. airlift pilots.

Robert E. Frye

white chickens." She still keeps Halvorsen's letter and calls it the jewel of her childhood.

Her own father had been a pilot and was killed over England. She had survived the bombing, and, understandably, was dead scared of airplanes. Until the age of fourteen, she was too terrorized of fire to even strike a match to light the gas stove. She had also lived through the two months of Russian occupation, and soldiers were not her favorites. But Halvorsen changed all that. "It was the best he could do for the Berliners. He opened the heart of the Berliners to the Americans," she says.

One boy sent a map and very precise instructions how to candy-bomb his home. "First you come down the canal. At the second bridge, turn right one block. I live at the house on the corner. I will be in the backyard every day at two o'clock." After several misses, in which the wind took his parachute, Halvorsen received another letter from the boy. "Look, you are a pilot. I gave you a map. How did you guys win the war anyway?" He, too, had a parcel mailed to him.

The kids in East Berlin had also heard about the chocolate bomber and were sending letters. Halvorsen decided that they, too, deserved some candy. Two weeks into that operation he was again called before his superiors to explain what he was up to. He told them. "You can't do that," he was told. "Why not?" asked Halvorsen. "The laws of gravity are the same on both sides of the borders." "The Russians have been complaining to the State Department that this is a dirty capitalist trick. They accuse us of trying to influence the minds of young people." "So I had to stop it," says Halvorsen.

Perhaps more than any other single action, Halvorsen's generous impulse established a bond between the pilots and the people of Berlin.[11]

▮ GROUND PERSONNEL ▮

The contribution of the ground personnel in the airlift often tends to go unrecognized, but if less glamorous than the pilots in the skies, the ground personnel were indispensable. Ground controllers had to direct the planes in all types of weather. To keep the planes flying, mechanics worked around the clock in eight-hour shifts. The planes had to be loaded, and intricate off loading routines had to be devised, using ten-ton truck trailers, so that the planes could be emptied and sent on their way again.

The weather can be lousy in Central Europe, and ingenious solutions had to be found to make up for this fact. To defrost the planes, a couple of giant jet motors, going full blast, mounted on a truck could do the job in a few minutes. To solve the problem of the many birds that congregated near the airport and represented a danger to the planes (by getting sucked into the propellers or smashed against the windshields), the British brought in trained falcons from the island of Malta.[12]

The airlift was a success, according to air traffic controller William Morrissey, in great part because of the development of the so-called Ground Control Approach. In 1948–49, airplanes were not supposed to be able to fly in bad weather. The Soviets did not block the air routes in part because they believed that winter weather would cripple the airlift. The Russians had some justification for this view. During the battle of Stalingrad, the German Luftwaffe had been unable to deliver three hundred tons of daily supplies to the German 6th Army, which was cut off and destroyed as a result.

A major problem was that there were no facilities for instrument landing in Berlin. Ground control facilities had to be built while the airlift was proceeding. "When I arrived a month or two after the airlift started, we did not have radar," says Donald Pastore, one of the Berlin air traffic controllers. He was eighteen at the time and was stationed in Las Vegas, Nevada, when he answered the call for volunteers for the Berlin airlift and found himself dispatched immediately. "I got to Berlin and they told me I was an air traffic controller. I said, 'What's that?' Then they gave me about a thirty minute briefing."

As the new controllers arrived, radar was being installed, a long-range artillery radar, which was modified for air traffic control, something that had never been done before. "Thank God, planes flew slow in those days, because the radar turned only five times a minute, so you only got a sweep every twelve seconds, which showed you where the plane was," says Pastore.

However, once it was up and running the radar was a lifeline for the pilots. Using information from the radar, the controllers would talk the plane down, telling the pilot whether he was left or right, high or low.

Landing in Tempelhof Airport was particularly tricky because the airport was in the middle of the city. Normally a plane has a glide slope, that is the angle the plane makes on final approach to landing, of about 2½ degrees. In Tempelhof, it was 4 degrees. To complicate matters, in the approach into Tempelhof, the pilots had to fly over a graveyard and then between the buildings. Inconsiderate as he was, Adolf Hitler had built the runway too short for U.S. pilots. Those in the control tower would actually lose sight of the planes as they approached.

"When the air controller told the pilot 'you are over touchdown,' they were actually a good distance down the runway. For many a pilot, when the Ground Control Approach operator said they were over touchdown, that's the first time they saw anything," says Pastore.

Ground Control Approach enabled planes to fly 'when birds walked,' as the saying had it. "In the fog, when the birds were walking, we were still flying," says James Spatafora, who was nineteen years old at the time and a mechanic PFC at Rhein-Main Air Base. "That is not an exaggeration. The birds were walking on the ramp, because they would not fly in that kind of weather, and we were flying in and out of Berlin."

How bad was the fog of Berlin? According to an air force communications command account, there were times when the fog was so dense that radar made it easier to land an aircraft than to navigate on the ground. One time, a C-54 aircraft had been directed to the Tegel airport in the French sector by mistake. The airport was closed due to dense fog, but the plane was nevertheless brought to a successful landing by ground control radar. The real problem came when the pilot called for a "follow me" jeep to lead him to the off-loading ramp. The jeep instantly got lost in the fog, and it took twenty-five minutes for it to locate the plane on the runway. The way back to the loading ramp took another half an hour as the jeep lost the giant cargo plane three times on the way.[13] That's how bad the fog could be. Says Halvorsen, "We never went to sleep on a weather briefing, I'll tell you that."

The 'round-the-clock airlift faced the most tremendous maintenance problems ever encountered in airplane operations. The facilities for support maintenance at Rhein-Main, which was the biggest air base in West Germany, were soon overburdened with requests for hangar space. The ground mechanics had to repair and maintain the aircraft outside in all kinds of weather with only make-shift windbreaks made of canvas on wooden structures to protect them from the elements. In the winter, their fingers would freeze to the cylinder heads.

"Especially early in the airlift, before we had sufficient crews and aircraft, the urgency of getting the supplies underway meant we would fly the airplanes with problems that normally we would not have flown," says Halvorsen. If the autopilot or the synchronization gauge, which shows when the engines are in sync, was out, well, so be it. Oil leaks higher than normal would be accepted, if they did not seem to present too much of a fire hazard. Gas leaks would also be accepted. There was a lot of stress on the wings from landing with large loads and often.

Finally, the landing gear took an immense beating. That's one item the crews had to take very seriously; particularly, they had to check for cracks in the nose gear. The landing strip at Tempelhof was built of pierced steel planking, huge sheets of steel, three feet wide by sixteen feet long, that interlocked to make it one big sheet. It was full of regularly spaced holes to let out water. It was very hard on tires. In dry weather, the braking action was pretty good. "If you got a little bit of water on it, before you knew it, you could lock a wheel, and then that thing would be like a potato grater," says Halvorsen.

Only basic maintenance was performed in Berlin. Every fifty hours of flying time, the planes were checked at the bases in West Germany. Two hundred–hour checks would be more complete: the planes would be flown to Burtonwood in Britain, where the controls were cleaned up and the spark plugs changed. After one thousand hours of flying time, the planes were returned to the United States for a complete overhaul.

James Spatafora recalls that some of the scenes were straight out of a Laurel and Hardy movie. "When you could not start the airplane, you tried to turn the propeller, just like you did on a model airplane, by having a big, heavy bungee cord attached to a little cup on the propeller tip. Then you would use a jeep to pull on the heavy cord to flip the propeller just like a model airplane to get the engine started." For the landing gear, Spatafora remembers, "we used to go out and beg for pieces of German lumber and use our belts and rope to tie the landing gear down so it would not collapse on takeoff." As for the hydraulics, a little over a month into the operation, the coal dust and the flour dust started clogging the planes' controls and the pulleys, forming a kind of hydraulic fluid paste. When that happened, the response of the control column became slow. "It was worse than dried chewing gum," recalls Spatafore.

First, the ground crews tried to sprinkle the coal with water to cut down the dust, but found that the airplane could hardly get off the ground, as this added too much weight. A better solution was to fly with the escape hatches out along the fuselage, which helped clean out the coal dust. On the ground, everything had to be cleaned out with brooms and mops, since they did not have vacuum cleaners.

"Our squadron used to have two 'suicide squads,'" recalls Spatafora. "If an airplane had severe troubles when it left Rhein-Main and lost its complete hydraulic system or it lost an engine, we used to get volunteers who would take turns to go up to Berlin and bring back the airplane to

Rhein-Main because the airplane was not safe to fly with a regular crew. We would volunteer to go up there with experienced crews, experienced pilots, and co-pilots, and they would try to figure out what was wrong and see if there was some way we could fly the airplane back to Rhein-Main to get the proper repairs."

In an enterprise the size of the airlift there will be accidents. Spatafora witnessed one of them at close quarters.

I had just come back around 4:30, and I had about an hour and a half to fix a worn-out nose wheel. I got the airplane jacked up, I changed the wheel and the tire. I had just filled out the paperwork, and had the airplane loaded with gasoline and cargo. It was all ready to go again.

It was late in the afternoon, and it was real hot. We were all tired. The airplanes were getting ready to take off. I ran across the taxi way, which was parallel to the runway, and I was just going to go up and get a cup of coffee and a doughnut. I was through for the day 'till the airplanes came back around 10:30.

Earlier in the afternoon, there had been a small brushfire at the end of the runway. Dry grass had caught fire, and the fire department had been called in to put out the fire so that the smoke would not obscure the 6:00 o'clock takeoff of the planes. By six, the fire was out, and the trucks were preparing to go back to base. The sun was low in the western sky and the airplanes were taxiing towards the east, so they had the sun behind them. They also had their landing lights on.

Then things started to go wrong. Blinded by the sunset and by the landing lights of the planes, the fire truck headed straight towards the leading airplane and almost ran into the number two propeller, right next to the body of the aircraft. At the last minute, the truck veered off, but didn't manage to clear propeller number one. The truck came straight into the propeller, which went through the engine of the fire truck and through the driver's compartment, killing the GI driver instantly and throwing out the German co-driver, leaving the rest of the German fire-fighters alone in the back of the truck.

Spatafora watched it all unfold.

Now you have three Germans in the back of a fire truck that does not have a driver. The fire truck continued on without a driver, down the ramp, with the engine still running. It went ahead and went under the wing of my airplane and tore out the bottom of my wing and tore off the left wing landing gear, and the airplane, once the landing gear was torn off, just sat down on the fire truck, which had the engines still running. I had just put twelve hundred gallons of gasoline in the airplane, and the gasoline just poured all over that hot fire truck.

By some miracle neither the airplane nor the fire truck caught fire. Police watched the airplane all night while the twelve hundred gallons of gasoline drained out of the torn wing, which is the gas tank of the C-54. When that was all drained and evaporated and the battery on the fire truck was absolutely dead, then we went ahead and used the big nylon bands to pick up the airplane and pull the fire truck out.

Loading and unloading had to be done with equal precision and speed. The coal was carried in army surplus dufflebags, which would be loaded, and then put on an Army tractor trailer that could carry ten tons. To accommodate huge, unwieldy machinery like earth-moving equipment and bulldozers, they were cut into sections with acetylene torches, put on board the transport planes, and then rewelded in Berlin.

Harold Nance was a corporal with the U.S. Army's 24th Transportation Battalion, stationed in Frankfurt, the primary ground support organization. Two of the battalion's units, with 104 vehicles, supported the airlift at Wiesbaden Air Force base, the remainder of the battalion, another three hundred vehicles, gave ground support to the Rhein-Main operation. "We worked seven days a week around the clock," recalls Nance. "Without leave or rest or recuperation period, working shifts of twelve to eighteen hours per day. We had a mandatory six-hour 'bunk fatigue.' That means you'd sleep for six hours. In the Air Force, they flew for six months and then got relieved and went back to the States. As ground troops, we had to continue to work."

From June 26 through November 1948, there was a shortage of heavy truck driver personnel to drive the tractor trailers in support of the mission. The battalion constantly took on light truck drivers from other units in West Germany and trained them to drive the heavy vehicles. Even qualified drivers had to be retrained to back up the tractor trailers on their blind side to avoid damage to the C-47s, due to the design of the wings of the aircraft. "All of the drivers were accustomed to backing up from the driver's side of the vehicle, rather than the blind side. There were some crunches," Nance says laconically.

There was an ongoing scramble to obtain truck parts from any and every source available. Mostly it meant cannibalizing parts from other trucks. Unfortunately, the vehicles had been designed for hard surfaces and had two-wheel drive and were thus not suited for the terrain at Rhein-Main, which was primarily mud. When the environment changed from summer to winter, to rain, ice, and snow, the vehicles were constantly bogged down in mud with snapped axles and had to be towed. The men also had to replace starters constantly. Special trailers carried nothing but replacement axles and starters. To cut down on the mud, engineers put down PSP surface, the steel matting surface that was also used for the landing strip at Tempelhof. Of course, none of the vehicles were equipped with heaters.

In Berlin, the freight handlers were Germans and displaced persons. The second the plane stopped at the ramp and the crew chief had run back and opened the back door, a semitrailer would back up to the door and people would pile in. It was dangerous work; a lot of fingers got caught. The record for unloading ten tons was under ten minutes, with the average running at fifteen minutes. The powdered milk and eggs were packed in cardboard drums of about thirty gallons. Recalls William R. Michaels, a flight engineer, operating out of Celle air base, "We always knew when the cargo was powdered milk or eggs because the hands, faces and pockets of the civilian personnel loading the cargo would be covered with a white or yellow powder due to an accidentally (!) broken container lid. The loaders were Yugoslav displaced persons. We made no complaint about that. We knew they were on short rations."

Pilferage, of course, was a problem. Personnel would find little parcels of food hidden all over in Tempelhof Airport. Shoes also had a way of disappearing. To remedy that situation, shoes were sent in shipments of all left shoes in one batch, and a week later a shipment of right shoes would follow. That stopped the theft of shoes.

Michaels' most unusual cargo was twenty thousand pounds of fresh green herring, packed in ice, which melted and was absorbed into his plane's plywood flooring. "I was very happy when it became time for my aircraft to be returned to the U.S. for major inspection," he says.

∎ THE BERLINERS AND THE AIRLIFT ∎

When the Russians imposed the blockade, every Berliner had to engage in some soul-searching. First he was asked to translate his savings into a new currency, the Deutschmark. Then he had to wonder whether the airlift would be strong enough to keep him from starving. And he also had to worry about the staying power of the western Allies. If the Allies moved out, it did not take too much imagination to see what would happen to people who had thrown their lot with the West and with democracy.

Throughout the airlift, Ernst Reuter worked tirelessly to remind his fellow Berliners why it would be worth paying the price for freedom. "With all the means at our disposal," he told a rally early in the blockade, "we shall fight those who want to turn us into slaves and helots of a party. We have lived under such slavery in the days of Adolf Hitler. We want no return to such times."[14]

During the blockade, the Communist propaganda machine switched into high gear. Soviet agents were busy spreading the rumor that Mongol troops would be returning to Berlin and that Berliners would experience a repeat of 1945 if they did not give up their futile resistance. The Russian "Radio Berlin" falsely reported on plane crashes and spread the word that West Berlin's population was in a state of revolt and that allied troops opened fire on the demonstrators.

At the same time, the Russians offered to give ration books to all Berliners who would like them, trying to break the solidarity of the West Berliners. Less than three percent, however, applied for East German ration cards.

In what was surely a small case of divine retribution, one of the first to experience the hardships of the Soviet blockade was Marshal Sokolovski himself, whose headquarters was in Babelsberg and derived its heating from a plant in the American sector. His heat was immediately turned off, forcing the marshal to find new living quarters. In a further instance of poetic justice, by mistake his belongings were routed through the American sector when he moved. They were immediately confiscated.[15]

For the Berliners, who had learned to fear the sound of airplanes during the war, bringing with them as they did a rain of death and destruction, the steady, around-the-clock drone of the airlift came to be a sound

Children play the new game in town: Airlift.

of reassurance, signifying the city's lifeline to the West. Now, the problem was those days when the noise stopped, as it did through some periods in November. Silence meant that no supplies were coming through.

For their part, to augment their outside supply of foodstuffs, Berliners took to gardening on a large scale. Every plot of soil was planted with vegetables, including flower pots on the window ledges. Some Berliners even covered their balconies with soil for gardening. Every fresh vegetable counted. Trees were cut down for firewood. Electricity was available only a few hours a day in most districts.

The seriousness of the food shortage in Berlin was perhaps best illustrated when, in March 1949, a British York, carrying a load of coffee beans and lard, failed in its approach at Gatow airfield in the British sector, and crashed, killing all crew members. Police had to hold Berliners back from the wreckage while the salvage crew got the bodies out. In the meantime, every head of family was allowed to stake a claim on the ground surrounding the wreck, which covered a considerable area. Every coffee bean was carefully picked up. The Berliners even cooked the surface earth in small pans over a fire so the melted lard could be drained off through a sieve.[16]

Though severely hampered by the blockade, local industry refused to give up. Production fell to between half and a quarter of its normal volume, and about 30 percent of the Berliners were left without work.[17] Still, some thirteen thousand tons of goods worth a quarter of a billion Deutschmarks were sent back to West Germany with the proud stamp "Made in Blockaded Berlin," showing a bear, the traditional symbol of the city, breaking its chains.

The hardships of the blockade and the shared danger encouraged a common bond between the American forces and the Berliners, a feeling of being in it together. "Immediately we became integrated into the German surroundings," says Teddy Mohr. "We all lived in German houses. When there was not coal enough to fire the electric plants, we had two hours of electricity out of 24. These hours were announced. What you had to do was set the alarm for two o'clock, because the electricity came on at 2:30 and you might have a lot of washing and ironing to do. That immediately made the Germans and the Americans closer to each other."

I remember going to our Commissary. There was always a box of candles at the door with a sign saying 'Take what you need.' You read by that or you did not read. Gasoline was rationed. Those of us who had privately owned vehicles got five gallons of gas a month. That was it. You did not drive your car empty—if you saw an American standing on the corner, you took him with you. There was a feeling of togetherness that only comes in a situation like that.

Again, RIAS proved itself a vital instrument for keeping the Berliners informed. During the periods when the electricity was out, radio vans and trucks were strategically located throughout the city, broadcasting the RIAS message.

At the hospital, Dr. Mattheis recalls, the long periods without electricity created their own problems. "We had to feed our babies by the light of small candles. The babies started coughing. First I did not know why until I realized it was due to these rather bad candles we used."

When an operation proved to be necessary during the dark period, the hospital had to call the electrical plant. "We have to do an appendectomy. We need electricity." "O.K., how long will you need it?" "Three quarters of an hour." Electricity for the hospital meant electricity for the whole neighborhood. Lights went on, and everybody looked at the hospital and was pleased. "When we neared the end of the three quarters of an hour, somebody said 'It will not do, we need another quarter of an hour more.' Again we called the electricity plant."

In Berlin, the intensified superpower conflict had meant that the new city government never actually got a chance to govern. While the Russians did not dispute the election results, they raised questions and started investigations of every one of the candidates they did not particularly care for, and used their veto power in the allied Kommandatura liberally.

Finally, because of the continued Soviet use of intimidation, including mob attacks on democratic-minded parliamentarians, such as the popular Ernst Reuter, the Berlin City Council ended up moving out of the city hall in the Russian sector and into the British sector. In December 1948, elections were authorized for West Berlin alone, and Reuter could finally take up his rightful position as governing Mayor.

Time and again, Reuter demonstrated what a remarkable politician he was, one of the rare breed who can demand sacrifices from his people and still retain their affection. When, in March, a severe cold spell suddenly came on the city; the military government was willing to grant another issue of coal, but Reuter denied the offer. His argument was that the Berliners knew they might need the coal reserves for other things, and, furthermore, they wanted to show that they would not give in.

The city now had two city parliaments, two police departments, and two universities. The intellectually repressive atmosphere of Berlin University led to a walk-out by students and teachers and the founding of the Free University in November 1948.* As one farsighted Berliner, Ruth Andreas Friedrich, noted in her diary in September 1948, "Perhaps by tomorrow we will have two city governments and along the sector boundary a Chinese wall with battlements and watch towers."[18]

▌ THE RUSSIANS GIVE UP ▐

As the months passed and it became clear that the airlift was successful in beating the blockade, the Soviets began having second thoughts about the matter. Before they initiated the blockade, the Soviets had been importing processed steel, large amounts of chemicals, and quantities of food from the western part of Germany. These goods were no longer

---

*Due to the repression of academic and democratic freedoms in the Berlin University in the Soviet sector, a group of students as well as leading political and academic figures took the initiative in the spring of 1948 to establish a new free university in Berlin. The Berlin City Council voted overwhelmingly in favor of creating such an institution in May, and *Freie Universitaet Berlin* was incorporated on November 4, 1948.

available, and without them, what was already a severe economic condition in Eastern Europe worsened with the East German workers unable to fulfill their quotas. Overall, the policy had been counterproductive. Rather than prevent the formation of a West German government, the blockade concentrated these efforts. And the resistance of the Berliners had been strengthened.

To drive the message home to the Russians, the Americans played their own little games. It was common knowledge that Berlin was crawling with spies paid by the Russians, many of them busily engaged counting planes in the airlift. Every plane had a parking space and the number of the parking place was painted on the tail of the airplane. James Spatafora's plane, for instance, had the number 9. Watchful spies would know that number 9 had made three runs that day.

"We thought we would have a little bit of fun with the spies," says Spatafora, recalling how the crew would change the tail numbers on the planes. It was a four-hour round trip between Frankfurt and Berlin, plus time to load and unload—roughly six hours total. One day, five planes might carry the same number, bedeviling anyone trying to make a record. "How the hell could the plane go empty back to Rhein-Main and in twenty minutes get loaded up and come back again? We'd just drive the spies crazy."

In the end of the spring of 1949, the Soviets started sending out signals that they might be willing to reconsider the blockade. Field Marshal Sokolovski provided a classic example of double-talk when asked about his feelings on the blockade. "There is not and never was a blockade of Berlin," he stated. "The expensive airlift transportation of food and coal from West Germany to Berlin by the Allies is an unnecessary measure for the sole purpose of propaganda. Its existence is not justified nor is it necessary."

At midnight on the night of May 11–12, 1949, the blockade was lifted, and the first trains and trucks started arriving, carrying fresh fruit and produce from West Germany. They were greeted with jubilation by the Berliners who had stayed up to greet them.

Just to make sure that the lifting of the blockade was not another Soviet trick, the Allies continued the airlift for another four months,

German Information Center

Victory celebration at Rhein-Main Airport in Frankfurt.

building up strategic reserves of raw material, fuel, and food. During the blockade, Kraftwerk West in particular had been in a shambles. Most of the electricity of the city used to come from the East. When that source of power was cut off during the blockade, it meant that the very old Kraftwerk West plant could supply only a few hours worth of electricity a day.

One piece of equipment essential for the repair was a large axle for a generator. During the blockade, that would have to be flown in, but there was no airplane big enough. General Clay, who was an engineer, even got himself a drawing of an airplane fuselage and tried to demonstrate how the axle could be flown in. Actually, it turned out to be impossible, and in the end the axle was one of the first pieces of equipment to be trucked in on the autobahn.

The airlift was a remarkable technological feat. On April 16, the so-called Easter Parade broke all previous records. Tunner had ordered a maximum effort for twenty-four hours; he was hoping to reach the goal of landing one aircraft in Berlin for every one of the day's 1,440 minutes. He fell two flights short and had to settle for 1,398 missions on that day, with 12,941 tons of coal and supplies delivered (the equivalent of 600 railway box cars) and 789,545 miles flown without a single incident.[19]

Altogether, over the fifteen months of the airlift, according to the Military Airlift Command's official history, a total of 2,325,509.6 tons of cargo was flown to Berlin—1,586,029.3 tons of coal, 536,705.3 tons of food, and 202,775.0 tons of other goods. Of this tonnage, the Americans were responsible for 77 percent, and the British for 23 percent.[20]

The experience gained during the airlift was crucial in the development of civilian flying. Notes Bill Morrissey, "A lot of the procedures that

What a difference a day makes . . . twenty-four hours after the Soviets lifted the blockade the first truck convoy with a shipment of CARE packages is greeted by Berliners.

were developed at the time were used to upgrade the air traffic control system in the United States," notably the Ground Control Approach.

Just one of the things today's air travelers take for granted is the torch that looks like a magic wand that's used in aviation to park the airplanes. "We invented those things at Rhein-Main in 1948," says Morrissey. "We took a regular GI flashlight and glued on some pieces of Plexiglas, so you could make a battery-operated torch that the pilot could see. It would be just like an elephant boy with a big elephant. The pilot had his head stuck out the window, looking for this dim glow that would lead him to the parking place," says Morrissey.

The safety record of the airlift was extraordinary. Tanner's tight organization paid off. Compared with the operations of the U.S. Air Force in all theaters, the airlift had an accident rate of less than half the air force average during its eleven months. Operation Vittles accounted for 5 percent of the total air force flying hours during this period, but only 2 percent of the major accidents during the same period. Despite this impressive safety record, the airlift also had costs. The airlift claimed seventy airplane crew members, thirty-one of them Americans, and eight German ground personnel.

One joint institution that did survive the airlift (the other was Spandau Prison, which housed convicted Nazi war criminals) was the Air Safety Center, which had been set up to guarantee safety in the air corridors, and which was staffed around the clock by a British, a French, an American, and a Soviet air controller. Before a plane would enter one of the air corridors, the controllers would notify the Soviet officer with a slip holding its number and route. The officer would relay the specifics to the Soviet military flight control and to the East Germans. The slip would be given back with a Soviet signature.

During the airlift, the Soviets would acknowledge the flights without comment. Later, in times of tension, as in the early 1960s, slips might come back with the ominous message, "Security not guaranteed," but the survival of the institution was seen as a sign that the Soviets did not want the situation to get out of hand.

The overall impact of the airlift was to bring the population of West Berlin and the occupation troops together in an enterprise of shared sacrifice. Up until then, despite a measure of contacts, there had been a clear division between Berlin's three million citizens and the thirty-thousand-strong western occupation force. More than anything, the shared fight for freedom brought to an end the division between occupiers and the conquered. As one contemporary historian puts it, "From this solidarity came a mutual respect and understanding, a working together, which never in history has followed so closely on the ending of a bitter war."

To commemorate the event, a giant sculpture of an arch, ending in three prongs, was erected in front of Tempelhof airfield, with a corresponding one in Main air base in Frankfurt, symbolizing the allied airlift. A plaque bears the names of those who gave their lives so that West Berlin would remain free.

The achievement of Lucius Clay cannot be overestimated, nor can the esteem the Berliners held him in. At a time when many in the State Department and in the Pentagon were inclined to give up Berlin as indefensible, Clay was adamant that the airlift would succeed. Says

Airlift Memorial in Berlin, nicknamed "Hunger Harke" (hunger rake) by the Berliners. A similar monument was erected at Rhein-Main air base in Frankfurt to symbolize the other end of the bridge through the air.

IN-Press/dpa/German Information Center

translator Robert Lochner, "How lucky we all were that, at such a crucial time, two men of the gigantic stature of General Clay and Mayor Reuter were in the responsible positions. On the day that Clay left Berlin in May 1949, he paid a call to Reuter to demonstrate his respect for him. Don't forget, this is military government. Clay's word was God in Germany."

The Harvard economist John Kenneth Galbraith, who worked closely with Clay during the war, later said that Clay was "the ablest politician ever to wear the uniform of the United States Army."

William Morrissey sums up the experience of being in the airlift.

I was nineteen years old when I started. I did not realize what was happening at the time. Like most people, you have a job to do, you do it and that's it. It was years later when I realized what had really taken place. In 1972, my wife and I were in Dahlem, and we rode the military train up to do some sightseeing. We went into a bar in West Berlin. 'You are American?' they asked. I answered in the affirmative. I told them I was in the air force. 'Very good.' Then I told them that I was part of the American airlift, die Luft-bruecke. *After that, the bar was mine.*

THE OTHER ALLIES

It is perhaps too easy to conclude that Berlin was an American-run show. It was that to the extent that without American support, there would have been no defense of Berlin. The French and the British contributions, however, cannot be overlooked.

The Allies' attitudes towards the Germans were widely divergent in the beginning. Arriving in Berlin in 1945, American soldiers found it relatively easy to let bygones be bygones. Unlike the French and the Russians, Americans had not had their territory occupied and ravaged. Unlike the British, they had not seen their cities and towns bombed relentlessly. Being protected by an ocean meant that Americans simply did not share much of the bitterness felt by the other Allies. Add to this President Roosevelt's view that the American boys had to be brought home as quickly as possible, preferably within two years.

"The British, when they went into Germany, were in a very bitter mood," says Lord Annan, who at that time was a key figure in the British military government. "They felt they had done all they could to help Germany get over the Treaty of Versailles, which was undoubtedly unjust, but what had been the reward? The reward was Hitler." In fact, Winston Churchill was not even in the mood for the Nuremberg trials. He would have preferred to shoot the lot.

According to Lord Annan, the attitude of the administrators could per-

haps be called colonial in style. The British Control Commission thought
Germany was going to be under occupation for twenty years. The British
envisaged the democratic re-education of Germany, starting at the bottom, with the *Kreis* level, then the land level, then finally, there would be
elections in the occupied zone.

Obviously the British thought they would be in Germany directing,
controlling, and helping the growth of democracy in the country for a considerable time, very much in the style of the British colonies in the period
between the wars, during which time it was planned that the colonies
would eventually become self-governing. This prompted an indignant
Kurt Schumacher to note that Germany should not be treated like an
African colony.

Even so, on the local level the British were perhaps more in tune than
the Americans with political developments, such as when in 1946 the
Soviets forced the merger in the eastern sector of the SPD and the Communist Party to create the SED and caused trouble in the subsequent
Berlin elections of October 1946. Though the Germans tried desperately
to interest the Americans in what the Soviets were up to, the American
attitude, especially General Clay's, was that Russia was still an ally and
still to be trusted.

It was undoubtedly significant that the British government at the time
was a Labour government that did not hesitate to throw its weight behind
its ideological soul mates among the majority of German Social Democrats, who were against a merger with the Communist Party.

Among other things, the British managed to find an old article in an
obscure German newspaper in Sweden, in which Walter Ulbricht had
praised the Nazi-Soviet nonaggression pact and claimed that the war
fought by the British and the French was an imperialist war. The British
immediately published it in Berlin to suggest that Ulbricht was not the
paragon of principle he professed to be.

What changed the British colonial attitude towards Germany was the
winter of 1946–47. It was disastrously cold. British finances were in desperate straits since the lend-lease agreement with the Americans came to
a halt as soon as peace was signed. Britain had started the war with
debts of 469 million pounds and plentiful gold and dollar reserves. By the

Field Marshal Sir Bernard Law Montgomery, Military Commander of British-occupied Germany, reviews British troops in Berlin with Soviet guest.

end of the war, Britain was 3.5 billion pounds in debt and barely any reserves. As Prime Minister Clement Attlee put it, prospects were "grim, grimmer even than the worst nightmares of most experts." The Americans did extend to the British over $3.7 billion in credits, but because of the harsh terms of the American loans, no sooner did the dollars flow, than they flowed out again owing to the insistence of the Americans on pound-sterling convertibility.

One major outlay was the cost of occupying Germany. The ironic fact was that the British had to tighten their own belts in order to feed their former enemies. In 1946, Britain had to introduce bread rationing, something that had never even been seen during the war. Britain was broke.[1]

By the end of 1946, it became clear that the British could no longer afford to go on in this way, particularly since they were, at the same time, involved in Greece, where Britain was supporting the royalist exile government against a Communist-led resistance movement. Since the British had large areas of German industry in their occupation zone, which included the Ruhr district, but not many food producing areas, a merger with the Americans made sense, and the bizone was born.

The French government initially was even more determined than Britain to remove Germany as a threat. French statesman Georges Clemenceau had stated at the beginning of the century, "The trouble with the Germans is that there are 20 million of them too many." Says Philippe Moreau Defarges of the French Institute for International Relations, "France after World War II was determined to punish Germany. At that time, it was believed that the first enemy of France was Germany."

The French saw a direct line running from Bismarck in the nineteenth century to Adolph Hitler in the twentieth. During World War I, Charles de Gaulle had been a prisoner of war in Germany. As he expressed it, "France has been invaded three times in a lifetime. I do not want ever to see the establishment of a Reich again."

The French emphasis was on reparations and on limiting German production. The French opposed the idea of a bizone based on the argument that such an arrangement would create a central government in Germany, and the French were still hoping that the country could be divided into four separate states. The French wanted a weak Germany or, rather, no Germany at all. Thus, in the early days, it was not just the Russians who obstructed the Four Power government, it was the French as well.

What brought the Allies together was the blockade, which made it clear that the country threatening Europe was not Germany anymore, but the Soviet Union.

During the Berlin Airlift, the British certainly did their part. They flew about one third of the flights (and a fourth of the tonnage) in the Hamburg/Berlin corridor. One of the young British pilots was the businessman Freddie Laker, who was twenty-six at the time.[2] "He had bought some tattered old Halifax bombers, and converted them to carry cargo. They were bent and ancient aircraft that looked like they could not survive another flight," recalls Jack Bennett.

"Our airplanes were all wartime airplanes," concedes Laker. They were not very reliable. "They were built for a wartime operation where they thought they were lucky if the could get six flights out of them. So they were not built to stay." Laker operated six old converted Halifax bombers he had bought from the government for 100 pounds each. He painted them silver, and hauled mostly oil drums, eight tons a flight. He was the first British civilian operator on the operation and the last off.

The British government had nationalized all air transport, and all its cargo planes were in use elsewhere. "Of course, because we were not allowed to have these fashionable aeroplanes and have our own airlines, we used government surplus bombers," recalls Laker with some irony. The government had to contact private cargo operators like Laker, who almost had the status of illegals, to rent their war surplus airplanes. The Berlin Airlift brought home to the British government that there had to be room for independent operators. "The Airlift was the catalyst that set off the need for Britain to have an independent airline operation."

"These airplanes really were not built for flying in icing conditions," recalls Laker.

The Old Halifax did not even have windscreen wipers. The windscreens were all iced up. You had to open the side windows and the little clear vision panels and keep them open to look out the side. To keep the ice off the wings we used to put paste on the wings. The hail and heavy rain would just blow it off. When the old girls were getting buffeted around and covered in ice, staying within the corridor was quite something.

Though their airplanes may have been rickety, the spirit of the British should never be underestimated. After all, this was the nation that produced the immortal lines

> *The mustache of Adolf Hitler*
> *Could hardly have been littler,*
> *Was a thought that kept reoccurring*
> *To Field Marshall Goering.*

For the British, the airlift was simply an extension of the war. Many of the pilots were RAF pilots who had flown bombing runs over Germany.

Recalls Laker, "All of the people who were flying had been in the Royal Air Force. It was the old squadron camaraderie that came over. They thought they were back in the Air Force. They went back to war."

Among the most famous pilots flying for the British was Donald Bennett, an Australian, who had been the leader of the Pathfinder Force during the war. They were planes that came in ahead of the bombers and marked out the target area with flares like lightposts. The difference this time was they were risking their lives on behalf of the Berliners.

On one occasion, Donald Bennett took off from Wunstorf airfield when the flying controls locked on his Tudor airplane: he could not move the controls, the rudder, the ailerons, or the elevator. As he had no parachute, he flew his Tudor fully loaded around the airfield and landed the plane without a scratch using only the trimming tabs and the engines. "Everyone else who has tried it has died," says Laker.

Altogether, Laker's company did just under five thousand flights. When Laker talks about it, one gets the impression of a true entrepreneur who is in love with flying. After the end of the blockade, he sold the planes for scrap metal, which was to be used to make pots and pans. Always a good businessman, he sold them for more than he paid for them.

The French contribution was smaller: The French had no airplanes, since they were all in Indochina. Actually, they did have one plane, which they used for supplying their own garrison. It didn't last long, however. As rumor would have it, a British pilot bribed a lorry driver to back into the French plane, which had proved to be quite a bit of a nuisance and kept interfering with the flight patterns.[3]

The planned new airport to supplement Gatow and Tempelhof was situated in the French sector, at Tegel Field. One obstacle to its construction was a Soviet radio antenna located in the French sector, blocking the airport. The Russian personnel, however, refused to leave or relocate when told the area had to be cleared. This problem was solved by the French in a rather blunt fashion: they let the Russians know that they were going to blow up the antenna, and that they would have five minutes to evacuate, which they immediately proceeded to do. When reproached by Soviet Marshal Koniev, who asked the French commandant General

Ganeval how he could do such a thing, the unflappable Frenchman answered, "With dynamite, of course."

There were, of course, moments of friction. During the airlift, U.S. flyers found out that they were flying in loads of wine for the French, which the Americans justifiably considered a luxury that took up space for more important cargo. When challenged on the point, the French responded that this was their national food. The Americans started muttering that their national food was Coca-Cola.

Looking back at this early period, it is ironic that France, which in the beginning was the odd man out, ended up having the vision that would shape the future of Europe, while Britain continued to cling to its empire and later its commonwealth. Having realized that its plans to divide Germany were counterproductive, the French moved quickly to create links with Germany, to integrate the country into a new Western Europe. If the Ruhr district could not be internationalized, at least it could be so closely intertwined with France and the rest of Europe that the Germans could not go to war anymore.

The result, in 1951, was the European Coal and Steel Community, the precursor of the EEC. "There they overtook the British," says Lord Annan. "The British threw away the leadership of Europe and the French moved in."

Each sector of Berlin had its own atmosphere. The differences between the three approaches are perhaps best summed up by Gerhard Kunze, who later became a high-ranking city official. "American policy was policy by heart, British policy was policy by brain, and French policy was policy by law."

THE BERLIN UPRISING

The end of the airlift brought on a new era in German history. Approved by the western Allies, a new *Grundgesetz,* or Basic Law, took effect on May 23, 1949, in the western zones, which were merged. The three zones officially became the Federal Republic of Germany in September of that year, a reluctant move by the West Germans, who feared that this would cement the permanent division of Germany. Politicians in the West were careful to stress that their new Basic Law was not actually a constitution as such, but a temporary measure, stating that "the entire German people are called upon to achieve in free self-determination the freedom and unity of Germany."

In October, the East German dictatorship founded its own German Democratic Republic, a misnomer if there ever was one. The move was delayed until after the foundation of the western state, which allowed the East German government to claim that the West Germans had betrayed the idea of German unity. They now claimed to represent the only true Germany, a communist Germany, of course.

The eastern sector of Berlin was declared the capital of the GDR and was increasingly integrated into the East German system, a clear violation of the Four Powers Agreement of 1944, according to which Berlin was to be jointly administered by all. The Federal Republic government, meanwhile, set up shop in the small town of Bonn.

West Germany was no longer under military government, which was replaced by an Allied High Commission. Thus General Lucius Clay was at this time succeeded by U.S. High Commissioner John J. McCloy, a former president of the United Nations Bank for Reconstruction and Development.[1] In Berlin, city government received wide authority to run the city in its day-to-day affairs, though liaison officers remained as the link between the governing mayor and the military commands. The purpose of the Berlin garrison would from now on be not to govern, but to deter aggression, prevent civic disturbances, and defend the city. The first U.S. Commander, Berlin, to serve under this new arrangement was Major General Maxwell D. Taylor.

The 1950s was the decade when the so-called economic miracle, the *Wirtschaftswunder*, took off in West Germany. The Bonn government proclaimed Berlin an emergency zone and the city thereby received major financial aid. Supported by the Marshall Plan and given clear direction by Federal Chancellor Konrad Adenauer's economics minister, Ludwig Erhard, who promoted private initiative based on market principles and benefited from a population that was willing to work hard, the standard of living rose quickly.

The disparity between the two Germanys was quickly becoming apparent. East Germany was coming to look like an armed camp. Barbed-wire fences, watch towers, and land mines lined the border between the two Germanys. Socialism was being imposed in the East with a vengeance, from the collectivization of agriculture to the fusion of state and trade union power.

While East German workers saw their wages fall and their prices rise, they were at the same time being asked to produce more, and of course they did not have the right to strike. To divert attention from the failures of the communist system, the East German propaganda machine shifted into overdrive. A particularly imaginative government pamphlet charged that American aircraft, as part of the general effort of *Dollarimperialismus,* were dropping potato beetles on East German fields to destroy the crops.

As the disparities grew between the two Germanys, so did tensions in Berlin. In 1952, Soviet MiG fighters got the spring off to a bad start by

Children accompanying the "Liberty Bell" to its shrine at the Schoeneberg Town Hall. This gift by the United States was presented to the citizens of Berlin by General Clay on October 24, 1950.

strafing an Air France passenger plane, wounding several passengers and leaving a hundred holes in the fuselage. The atmosphere was so tense that Ernst Reuter proposed a children's airlift to provide a few weeks of carefree vacation in West Germany for the cooped-up children of Berlin.* The following year in March, the Russians shot down a British military plane in the Berlin air corridor.

---

*Ernst Reuter recognized that if life in Berlin could be hard on adults, it was even more so for the kids. From that developed the idea of "the children's airlift."

"At the beginning the American diplomats were not so happy about the idea. They were afraid it would create further difficulties with the Russians," says Peter Boenisch,

Helga Mellmann

A plane load of sun-hungry Berlin youngsters leaving for a one-month vacation in West Germany, compliments of the U.S. Air Force.

one of the forces behind the initiative at the time. At the U.S. Air Force in Heidelberg, there were people who got behind the idea immediately, particularly Lt. Col. Davenport who worked out all the plans. But without the OK of the generals, it went nowhere.

Then, suddenly, the situation changed. During one of Boenisch's numerous meetings with Davenport, the door opened and a general came in. All he needed was to hear the word "airlift," and the thing was decided. This, of course, was Gen. Tunner, the man behind the original airlift, and in his book the worries of the diplomats did not count for much.

In practice, it was a simple operation. The northwest German radio stations asked listeners to host kids from Berlin. Listeners called in. The German Red Cross and other charitable organizations checked out the homes and gave their approval. Then the children were flown out of Berlin by the thousands. The "stewardesses" on the DC-3 planes were German Red Cross nurses and the pilots were Americans; no pilot was lower than the rank of major. "They really had fun flying the kids to the West," says Peter Boenisch, who later became one of Germany's best known journalists and speaker of the federal government.

Mellmann

*Major General Royden E. Beebe, Deputy Chief of Staff
USAFE, accepts a bouquet of wildflowers hand-picked
by a young Berliner, July 6, 1955, the start of the third
year of the children's airlift. The president of the Red
Cross section Berlin, Dr. Dietrich Blos, looks on.*

▌ THE BERLIN WORKERS' REVOLT ▌

On June 17, 1953, the situation in East Berlin reached the breaking point.
The East German government had demanded a 10 percent raise in production norms after attempts to obtain "voluntary" increases in production had failed. The reaction of the workers was prompt. On June 16, they
had put down their tools and marched on the House of Ministers to
demand a reversal by the government. Before long, however, their list of
demands had grown: They wanted free and secret elections, the release
of political prisoners, and a lower cost of living. What started as a

133

demonstration assumed by the next day the character of a general uprising. The fact that Joseph Stalin had died on March 5 no doubt encouraged the demonstrators.

One delegation of East German workers went to RIAS, the Radio in the American Sector, and asked to have their demands broadcast. RIAS was in a rather difficult position, given the volatility of the situation. The director of RIAS, Gordon Ewing, was already under fire from anticommunist crusader Senator Joseph McCarthy because his wife had lived for a number of years in the Soviet Union when her father moved the family there in the 1930s. Ewing chose to keep people informed, but avoid anything that would incite rioting. RIAS broadcast the strikers' demands—with the exception of the appeal to a general strike the following day.

"The importance of RIAS cannot be underestimated, because RIAS could really have started a revolt and a blood bath at that time," says Karl Mautner, who was the liaison officer between the U.S. mission and the mayor's office.

While commiserating with the plight of the East Germans, the West German Minister for German Affairs, Jakob Kaiser, similarly stated in a radio appeal: "Nevertheless, I exhort every single East Berliner and every resident in the Soviet zone not to be carried away, either by deprivation or through provocation, to commit thoughtless acts. No one should endanger himself or his surroundings. The basic change of your existence can and will be changed only by the restoration of German unity and freedom."

Despite the western pleas for calm, on June 17 the strikers' demands spread to 272 other cities and towns, from the Baltic coast to the mountains of the Czech border. In Berlin, fifty thousand demonstrators gathered; some climbed to the top of the Brandenburger Tor and removed the Soviet Red banner, substituting the black, red, and gold flag of the German Federal Republic.

Edward De Fontaine was a young corporal working for Allied Forces Network with Wladimir Benz, his German interpreter. De Fontaine had been in Berlin only six months when the situation blew up. For several days, there had been reports of trade union meetings in East Berlin—the workers had not received an adequate response to their demands and arrests had been made.

Protesting workers from East Berlin march through the Brandenburg Gate on June 17, 1953.

"Early in the morning we went in an army staff car to an area just 'round the corner from Brandenburger Tor. After filing a couple of phone reports from a nearby store on how thousands of people had gathered there, we heard shots. We had a continuing story at hand, and we needed to do something more complete and in depth."

The reporters raced back to AFN in Podbielskiallee, picked up tape-recording equipment and amplifiers and a soldier technician by the name of Tony. They returned to the area and parked where they thought they would be far enough away from the fighting to be protected from the rush of people who might cross the demarcation line. "It was a military vehicle which I had signed out," says De Fontaine, "and I did not have the few thousand dollars to pay for it if it were destroyed." In the army, such considerations are important.

Among his impressions, Benz recalls seeing people setting fire to newsstands and the fire brigade rushing in to hose them down. One spokesman for the regime tried to talk to the crowd. "They ganged up on him and beat him to a pulp. He had to be saved by the police," recalls Benz.

They proceeded to take the equipment across Potsdamer Platz. Tony the technician was carrying two suitcases full of equipment when a man running in front of him seemingly stumbled and fell to the ground. When Tony leaned over to help him up, he saw that the man had been shot through the throat. "Tony had never been in combat and neither had I. He was extremely upset for a while; he had never seen a man hurt like that."

The AFN newsmen set up their observation post in an apartment above a wholesale wine merchant on the third floor of a building on Potsdamer Platz, giving them a vantage point from which to observe the events and record them, as they had no line back to AFN headquarters. Then, they spotted a Soviet troop convoy in the distance. Realizing that their East German puppet regime was quickly losing control over the situation, the Russians had declared martial law and dispatched an entire armored division into East Berlin. Gunfire was heard across the city.

Benz and De Fontaine could observe the Soviet troop convoy as it came in. The East Germans threw stones at the troops as they went by in their trucks. The troops did not respond.

One of the young men throwing stones that day was Joachim Maitre.[2] At the time, he was nineteen years old and a member of the FDJ, *Freie Deutsche Jugend*, the communist youth organization. On that day, he happened to find himself on his bicycle on Potsdamer Platz just at the moment the Soviet tanks came rolling in.

Instinctively, he left his bike on a corner and, together with another passer-by, an apprentice electrician by the name of Erwin Kalisch, started bombarding a Russian T-34 tank with stones. "It was a spontaneous reaction," recalls Maitre. "There was nothing planned about it." In retrospect, Maitre dismisses the act as a piece of youthful folly that placed others in jeopardy. "Our action could easily have led to a mass shooting. If the tanks had opened fire, hundreds could have been killed." At the time, of course, it was seen as much more than a case of youthful impulsiveness, and rightly so. A photographer managed to capture the stone-throwing episode on film. The picture was carried by all the Berlin newspapers and flashed around the world, the symbol of resistance against Soviet oppression.

After the event, Maitre found that his bike had been stolen. Acting on an endearing if somewhat literal-minded respect for the law, he went straight to the closest police station in Wilhelmstrasse to report the theft, where he was immediately arrested. The people who had nicked his bike turned out to be East German security personnel. Due to his membership in the youth organization, he was sentenced to one year in the penal battalion of the *Volksarmee*. In 1954, as a noncommissioned officer, he led fifteen of his men over the Czech border, where they sought asylum in the Canadian embassy in Prague. Erwin Kalisch fared worse. He was tortured for weeks and spent three years in prison.

Countless demonstrators were arrested, a step that was repeated in cities throughout East Germany. By 9:00 in the evening, the streets of Berlin were empty of demonstrators. The uprising had been crushed. According to East German official figures, nineteen demonstrators and four *Volkspolitzisten* were killed, but the actual figures are thought to be considerably higher, more than three hundred dead. Soviet military tribunals condemned nineteen participants to death, sentences that were mostly carried out without delay. Some fifteen hundred demonstrators were sentenced to prison, some for life.

At the end of the day, U.S. soldiers were under orders not to enter East Berlin during the riots so as not to provide an excuse to the Soviets for further repression. It also reflected the reluctance on the part of the western Allies to support the East Germans in the uprising. Afterwards there was a ceremony in the city assembly for the victims. "We liaison officers had our own seats," says Karl Mautner, "but I was the only one there. The British and the French did not come."

At the ceremony at the Schoeneberg City Hall, at the Liberty Bell donated by the people of the United States to Berlin in 1950, Konrad Adenauer was present, but the allied commandants were reluctant. They did not want to come in uniform. "Our Mission Chief, Cecil Lyon, told me to take his big Chrysler and be the American representative in the funeral

AP/Wide World Photos

Growing unrest in East Germany erupted into open rebellion as 50,000 East Berliners revolted against communist rule. But on June 17, 1953, stones could not defeat the armored giants of the oppressors.

cortege. We ran up the American flag on the car and went along with the funeral procession," says Mautner.

Despite Soviet attempts to portray the uprising as a revolt engineered by sinister forces in the West working together with "fascist bums from West Berlin," or a "putsch carried out by imperialistic subversive organizations which succeeded in leading the workers of the GDR astray," as the East German propaganda poetically put it, this was no centrally planned revolt. It was a spontaneous reaction to an increasingly repressive regime. The lack of planning among the protesters was exactly one of the reasons the Soviets had so little trouble putting down the revolt.

Another reason, of course, was the lack of response from the western Allies. It showed very clearly the limits of their commitment.

"1953 was a time when the western commandants and their deputies were not at their best," says Mautner. "There were a lot of new people there. They were concerned that it was after all an uprising against an allied force, and that it might spill over. They were a little worried. I do not think we really understood the importance of this at the time. Some of us on the ground level knew it, but maybe we got a little bit too close to this whole business."

One problem was that Mayor Ernst Reuter, the man whose moral authority had guided the Berliners through the hard days of the blockade, was out of town. He did not get back until the following day.

Reuter's radio remarks from West Berlin on June 18 painted a tragic picture: "What I saw today at the Potsdamer Platz of these wastes, this dead, empty city, reminded me of my first impression at the end of 1946, in that terrible winter when I first returned to Berlin and saw the Tiergarten. A man's heart could have stopped, and it could stop today as we see this city murdered by the forces of history in which we have all been torn."[3]

The revolt put the just-inaugurated Eisenhower administration in a bind. During the 1952 campaign, the Republicans had been critical of the Truman policy of containment, which they characterized as "negative, futile, and immoral." What conservatives had advocated instead was "roll back" and "liberation," the actual reversal of communist wartime gains. The main promoter of the "roll back" concept had been John Foster Dulles, who was now Eisenhower's Secretary of State.

However, when contacted by the press on the matter, the State Department had "no comment." When asked about events in East Germany, President Eisenhower likewise avoided reporters' questions, claiming that he was not sufficiently informed to make a comment on the situation.

On July 1, when it was all over, Eisenhower told reporters at a press conference at the United Nations, that the United States "planned no physical intervention on the Soviet Union's side of the Iron Curtain,"[4] which was what the Soviets wanted to hear. He later amplified this statement by stating that the United States would do nothing that could be interpreted as "forceful imperialism." These assurances, some people felt, went a little too far in trying to please the Soviets.

But the message was clear: The policy of the United States was still containment, not roll back. The Allies were prepared only to defend West Berlin. Moreover, the United States was still engaged in Korea at the time and did not want two simultaneous military conflicts.

For the Germans, June 17 became a day of national commemoration, and one of Berlin's main stretches, Berliner Strasse/Charlottenburger Chaussee, leading to the Brandenburger Tor, was renamed Strasse des 17. Juni in honor of those who fell.

The death of Mayor Ernst Reuter in 1953, four months after the East German workers' rebellion, left a void. His immediate successors did not have his stature, though CDU mayor Walter Schreiber was a competent man. He was followed by Otto Suhr, an intellectual Social Democrat, a decent man but with limited resonance.

▌ REBUILDING BERLIN ▌

Through these tense years, the German economic recovery was proceeding apace. "The 1950s in Germany was mostly concentrated on rebuilding, on economic recovery," says Mautner. Delayed by the blockade, the European Reconstruction Program (ERP), better known as the Marshall Plan, was finally set in motion in Berlin in 1949. The start was slow, but the program soon gained speed. The Berliner Industriebank had been set up with the express purpose of dispersing Marshall aid money in Berlin.

According to Werner Minzlaff, who for decades worked as an economist for the bank, Berlin was in dire need of help. As a result of losing its status as capital, the city was estimated to have lost about half of its economic power. In 1950, unemployment was over 30 percent in Berlin. There was only one way to rebuild West Berlin and that was to reconstruct its industry. Berlin received 1.1 billion marks in original Marshall Plan funds, mostly in the form of low-interest loans. From this 1.1 billion, industry got about 80 percent, and more service-related parts of the economy the remainder.

In January 1950, the Berliner Industriebank got the first portion, some 90 million marks. Home construction was given a boost, and rubble removal accelerated. Big projects like power plants, industry, and communications systems were started with ERP money. When the original ERP aid for Berlin ended in 1953, the reflow from the credits made to industry were sufficient to finance a further 200 million a year in credits to industry.

Berlin had a large electrical industry, including companies like Siemens, AEG, and Standard Electrik Lorenz, which employed about one third of the work force. Machine tools and pharmaceuticals were also important. But small factories, from subcontractors to the big firms all the way down to arts and crafts workshops, also received Marshall Plan money.

The KaDeWe, Berlin's no. 1 shopping center was rebuilt, and new hotels shot up. The first hotel erected with Marshall Plan money was Hotel Berlin on Luetzowplatz 1955, while the famous Kempinski corner was rebuilt. In the 1960s, swank places like the Hilton (now the Interconti) and the Schweizerhof were to follow. Private money also played a part. In 1957, the *Kongresshalle* was built with funds from the American Benjamin Franklin Endowment and was promptly nicknamed "the pregnant oyster" by the Berliners.

By the end of the 1950s, the unemployment rate had been brought down to 4 percent. "With the help of Marshall aid, about 270,000 jobs were rebuilt in West Berlin," says Minzlaff. Throughout the process, the Americans limited themselves to a discreet oversight function. "We had some supervising people, but they were smart enough to let the Germans alone," says Mautner.

■ THE POLITICAL DEBATE ■

For a nation that had tried to conquer all of Europe *und Morgen die ganze Welt* ("and tomorrow the whole world"), there was a strong temptation to concentrate on practical issues such as rebuilding and turn its back to the world. A popular slogan at the time was *"ohne mich"* ("without me" or "leave me out"). Basically that meant that whichever way the world was going, it should not count on the Germans to go along. The slogan was specifically directed against the enlistment of Germany into a new European security cooperation, a new European army, and later on against membership in NATO.

But without popular engagement, the outward form of democracy is not enough. The Weimar Republic was democratic in a political sense, but there was no democratic culture. A democratic culture had to be encouraged, with emphasis on constitutional law and civil liberties. And there had to be a willingness to defend these principles, if need be, with an army. The West needed to contain communism, diplomatically, culturally, and intellectually.

At *Der Monat*, Melvin Lasky's efforts to encourage the Germans to be engaged in the world continued. "We did not preach for an army to go to war, but we preached for an army as a deterrent to communism," says Lasky. "The point was that it would not get to war if everybody did their duty and stood together."

These sentiments were very much in tune with Chancellor Konrad Adenauer's vision. He saw that his country's interests lay in a secure relationship with Western Europe and the United States and sought close economic and political ties with Germany's neighbors, particularly France. Germany's future would be built on the twin pillars of the European Coal and Steel Community (later the European Community and now the European Union) and the European Defense Community (EDC), its military arm.

The EDC, a more limited concept than NATO, would have allowed Germany limited rearmament within the context of a European army. Adenauer worked hard to promote the initiative and was devastated when it broke down over a vote in the French parliament in 1951. Instead, the British and the Americans offered Germany NATO membership, which Adenauer eagerly accepted.

The Social Democrats, led by Kurt Schumacher, advocated a course that focused instead on the reunification of Germany, but the elections of

1953 gave Adenauer a broad popular mandate, and Germany gained NATO membership in 1955. (The SPD would later come around to backing NATO membership as well.) Adenauer's unwavering commitment to a Germany integrated into Europe served to ease the concerns of the western Allies and allowed a more speedy establishment of the West German state as well as German rearmament than would otherwise have been the case.[5]

The impact of events in Hungary in October 1956 was especially strong in Berlin. A crowd of one hundred thousand gathered in front of the Schoeneberg City Hall the evening of November 4. Mayor Suhr seemed out of his depth dealing with the situation, but the forty-three-year old Willy Brandt, president of the city assembly, made his mark. When the demonstrators threatened to march to the Brandenburger Tor to protest the bloody suppression of the Hungarian Revolution in Budapest, Brandt redirected them to the Memorial of the Victims of Stalinism on Steinplatz in the British sector, quite a way from the Brandenburger Tor, thereby defusing the situation. This was one of the early instances of Brandt's talent for taming crowds. When, in August 1956, Suhr died, Brandt succeeded him as mayor.

THE COLD WAR GETS COLDER

As an outpost in the Cold War, Berlin (as well as Vienna) became one of the primary focal points for superpower espionage. Spies, counterspies, spy swaps—all were part of the distinctive character of the city, the *Agentensumpf* ("swamp of agents"), as the Berliners affectionately called it. One of the most famous episodes in this high-stakes game was the building of the British and American spy tunnel in 1954–55.[6] The idea was to place listening equipment in a five-hundred-yard-long tunnel, dug twenty-four feet below ground, to allow them to tap Soviet and East German communications over the telephone lines. The operation, code-named "Gold" by the Americans and "Prince" by the British, placed the tunnel entrance in Alt Glienicke in southeast Berlin close to the boundary of the American and Soviet sectors, and ran along the phone lines to the Soviet headquarters at Karlshorst. It provided eleven months of fascinating information. To confuse the Soviets and the East Germans if they should chance upon the tunnel, in an especially ingenious touch, William K. Harvey, the tunnel's CIA originator, placed a large sign that said: STOP. NOT TO BE OPENED BY ORDER OF THE COMMANDANT in Cyrillic and German.

"It was a great score for the United States that allowed them to listen in on Soviet communications," says Mautner, "if it had not been for one unfortunate detail: The Russians knew about the tunnel almost from the beginning." In fact, it turned out that the secretary of the joint committee that had studied and planned the project, George Blake, had been a

UPI/Bettmann

The Soviets spotlight a CIA stunt. Red Army officers show reporters the Soviet underground communication cables that had been tapped by the United States. The CIA had placed a sign reading STOP. NOT TO BE OPENED BY ORDER OF THE COMMANDANT *in Cyrillic and German, a ploy that was not to be successful.*

Soviet agent! But it took the Soviets some time to set up an alternative phone network and track down the tunnel's location. They were able to feed the CIA and M16 some disinformation and sought to make the tunnel into a public relations bonanza for the USSR when they uncovered it with much fanfare April 26, 1956.

In other areas, the Soviets were flexing their muscles as well. In 1953 they exploded their first hydrogen bomb, and in 1957 the Soviet space program succeeded in launching Sputnik, the first man-made satellite, into orbit around the globe. The unpleasant message of the beeps from space was clear: Sputnik meant that the Soviets would soon be able to hit U.S. territory with intercontinental ballistic missiles.

Emboldened by the Sputnik success, on November 27, 1958, Soviet leader Nikita Khrushchev embarked on a new Soviet attempt to rid Berlin of the western powers. In fact, he declared the Four Powers Agreement of 1944 null and void. According to the Khrushchev ultimatum, western powers were to withdraw from the city within six months, which would transform Berlin into a "neutralized" city. If the three western Allies did not comply, Khrushchev threatened, he would conclude a peace treaty with the East Germans and leave the western Allies to negotiate their rights in Berlin and their own access to the city with an East German government they did not recognize. The Soviets were claiming that the city's ties with the Federal Republic were incompatible with Berlin's legal status.[7]

One of the events that may have emboldened Khrushchev, according to Karl Mautner, was an incident in which a U.S. helicopter, on its way from Bavaria, developed engine trouble, came down in East Germany, and was held by the regime. In the negotiations that followed, the Soviets referred the Americans to the East Germans. For the American side to talk to the East Germans was a diplomatic no-no. Eventually, however, instructions came from Washington to do just that, and the helicopter was released. "We were quite upset about it; we thought it was a mistake. If we had waited a little longer, we would have gotten it back," says Mautner. "Willy Brandt, who was already mayor, was of the same opinion that it would set an unfortunate precedent. That may have encouraged Khrushchev to think he could get away with a little more."

The United States and its allies rejected Khrushchev's ultimatum on Berlin, and the deadline passed without incident, but the level of harassment on the access routes to Berlin intensified. Trucks were stopped for lengthy periods on the autobahn, an American cargo plane was buzzed in the air corridor, and barge traffic was interfered with.

Influential politicians like William Fulbright, chairman of the Senate Foreign Relations Committee, had lashed out violently against the administration's line on Berlin, which he regarded as far too confrontational with the Soviets.[8] In fact, Fulbright and Senator Mike Mansfield publicly demanded the resignation of Secretary of State John Foster Dulles. (Dulles, who was ill with cancer, resigned on April 15 and died a month later.) In negotiations with the Soviets in Geneva from May 11 to August 5, the United States did offer a number of concessions, including a reduction in troops stationed in Berlin, but for Khrushchev and his Foreign Minister Andrei Gromyko the concessions were not enough and were rejected out of hand.

While the pressure that was brought to bear by the Soviets was reminiscent of the blockade, the circumstances were different for West Berliners. The city was still dependent on outside help for its existence, but unlike in 1948–49, the Communists could no longer put pressure on the Berliners by shutting off gas, electricity, and water. In these areas, the western part of the city had become self-sufficient.

The East German politician who in large part contributed to the ongoing confrontation over Berlin was Walter Ulbricht. Ulbricht was a communist of the old school, one of the original members of the German Communist Party. He had his political roots in Weimar Germany and truly and deeply believed in the superiority of socialism over capitalism.

Ulbricht was a pesky sort who did not hesitate to remind his Russian friends in that piping Saxon accent that Karl Marx was a German. And he would also describe his own meeting with Lenin (he had met the great man as part of a German delegation) as a kind of personal anointment of almost religious significance. He was more Marxist than Khrushchev, to Khrushchev's infinite irritation.[9]

Ulbricht, who in 1953 was appointed First Secretary of the SED Central Committee, that is, the country's de facto leader, desperately needed to consolidate his grip on the country. But as long as escape from East Germany was possible through the open doorway of Berlin, he could not achieve this. Always pestering the Russians for more money, he constantly reminded Khrushchev that one reason East Germany was not doing better was that the country had been bled dry by war reparations to Russia, while the western Allies had started early reinvesting in their zones. East Germany could not compete with West Germany on equal terms. It was therefore up to the Russians to make those terms more equal. Thus at one point he included among his requirements a demand for sixty-two tons of gold.

In Khrushchev's memoirs, the Soviet leader's frustration with Ulbricht is palpable. At one time, when Ulbricht had been asking Khrushchev for Soviet workers to do unpleasant jobs in East Germany because he was losing all his workers to the West, Khrushchev brusquely informed him that, considering the horrors of World War II, he could not possibly be expected to send Russian citizens to clean East German toilets.

There was also considerable concern among the Soviet leadership that Ulbricht might freelance in his moves against the western Allies and go further than the Soviets would like. At times during the Berlin crisis, starting in November 1958, with Khrushchev's ultimatum to the West, the East German tail indeed seemed to be wagging the Soviet dog. The Soviets did not want the East Germans to get out of control. If there was going to be harassment, they intended to be in charge, if not necessarily to implement it themselves.

When Khrushchev did not follow through on his ultimatum to force the western Allies to negotiate access to Berlin with the East German government itself, Ulbricht got furiouser and furiouser, trying to goad Khrushchev to live up to his rhetoric. By the fall of 1960, two years later, Ulbricht was still trying to force the issue, insisting that the communist side would look weak if the threat was not followed through. At this point, Khrushchev was still not ready to comply and warned the East Germans against taking unilateral action.

However, Ulbricht would not have to wait much longer. In 1961, the United States had a new president, John F. Kennedy. Khrushchev was clearly of the view that he could bully the young and inexperienced president, who had just messed up the CIA-engineered invasion of Cuba, into making concessions. At their summit meeting in Vienna in June, the Soviet leader presented Kennedy with another six months ultimatum on Berlin. After the summit, Kennedy confessed to *The New York Times* that the meeting with Khrushchev was "the roughest thing in my life. He just beat the hell out of me." Afterwards, Khrushchev celebrated his triumph at a reception at the Indonesian Embassy by singing and dancing and banging noisily on a ceremonial drum.

The force that the western Allies in Berlin were up against was formidable. The Soviets had twenty motorized infantry and armored divisions and eight hundred aircraft in the Soviet zone of East Germany, a force totaling some four hundred thousand men. In addition, the East German National People's Army numbered 160,000. In Berlin itself, the Russians had nineteen garrisons and airfields. There was also an assortment of East German emergency People's Police, some seven thousand men, and thirty-five thousand members of the so-called "workers fighting squads," ie, paramilitary units.[10]

To warn the Soviet leader against making any miscalculations about America's commitment to West Berlin, Kennedy a few weeks later enunciated the three essentials for West Berlin: free access, the presence of the western powers, and freedom and security for the West Berliners. On June 21, he directly responded to Khrushchev's challenge.

West Berlin . . . has now become, as never before, the great testing place of western courage and will, a focal point where our solemn commitments, stretching back over the years since 1945, and Soviet ambitions now meet in basic confrontation.

It would be a mistake for others to look upon Berlin, because of its location, as a tempting target. The United States is there. The United Kingdom and France are there, the pledge of NATO is there and the people of Berlin are there. It is as secure, in that sense, as the rest of us, for we cannot separate its safety from our own.

I hear it said that West Berlin is militarily untenable. And so was Bastogne. And so, in fact, was Stalingrad. Any dangerous position is tenable if men—brave men—will make it so.

The speech, however, pointedly made no mention of East Berlin.

Khrushchev went ballistic when he heard the speech. He told John J. McCloy, formerly U.S. High Commissioner in Germany and by then the chief U.S. disarmament negotiator, who was visiting the Soviet leader at his retreat of Sochi on the Black Sea, to "Tell Kennedy that if he starts a war he will probably become the last president of the United States." And just for good measure, at a night in the theater, he rather recklessly told the British ambassador that it would take only six nuclear bombs to wipe Britain off the map, while France would require eight.

Equally importantly, banking on Khrushchev's respect for deeds rather than words, the Kennedy administration undertook a number of concrete measures to show that they were serious about Berlin. Secretary of Defense Robert McNamara requested placing an additional 133,000 men on active army duty, which would raise overall U.S. army strength to one million. He also suggested that he might have to order more reserve forces for active duty and increase the draft levels, altogether an overall troop increase of some 225,000 men.[11] As a show of force it was impressive, and it told Khrushchev that he would not succeed in his plan to dislodge the western Allies from Berlin. But it was not enough to prevent the East German crackdown that was to come only two months later.

THE WALL

Having failed to drive the western powers out of Berlin, the East German Communists and their Soviet backers did have the power to do something about their most urgent problem: the exodus from East Germany. In what came to be known as *Republikflucht*, or "flight from the republic," many of the country's most educated and youngest citizens chose to vote with their feet and go to the West. More than three thousand doctors had fled the GDR since 1954, which was about a fifth of East Germany's practicing physicians.[1]

While an Iron Curtain may have come down in Europe, the sectoral border in Berlin was still open and constituted the main escape route for refugees from the GDR. In 1961, some 60,000 East Berliners still had jobs in West Berlin and crossed over every day.[2] Between 1949 and August 13, 1961, 2,686,942 East Germans left for the West, and of them 1,649,070 came through Berlin.[3]

After a particularly inspired East German propaganda offensive in 1961, Walter Ulbricht, known among U.S. soldiers as "Pointy Beard," claimed that the Federal Republic was preparing an attack on the GDR, in which case East German militia groups would be left to defend their factories while the workers would be transported to the Soviet Union to Soviet factories to make it possible to draft Russian workers. This prospect did not much appeal to the East Germans. The exodus grew to flood proportions.

Thus in the first twelve days of August 1961, 21,828 refugees arrived in West Berlin,[4] introducing the prospect of a GDR peopled only by hard-line Communists and old-age pensioners. This, despite the GDR's warnings that young women who fled to the West would end up in bordellos for allied soldiers while the young men would be kidnapped straight into the French Foreign Legion. Refugee camps were set up throughout West Berlin to cope with the flood.

In what came to be known as "Operation Chinese Wall" among western intelligence services, on August 13, 1961, just after midnight, East German troops sealed off the sector boundary, and engineers, under the supervision of Erich Honecker, the head of state security who later became East Germany's leader, started stringing barbed wire across the city. They tore up paving stones on intersector streets and broke up the road surface with pneumatic drills. Spanish riders and light obstacles were put in place.

Rene Burri/Magnum Photos

In front of the Brandenburg Gate—a black and white document of the brutality and failure of a system called German Democratic Republic, August 13, 1961. Of the GDR Berlin Mayor Willy Brandt said: "They are neither German, nor democratic, nor a republic."

The S-Bahn and the U-Bahn were also stopped. East-West S-Bahn trains ended their journey at Friedrichstrasse, the last station in the Soviet sector.

At the same time, ADN, the East German News Agency, carried a communiqué from the Warsaw Pact countries exhorting the East German government to take action to put an end to subversive attempts by the western powers "to undermine the GDR's economy," which constituted a threat to the Warsaw Pact as a whole. The communiqué was careful to state, however, that these steps would only affect the eastern part of the city and that they would not "affect the existing order of traffic and control on the ways of communication between West Berlin and West Germany."[5]

East Berliners who worked in West Berlin were prohibited from working in West Berlin. They were asked to report either to their last workplace in East Berlin to resume work there or to the appropriate labor registration office in East Berlin.

James Atwood, at that time a captain, was a member of what was known as Detachment M, a special security detachment world-wide. He was the station chief in Berlin from 1959–64, and he was on duty the night of August 12–13. "I was called in at 8:00 at night to analyze a report. It came from the chief of the U.S military liaison mission who had been over in the east." The report stated that scores of Soviet divisions had formed a ring around Berlin. East German divisions had formed a second ring. "This was rather bizarre and most unusual," recalls Atwood. Just three days earlier, the troops in the Soviet zone had been taken over by Marshall Ivan S. Koniev, the veteran commander who had conquered Berlin in 1945.

About four hours later, another report came in from intelligence sources that East German police were stopping traffic at the eighty crossing points between the eastern and the western sectors of Berlin. They were stringing barbed wire and putting barriers in place.

There are certain categories of what constitutes a threat to the interests of the United States government and requires immediate notification of the White House. A threat to allied control in Berlin was one of them.

Having notified the chief of staff, Atwood got permission to send a

East German border guards build the fence around the
prison for their 16 million compatriots.

flash message to the effect that serious threats were being made to the
flow of traffic in Berlin and that Soviet divisions were moving.

Says Atwood, "The Wall on 13 August started on a weekend. Anybody
who attempts to take on the United States would be wise to do it on a
weekend. Because everybody is on the golf course, everybody is on leave,
everybody is sleeping, nobody can be cranked in, and we are at a 20 percent state of readiness."

Brigadier General Frederick O. Hartel, who was the commanding general of the Berlin Brigade at the time, vividly recalls the beginning of the
Wall crisis. Around midnight, Hartel was awakened by a call from a
Washington newspaper reporter who wanted to know if it were true that
Russian troops were coming through at Friedrichstrasse. "I cannot hear
a word you are saying. The transmission is very, very poor," Hartel yelled
back and hung up, not wanting to commit himself to something he knew
nothing about, especially not at a time as tense as that.

"So I dressed and tore down to Friedrichstrasse and, of course, there were no Soviet troops coming through. But there were the Vopos and the East German army troops with bayonets on their rifles, preventing people from moving across the sector boundary."

Despite the late hour, there was quite a crowd, people who had returned from a late night in the East. (Many Berliners would go to the East in the evening because many of the good theaters and other places of culture were in the East.) On this evening they witnessed the extraordinary sight of a city suddenly armed to the teeth. Says Hartel,

Leap into freedom. Border guard Konrad Schumann crosses the border to join his family, which had fled East Berlin a few days earlier. This award-winning photo made the cover pages of many newspapers around the globe.

You can imagine the traumatic occasion. At this point, there was no wall. They had some wire, concertina wire, but most of it was just a wall of soldiers, East German troops and the Polizei.

While I was watching this scene, I knew nothing could be done right then and there. People were all excited, they weren't thinking clearly. This had to be considered at a much higher level than my standing there doing something about it. All I did was observe what was going on.

The allied commandants had to get together and discuss the event; the German mayors from the twelve western boroughs had to be called in, and direction had to be obtained from Washington. In the meantime, notes Hartel, "There was not much we could do now. We were waiting for words from our governments."

At about 5:00 in the morning, when it was becoming light, the chief of staff, Col. Roy Murray went down to see what was going on. What he saw confirmed what he had been told by intelligence. "We saw them putting up barbed wire in some places, like the Brandenburg Gate, and along the American sector. I just made a quick inspection." Murray noted that the East German army was stringing out the concertina wire and setting up the obstacles. He came down again around 9:00 A.M.

At 10:00, when Murray's wife Donna came down, the scene was tragic. People were using sheets to escape from buildings along the new line. "My husband's driver took me down in a little black Volkswagen to Bernauer Strasse and we got out of the car," Donna Murray recalls.

It was such a devastating scene that we ended up just clutching each other and crying. There was hysteria, utter confusion. It was such a cruel thing to see husbands separated from wives and mothers from children. It was the most horrible thing I had ever witnessed. People were hanging out of windows. Obviously, we could not stay very long. But Kurt, our driver, could only drive a couple of blocks before he had to pull over, and we both had to sit and compose ourselves.

There was of course the simple option, which the Berlin politicians were urging the U.S. commanders to take: Remove the wire by force. Chief of Staff Murray wanted to breach the East German line and penetrate East Berlin to remind the Soviets that it was still an occupied area and that the United States had lawful and legitimate access anywhere in East Berlin.

Murray had already called U.S. Army Europe's headquarters to send up thirty-three bulldozer blades that would fit on the thirty-three U.S. tanks they had in the city. "Since the East German army was in there illegally, I thought we could just go along the line of the concertina wire and cinder blocks and knock 'em down with the bulldozers," he says wistfully. "I never got to do that." The two American generals in charge did not agree, nor did the younger State Department officials.

Says General Hartel,

*I tore that one down right away. That would not have done it. The line they drew was always a couple of meters in the East, not on the line. Sure, I even practiced that at Tempelhof with some of my tanks later on when the Wall was there. I could put grappling hooks on the tanks and tear the Wall down. But we would have been the aggressor. We would have to go into East Berlin to do it.*

Meanwhile, there was still no word from Washington. "We got stunning silence for a while," remembers Hartel.

Everybody seemed to have been caught napping, fishing, shooting, or sailing: British Prime Minister Harold Macmillan was somewhere out on the Scottish Moors, having spent the day blasting grouse out of the sky as the British upper classes are prone to do. Charles De Gaulle had been enjoying his cheese and pear in the French countryside. John F. Kennedy was in Hyannis Port sailing, while Berlin Mayor Willy Brandt, as the Social Democratic candidate for German chancellor in the ongoing election campaign, was rattling along in a wagon-lit somewhere between Nuremberg and Kiel.

For Washington, part of the problem was to decide precisely what was going on. "The problem was that it took a while to figure out what would be the appropriate response," recalls McGeorge Bundy, who was National Security Advisor to President Kennedy at the time. Most administration officials had expected the East Germans to take some kind of action to stop the hemorrhage of their citizens. What they had not expected was the drastic measure the East Germans resorted to. It is important to remember that the Wall did not start out as a wall, but as strands of barbed wire, as can be seen from the famous photo of the escaping Vopo leaping over the barrier with his burpgun. The true significance of the move took a while to sink in.

On the question of Berlin, the Kennedy administration had over the past months split into two camps over how to deal with the Soviets.[6] A cautious camp was committed to negotiations with the Soviets; avoiding a nuclear confrontation was paramount. They believed that the Soviet Union had matured as a nation and become less revolutionary, more like a normal world power. They saw the Soviet actions in Berlin as mainly defensive, an attempt to stabilize an inherently unstable Eastern Europe. As long as the western Allies had access to West Berlin, they tacitly conceded the Soviet sector to the Soviets. This school of thought included U.S. Secretary of State Dean Rusk and head of the U.N. mission Adlai Stevenson. According to this view, hateful though the symbolism might be, the East German measures would stabilize the situation in Germany.

The other group comprised the hard-liners who saw the Soviet Union as an offensive power, still bent on world conquest, even if it may have extended its time schedule a bit. For them, the Soviet Union was constantly probing, trying out ways to further its influence. And Berlin was a key testing ground. Hence they were opposed to any concessions. This group included former secretary of state under President Truman, Dean Acheson, Paul Nitze, Secretary of Defense Robert McNamara's key aide on Berlin, and the Joint Chiefs of Staff. However, in the wake of the botched invasion of Cuba, this latter group's influence had been waning.

When U.S. Secretary of State Dean Rusk finally came up with an official reaction, at noon Sunday, Washington time, that is, seventeen hours after the East Germans had closed the sector boundary, it was with a statement that recognized the obvious fact that the East Germans were closing the border to its citizens. He noted with some relief, however, that allied rights of access seemed not to be affected. Rusk promised vigorous protest against the East German deed through appropriate channels.

To its domestic audience, Washington made a feeble attempt to describe what had happened as a propaganda victory for the West, a sign of desperation on the part of the Communists who had become so desperate that they had to lock up their own citizens. But it was clear that the United States had no intention of going to war over the rights of the East Berliners.

Meanwhile in Berlin, Mayor Willy Brandt, who had hastened back from his campaign trip, expected the Americans to use their tanks to prevent Walter Ulbricht from building his wall. He pestered the U.S. commanders to take action. Brandt also asked Chancellor Adenauer to stop the campaign for the time being and come to Berlin.

Brandt was keenly aware of the danger the communist move represented to the city's morale. To Brandt, the communist action meant that the Communists would consolidate their grip on East Germany. It meant that West Berlin might simply wither away. And, as had shown in earlier confrontations, the citizens' morale was vital for being able to hold the city.

Brandt's initial efforts were not particularly successful. The U.S. troops were on alert and Brandt's views were forwarded to Washington. But the U.S. commanders made clear that authorization for action would have to come from Washington.

The reaction from Bonn was not too impressive either. Clearly not his normal, decisive self, Chancellor Konrad Adenauer issued an official statement that did little to buck up the spirit of the Berliners. "It is the law of the hour," he said, "to do nothing that can worsen the situation." And instead of coming to Berlin, he set out on a campaign trip and even delivered a harsh personal attack on Willy Brandt for good measure. (It was not until August 29 that Adenauer finally took action and wrote President Kennedy that the uncertainty of the situation was stirring neutralist sentiments in Germany, spurring a desire to find some sort of accommodation with the Communists.[7] Some West Germans even began to question the purpose of NATO membership.)

Monday, August 14, the East Germans proceeded to cut all telephone and postal links with West Germany, though they did not cut the trunk lines between West Berlin and West Germany. They closed the Brandenburg Gate, and reduced the number of crossing points to twelve. On Monday afternoon, protesters, some three hundred thousand of them, assembled in Berlin in front of Schoeneberg City Hall. The mood among the demonstrators was such that there was a real possibility they might march against the Wall. Willy Brandt had to calm the crowd, assuring them that West Berlin was still supported by the Americans.

On Tuesday, three days after the beginning of the operation, the Allies delivered a protest to the Soviet military headquarters. But the protest was sent by messenger, not delivered in person by a western commandant. Again, no demands were made, just protests.

Looking back, the main initial failure on the part of the Americans was a lack of understanding of the psychological effect the Wall had on the West Berliners in particular and the Germans in general. Says Martin J. Hillenbrand, who was at the time deputy director at the State Department's Task Force on Berlin, "The one thing that was not anticipated, at least not in the initial reaction, was the enormous impact on Berlin morale." Though only a few days had elapsed, in Berlin it seemed an eternity.

On Wednesday, August 16, another huge crowd assembled before the Schoeneberg City Hall. Willy Brandt informed the crowd that he had written a letter directly to President Kennedy, including a number of suggestions for action. The most important of these were: reinforcement of the Berlin garrison, the dispatch of a U.S. cabinet member to Berlin, the return of Lucius Clay as American commandant in Berlin, a ban on goods coming from East Germany, stationing of allied troops along the sector border. By no means extreme in its suggestions, Brandt's letter nevertheless caused some bitterness in Washington. Some in the White House were furious with Brandt for writing the letter. They tended to see Willy Brandt as a dreamer and a hotspur out to garner votes in the upcoming German elections.[8]

Looking to the other western Allies for ideas did not lead to a consensus. Charles de Gaulle was firmly of the opinion that one should not make concessions to the Soviets; he thought the Soviets were bluffing on Berlin and that they were not prepared to go to war over the issue, but the French did not have the troops and deferred to the Americans. And Britain's Harold Macmillan was notoriously wobbly on Berlin. "The British were broadly speaking a little less eager to demonstrate reassurance than we were," recalls McGeorge Bundy.

On Friday, August 18, as the western Allies had shown they would not risk a war with the Soviet Union over the new barrier, the East Germans began pouring concrete along Berlin's dividing line. The Wall itself began to take shape. Entrances to houses immediately on the boundary facing West Berlin had been walled up, and now windows were closed as well.

Architecture communist style. Barricaded house on the eastern side of the border.

The Vopos began forced evictions from the buildings. Their inhabitants were told to pack their furniture and rush it into vans.

On August 22, the Wall was virtually complete. A concrete barrier six feet high, one foot wide, and twenty-eight miles long now separated the two parts of the city. The limits of the western commitment had been clearly demonstrated. Walter Ulbricht's calculation that America would not interfere had been proved right.

On August 23, the East Germans announced that they would be further reducing the crossing points from twelve to seven, of which four would be for West Berliners, two for visitors from East Berlin, and one for foreigners. The East Germans also announced that they would prohibit anyone from coming closer to the barrier than one hundred meters "in the interest of their own safety."

This, finally, was where the East Germans overstepped.[9] A reaction was immediately forthcoming from the western allied military leaders, who dispatched one thousand troops with tanks in battle order to the Wall. They did this without waiting for clearance from their respective capitals. Says Brig. Gen. Hartel, "We went right up to the point where we knew the line was. We stayed on our side, but we were not any one hundred meters away."

The sheer confusion in the western camp in the very early days of the Wall is clearly recalled by Harry V. Daniels, Jr. Daniels, from Hawaii, was a young lieutenant at the time. He was assigned as operations officer for the autobahn at the Provost Marshal's Office, that is, the chief of the military police. In that capacity, he was also responsible for the investigation of border incidents. When the East Germans closed off the border on August 13, that fell within his purview.

"It took a few days for us to determine that Friedrichstrasse was going to be the international crossing point," recalls Daniels. "On August 22, I was instructed to set up an individual checkpoint at Friedrichstrasse." Daniels had just one private working for him whom he hurriedly posted at Friedrichstrasse. At this time, there was nothing there, except a local bar and an S-Bahn station not too far away. Later, they set up a team that would serve as military police at the crossing point.

Many a tourist in Berlin has wondered how Checkpoint Charlie got its name. The explanation is simple.

Somebody came up and asked me, 'Well, what do you want to call this? I am from the post engineers, and I am a sign painter. What do you want to call this?' I thought, 'There is no sense in calling headquarters, I am not getting any support there.' So I thought, I had Checkpoint Alpha in Helmstedt, Checkpoint Bravo in Babelsberg, and this was going East, so 'Let's call it Checkpoint Charlie.' That's how Checkpoint Charlie got its name.

But that's not the end of Daniels' part in the story. When the East Germans started constructing the cinder-block Wall, he was there as the officer on duty.

I am six feet three inches tall. I had duty there all the time because it was my checkpoint. I would walk along the Wall and look over into East Berlin, and the Vopos did not like that. I will say I learned a number of German cuss words from the Vopos. I would ask the German police what the Vopos were saying, and the police would say 'Lieutenant, that's bad. You do not really want to know.'

And so the Vopos came along and put another row of blocks there, but I could still look over that, so they came over and put two more rows of blocks and by this time, I could not see.

Lieutenant Daniels' height, of course, cannot wholly be blamed for the size of the wall. Eventually, it was to grow to an average height of eleven feet.

In early September 1961, the Commander of the U.S Army in Europe, General Bruce Clarke, was to come to Berlin, and unbeknownst to Daniels, the provost marshall had instructed the engineers to build a shed to make the checkpoint look more official. The morning that the general was to arrive, Daniels was at his post in Friedrichstrasse. By that time, a squad of military policemen was stationed there twenty-four hours a day.

Cartier Bresson/Magnum Photos

The Wall as an inner city playground.

"This engineer van pulls up with this big white shed on it. And the German employee asks me, 'Lieutenant Daniels, where do you want me to put this?' I said, 'What is it?' He said he did not know, but 'Lieutenant Colonel Newman [who was the post engineer] told me to deliver it to you. Where do you want it?'"

"I did not even know this was coming," says Daniels. "So I called back to our headquarters and talked to Major Luce, and he did not know either where it was supposed to go. So he said, 'Well, put it in some place that you think is appropriate.' So I thought, 'I'll put it in the middle of the street.'" And put in the middle of the street it was.

Daniels served as the officer in charge of Checkpoint Charlie until July 1962. Did he know at the time that he was part of a historical event? "I don't know if it was historical, but at the time, I can say, I was almost hysterical because I was looking for guidance, and nobody would give it to me."

▌DAMAGE CONTROL ▌

Five days into the crisis, damage control started. Realizing that something drastic must be done to shore up the West's crumbling position, President John F. Kennedy announced that Vice President Lyndon Johnson and General Lucius Clay would go to Berlin. "It was a brilliant stroke, whoever thought it up, because it was Clay, not Johnson, who reassured the Berliners. This was awkwardly obvious on several occasions when I acted as interpreter for both again," recalls Robert Lochner.

"At Johnson's big speech in front of the City Hall, General Clay modestly did not want to steal the vice president's thunder, so he wasn't planning to speak at all. Only when Johnson mentioned Clay's name, and there was a roar from the tens of thousands in the crowd, did Johnson reluctantly call him out from behind him to have him say a few words," says Lochner.

At the same time, to reinforce the Berlin garrison, Col. Glover S. John brought a battle group of some fifteen hundred men motor marching up the autobahn to Berlin where they were welcomed by the vice president.

William Bentz was a rifle platoon leader in the infantry and one of the soldiers in the battle group that motor marched through the corridor into Berlin. He compares his reception to old newsreels from the liberation of Paris.

 Many of the small villages we passed were filled with waving [East] Germans. When we pulled into Berlin proper, the streets looked like pictures I had seen of cities and towns in Europe when the Allies rolled the Germans back. The streets were filled with Berliners applauding, running up to our trucks and giving us flowers, flags and candy. It was just overwhelming.

Within a few weeks, on August 30, Kennedy announced that Clay would be back in Berlin, under a formal arrangement that made him, a retired four-star general, an advisor to the U.S. Commandant General Albert Watson II, the two-star major general responsible for the American sector. "Of course we at the mission knew that the one who was really pulling the strings was General Clay, and there is no question it gave a tremendous boost to the Berliners to have him back in Berlin," says Lochner.

That boost was badly needed. "At the time of psychological angst, between the Wall and the tank probes, the worst time, there was a steady procession of moving vans going down the autobahn. I remember seeing it on East German television," recalls John Mapother, a CIA officer who was stationed in Berlin from 1961–66. "The East Germans really played it up and referred to it mockingly as *Der Grosse Transportations Erfolg*" (the great transportation success), poking fun at the *Wirtschaftswunder*. Businesses were busily relocating to West Germany.

"Clay came to Berlin with the purpose of stopping the encroachments the East Germans were making, mainly on their own authority. He knew the Soviets were not going to back them up," says Mapother.

Clay knew that the Soviets, if they thought they could get away with it, would stand aside and pretend that there was nothing they could do about the actions of the East German government. Says Mapother, "Clay's plan was to in effect provoke the East Germans to the point where the Soviets had to rein them in." The great game in Berlin was to force the Soviets to reveal themselves as the real power controlling the situation.

As part of his plan to restore credibility, Clay came up with the idea of bolstering the village of Steinstuecken.[10] Steinstuecken was a small exclave that belonged to West Berlin, but which suddenly found itself surrounded by East German territory on all sides when the Wall went up. And East German soldiers were making life miserable for the three hundred families living there. Clay wanted to send a platoon of American troops down the road to Steinstuecken, but General Watson, the U.S. Commander of Berlin, did not think it a good idea. He called General Bruce Clarke who definitely did not want to do it. Even General Lauris Norstad, Supreme Allied Commander in Europe, opposed it.

On September 21, Clay got presidential authority to fly into Steinstuecken and talk to the mayor to assure the residents of Steinstuecken that they had not been forgotten. He stationed three MPs there permanently with a helicopter link to West Berlin.

Then, in October, the East Germans demanded that the Allies show their identification cards when they passed from West Berlin over into East Berlin, thereby seeking de facto recognition. On October 22, 1961, they singled out a U.S. State Department vehicle and stopped it, demanding that the passengers show their identification papers. They refused and returned to West Berlin.

Clay decided to mount an operation to force the East Germans to let them in. A platoon of infantry was brought in, as well as MPs with a .50-caliber machine-gun on a jeep. Allan Lightner, the senior State Department official at the mission in Berlin, played the role of guinea pig to be escorted into East Berlin. As expected, the State Department car was stopped. Immediately the jeeps and the contingent of American infantry was brought up with fixed bayonets, and the East Germans stepped aside. The troops escorted the car a hundred yards into East Berlin, whereupon the car continued into the East.

Three days later, word came that when the East Germans stopped a British foreign ministry vehicle, the British diplomat showed his identification papers, whereupon he was let through. Recalls Atwood, by then a major, "Clay was furious: 'Dammit, we are prepared to go to war over this issue, and how in the hell can one of our allies not be in communication and in total unison with us on this issue?'"

The Americans decided to mount another probe on October 27.[11] This time, a unit of tanks was brought up and placed in a hidden strategic reserve about a quarter of a mile away. A sizable infantry unit was also placed in reserve.

The State Department car drove up as scheduled and was stopped. At this point, the operational plan was immediately put into effect. The infantry moved in front, and the MP jeeps came up. The car drove in, and again the East Germans had to step aside.

Recalls Atwood, "I remember everybody laughing in the command room. The operation had gone just as we anticipated. Everybody finished their cup of coffee." General Clay asked Atwood to draw up a summary of the day's events to send back to the White House, so Atwood sat down to draft the chronological sequence of what had happened.

Ten minutes later the phone rang in the operations center. Atwood was the only person there. It was the officer on duty at Checkpoint Charlie. He wanted to be put through to the general—now. "There is nobody here except me," said Atwood. "Holy shit," shouted the voice at the other end, "get everybody back up there, there are Russian tanks at the checkpoint. The shit has hit the fan."

"I went charging up to General Clay's office," says Atwood.

We had already sent the tanks back to their command, and the infantry troops had also been sent back. Everybody came back into the operations center and it started to get very tense. Our tanks rolled up. We were muzzle barrel to muzzle barrel. Everyone went on alert. We frankly anticipated that a shooting war may start here soon. All you needed was a trigger happy NCO on either side, to just accidentally or deliberately squeeze off one round, and it would have cut loose.

American Forces Network correspondent Dick Rosse was on the scene in Friedrichstrasse that day.

Friedrichstrasse is a very narrow street. They were two to three abreast, and eight to ten deep, at point blank range, on the east side of Checkpoint Charlie, and we on our side. I had never experienced a showdown between Russian and U.S. tanks like that. One of my enduring memories is weaving myself in and out between the tanks. I saw a corporal sticking his head out of the turret of one of the Pattons on the front line. I asked, 'You are just bluffing aren't you, you do not have a round in the chamber, you are not loaded.' 'We sure are,' he answered. 'All we have got to do is pull this thing,' pointing to his lanyard.

The Russian tanks seemed to come out of nowhere, but they had in fact been in readiness for some time. The Berlin Brigade's regular patrols had previously noticed some tanks parked in the crater of an old bombed-out palais on Unter den Linden, according to John Mapother, but they could not make national identification. The unit markings on the tanks had been smeared over with grease, and the crews were dressed in tank overalls with nothing to indicate their nationality. Not until the tanks were actually in Friedrichstrasse did their nationality become clear as Soviet officers directed the positioning of the tanks in a herringbone pattern down through the street.

At a news conference, General Clay pointedly announced the significance of what was taking place: The fiction that it was the East Germans who were responsible was now destroyed. The fact that Soviet tanks appeared on the scene in Friedrichstrasse proved that the harassment all along could not have been undertaken by the self-styled East German government, but ultimately had the backing of its Soviet masters.

At headquarters, the tension grew. Protests were being made at the highest level. Darkness came. Suddenly, word came to the command center that the Russian lead tank had elevated its gun barrel to a nonhostile, nonthreatening position. Atwood recalls General Clay calmly addressing General Watson: "I think, Sir, that you might wish to advise your troops to do the same thing. Let's de-escalate this thing now they have made the first move. We are not bending to them, we are not yielding."

So General Watson issued the instructions, and the American tanks elevated. A short time after, the Soviet tanks backed up twenty yards in a nonthreatening position. Watson proposed that his tanks do the same, and Clay concurred.

We sensed the situation had been defused. And the Soviets blinked first.

At this point, General Clay turned to me and he said, 'Jim, get the White House on the phone.' Now, I had had my eardrum shot out in Korea, so I do not hear too well, and I heard him say 'Get me Judge Bundy on the telephone.' I asked, 'Who, sir?' and he said, 'Judge Bundy.' So I picked up the phone and I got the White House on the hot line. It was late at night and this voice says, 'Hello, who is this?'

'This is Berlin calling. I wish to speak to Judge Bundy for

General Clay. Who is this?' 'This is President Kennedy,' and he laughed. 'And you mean McGeorge Bundy. We don't have a Judge Bundy. Let me speak to General Clay, please.' So I handed Clay the phone, and he said, 'Good morning, Sir. It is all part of the war of nerves, and I think we are winning. In fact, I think we have won. No, no, I am not going to get you in any trouble. We have got it under control. I'll keep you apprised, but I think the worst is behind us now.' So it kind of settled down, and everybody drank their forty-fourth cup of coffee. They all left, and again General Clay said, 'Jim, if you would, please summarize some times and things and bring it to my office.'

The crisis was over.

By this time, General Clay knew that a lot of people in the White House were nervous about his way of handling the Russians; if polled they would probably have come out 90 percent against him. A good many of the army brass thought him reckless. Yet, Clay stayed on until May, after Marshall Koniev had left, in other words, until the immediate danger had passed.

"I think that the October standoff at Checkpoint Charlie with the tanks was the closest that the West came to World War III. This is the only case, to my knowledge, where Russian and American tanks were barrel to barrel," concludes Atwood.

That the issue still continued to play in the background, however, was clear two months later during the Cuban missile crisis, when President Kennedy had to consider what repercussions might occur in Berlin. Recalls Pierre Salinger, Kennedy's press secretary, "The general feeling of the experts was that if we attacked Cuba, there would obviously be a return attack by the Soviets, but that that attack would be against West Berlin."

Even today one is left with the question, why did the Wall come as such a surprise for the West? After all, an undertaking of that magnitude is hard to conceal, involving as it does thousands of men and tons of material. In a key trouble spot in the world, U.S. ignorance of this constituted a massive intelligence failure.

Certainly, the Americans were expecting something to happen. It was

AP/Wide World Photos

Checkpoint Charlie, October 28, 1961. For more than 16 hours, battle tanks of the two superpowers faced off at a 200-yard range, ammunition chambers loaded. It was the hottest confrontation of the Cold War.

clear the Communists would have to do something to stop the population drain from the GDR. What they had expected, according to Martin Hillenbrand, who was on the State Department's Berlin task force, was that rather than cutting the city in half, the East Germans would take action to try to seal off East Berlin from the rest of the GDR, which would have been a less drastic solution, but also a less efficient one.

In retrospect, says Mapother, "there were a few people who told me things that I should have realized were important." Certainly, there were some early indicators: In July, during a television interview, East German leader Walter Ulbricht had explicitly denied his intention of building a wall, a curious statement since nobody had brought up the subject. Then there was the appointment of Soviet Marshal Ivan S. Koniev to supreme commander of the Soviet forces in East Germany, a posting that would normally be considered below a senior military figure of his stature, unless the Soviets were up to something serious. (The task had initially been offered to Marshal Georgi Zhukov, who had begged off because of old age.)

At the same time, it appears that the Russians may have been trying to send an early signal that Soviet intentions were not directed against the West. On the morning of August 10, the military liaison mission in Potsdam, then headed by Col. Ernest von Pawel, received an invitation for a party at Zossen-Wuensdorf, headquarters of the GSFG, the Group of Soviet Forces in Germany. They had to scramble into their dress uniforms to get there on time. It was a celebration to announce the turnover of command from Jacobovski to Koniev. Jacobowski was a big bear of a man; Koniev was a little guy, but he looked tough as nails. Despite his limited size, he was clearly in charge.

The Soviets made the announcement and poured glasses of wine. Koniev asked Von Pawel if any of his men had been at the Elbe. Von Pawel answered that neither he nor any of his staff had been there, but that his commander in Heidelberg, General Bruce Clarke, had been on the Elbe. "The next time General Clarke comes to Berlin, we must have a reunion," said Koniev.

Then the toasting began. The officers were toasting in different languages—"Skaal," "Down the hatch," "Na cdorovye." Nobody toasted in

German. So Koniev looked at Jacobowski and asked, "How do they say it here?" Jacobowski raised his glass and said, "Marshal, you know how they say it here" and proceeded to toast in Russian. In other words, the East Germans would do whatever the Soviets tell them to. Von Pawel afterwards stated in an intelligence debriefing with Mapother that this had surprised him since he had never seen the Russians make fun of the East Germans at official occasions.

Looking back, Mapother notes, Koniev's remarks at the party could be interpreted to mean that the Soviets were signaling to the Americans that whatever might follow over the coming weeks, they did not want to get into a serious confrontation with the United States.

Most western intelligence analysts give the East Germans high marks for the way they managed to conceal the project. The East Germans kept the staff involved in the planning of the Wall to an absolute minimum. As part of their elaborate camouflage for the Wall, the East Germans had pre-positioned the wiring and some building materials at construction sites, seemingly as part of ongoing construction programs. The East Germans had to ship large numbers of building blocks for the Wall, and a year later, Mapother found out how they did it. As part of the effort to build their own heavy industry to compensate for the lack of access to the Ruhr District, the East Germans had built a town on the Oder originally called Stalinstadt and later Eisenhuettenstadt.

In Eisenhuettenstadt, they had a plant that as a by-product of smelting made building blocks out of slag. According to one of the plant's top accountants, who managed to escape to the West about a year after the Wall had gone up, the factory had a whole field of reject building blocks just sitting there. Sometime in the mid-summer of 1961, they received an order to load them all on rail cars and send them to a building site in Potsdam. Asked by Mapother how the employees felt when they learned that they had been sending bricks for the Wall, he gave the answer that might be expected from the archetypal accountant: "From the viewpoint of the firm, we were not at all displeased."

To this day, though, there are Germans who believe that the United States must have known in advance. For instance, they seize on the fact that the legendary CBS newsman Ed Murrow, then director of the United

States Information Office, arrived the night before the construction of the Wall began. Ed Murrow was famous for always being where the action was, they argue, and he would surely not show up on the evening of August 12 by coincidence.

But that is exactly what it was, says Lochner. "He had been appointed director of USIA in April, and this was his first overseas trip, starting with the biggest USIA overseas operation, namely RIAS in Berlin." However, adds Lochner, "Even on our side, there are still people who can't believe it."

It has often been said that the Allies should never have allowed the Wall to go up. Later, intelligence reports revealed that the East German Vopos were under orders to yield if the United States pressed forward.

But what would have happened if U.S. forces had brought down the initial barriers, and the East Germans had simply pulled back one hundred yards and started all over? Or another hundred yards? General Clay once put the Allies' dilemma in terms of a dispute between neighbors fighting over a fence, Atwood recalls. If your neighbor starts building a fence on your side of the property line, you have a perfect right to knock it down. If he puts it on the line between his garden and your garden, you had better check with your lawyer before you knock it down. But once the neighbor builds the fence well into his own property, there is not much that can be legally done. The Wall was well within the property line of the GDR. Atwood recalls Clay's point: "We can talk morals, we can talk about whether they should have done it, but nobody ever made any recommendation that we knock it down."

Altogether, although it may be morally and emotionally unsatisfactory to say, notes Mapother, "If it had gotten out that the Allies were moving and pushing the East Germans back, I hesitate to say whether public order could have been maintained. I have never doubted that the American response, with all the criticism it caught, was the only one they could come up with."

In his memoirs, Hans Kroll, a former West German ambassador to Moscow, quotes from a conversation he had with Nikita Khrushchev.

I know, the Wall is an ugly business," Khrushchev said. "It will disappear one day, too, but only when the reasons that led to it being built no longer apply. What was I to do? Over thirty thousand people, among them the best and hardest working people in the GDR, left the country in July. It is not hard to work out how long it would have taken for the East German economy to collapse if we hadn't taken immediate action against the mass exodus.

But there were only two kinds of countermeasure: either a blockade or the Wall. The former would have brought us into serious conflict with the United States, possibly leading to war. I could not and did not want to risk that. So that left only the Wall. I am not going to deny to you that it was I who, in the final analysis, gave the order to go ahead and build it. Ulbricht had pressured me for some time, and in the final months, with growing urgency, but I should not like to hide behind his back. It is far too narrow for me.[12]

▌ THE ESCAPES ▌

In the few days after the crackdown, some of the first miraculous escapes took place. People jumped out of fifth-story apartment windows into the nets of the fire department on the western side. One bright East German youth made a theatrical copy of a U.S. uniform, including insignia and rank and a shoulder patch for the Berlin Brigade, hung a portable radio around his neck, got a mouthful of chewing gum, and walked straight through Checkpoint Charlie. He did not speak a word of English, he just waved at the Vopo. He did not even wear a hat, which should have been a dead giveaway. He walked through and it worked.

In another case, four Soviet "officers" were let through, while the girls who had tailored their fake uniforms hid in the bottom of the car. Another escapee drove a low-slung sports car under the barrier. After that, the East Germans lowered the barrier another foot. Several GIs had girlfriends they brought out clandestinely.

But the successful escape attempt was the exception. As anyone who has been inspected by East German officials can testify, they were among the most thorough on earth. They might even inspect your necktie for hidden foreign currency. Special wheel carts with mirrors were used to check underneath cars and trucks. In the first year alone, from August 1961 to August 1962, thirty-two people were killed making a run for freedom.

William Bentz who had come up with Col. Glover S. John's reinforcements, was stationed for a while at Checkpoint Charlie. "We would hear a lot of shooting along the Wall, but rarely would we see the results of it. We would just see lights and hear shooting on the east side of the Wall. There was no way to determine what had happened."

Later during his stint in Berlin, Bentz was appointed to be a so-called "flag tour officer." "We maintained all those years that we had equal rights to travel wherever and whenever we would in the Soviet sector of Berlin, as did the Soviets in our sector."

To exercise that right, the Americans had "flag tour" sedans, named for the American flag painted on the fenders. The purpose of this flag tour operation was to demonstrate to the people of East Berlin that the U.S. Army had a right to be there.

"I would have a driver and a sergeant in the front seat, and we would travel all over the Soviet sector at all hours, day and night," recalls Bentz. "We had certain rules we had to follow that we could not pick anybody up. It was heartbreaking because we would get off in some of the back roads and alleys in the Soviet sector of Berlin, and children and old ladies would come out with signs saying "Take Me With You." We could not do that because if we were caught, the whole U.S. presence in Berlin would be jeopardized."

Bentz had been on this mission for six weeks or so, traveling sometimes during the day, sometimes at night. At the time, Friedrichstrasse was the entry and exit point for the American flag tour cars. As the East German guards saw the flag car approach, they would lift the wooden railroad gate to let it through.

One evening, however, when Bentz came back after a two-and-a-half-hour tour, he ran into a problem. At the checkpoint, a group of Soviet officers were standing around, a very unusual sight since the post was always manned by East Germans. And as the car pulled up to the barrier, the guards refused to open it. A Soviet officer demanded that Bentz get out of the car, but he declined.

"Then they surrounded the car and got up on the trunk and started jumping on the back of the car," says Bentz. "By that time, I had had enough. I told the driver, 'We are outta here.' Boy, he loved it. He put it in low, and drove through the barrier with wood splinters flying everywhere, and away I went."

Bentz made for the American headquarters, the Clay Compound, where his normal debriefing took place. Everything that happened at Checkpoint Charlie was monitored by closed-circuit television at the American operations center.

The officer in charge came out and said, "Lieutenant, you had a little problem down there. Come over here." He took Bentz behind one of the buildings at the headquarters, where Bentz found—to his astonishment—his own car, or something very close to it.

There was a duplicate car, just like the one I was driving. It was an Opel, olive drab. We had a radio dome on top of our cars. This car had a radio dome made out of tin cans. 'For official use only' along the side of the car was on there. I think the only place they had messed up was the license plate. Ours had U.S. Forces, and they had put something slightly different. But other than that, it was perfect.

Three East Berliners had somehow made uniforms for a driver, a sergeant, and a lieutenant. They obviously had been watching me for months. And so, while I was driving around in East Berlin, after about an hour and a half or two hours, this car came to the Checkpoint, with those three people in the car, and seven people in the trunk. And when they arrived the East Germans opened the gate, and they just drove through. I can imagine what their hearts must have felt like.

So when Lieutenant Bentz arrived, his car had already passed. "That's why I ran into all that trouble. I thought it was wonderfully gutsy. It gives me goose bumps just to think about it. That's one successful escape story that I know very vividly about."

Horst Erdman remembers exactly what it was like. A student in the small university town of Greifswald, he had been captured by the Stasi (East Germany's secret police, *Staatssicherheitsdienst*) in 1953 for distributing leaflets demanding free elections. His sentence was eleven years in the jails of Bautzen and Brandenburg for "anti-Soviet activity and sabotage." Through it all, the prisoners would focus all their hopes on West Berlin. "It was a beacon of light for us all," says Erdman.

Consequently, when the Wall went up, the blow was felt especially hard in the East German jails among the political prisoners. "I experienced the building of the wall in the jail of Brandenburg. It was a terrible day, the guards in the jail told us that we could no more leave the GDR." The guards mocked the political prisoners with the taunt that they would now have to stay and build socialism in the GDR.

In 1964, when Erdman was released, friends of his arranged a crossing through Checkpoint Charlie. "I was snuck in between the backseat and the engine in a French Renault with the engine in the back; it was a very small space. They had installed too little insulation. The heat of the engine became so high that my skin was scorched, but strangely enough my shirt remained whole."

One of the saddest moments at Checkpoint Charlie came on August 17, 1962, when Peter Fechter, a young East German bricklayer, tried to scale the Wall. He was shot by a guard and fell, heavily wounded, at the foot of the Wall.[13] His cries for help could clearly be heard on the western side. American GIs just stood by, unable to help; they were under strict orders to avoid any kind of confrontation over escapees. According to one intelligence source, U.S. Commander Albert Watson II could not make up his mind whether to risk sending in an unarmed U.S. medic in uniform; chances are that the East Germans would not have shot. In the meantime, Fechter slowly bled to death and was finally carried away by border guards.

This incident caused a real collision between the Germans and the Americans. There were demonstrations against the lack of American response, and in the following days angry West Berliners stoned Soviet

German Information Center

More than 200 refugees were shot and killed by the GDR border guards at the Berlin Wall. Peter Fechter, an 18-year-old construction worker, was one of the victims. Already hit by the fatal shots, he is carried away by border guards. August 17, 1962.

buses as they brought their guard relief through Checkpoint Charlie en route to the Soviet War Memorial in the Tiergarten, which happened to be in the British sector. The Fechter incident led to the stationing of an ambulance on permanent standby at the Wall.

In September 1964, Hans Puhl, who was German-born and from Bremerhaven, but whose family had emigrated to the United States, was back in Germany serving in Berlin as an MP. One day when he was on patrol at a point just east of Checkpoint Charlie, an East German tried to escape. The East Berliner, a jockey by profession, made it over the few obstacles and got close to the Wall when Vopos began to fire on him. He fell to the ground just on the other side of the Wall.

Puhl realized immediately that the man was wounded. He ran into a nearby building and from a second story window threatened to shoot if the Vopos came any closer. Firefighters threw a rope over the Wall to the wounded man who managed to get it around himself, and he was hauled to safety. The East German lived despite having been hit by five bullets.[14]

Predictably, the U.S. State Department demanded that Puhl be court martialed. But the commandant at the time, General James Polk, intervened. Puhl was quietly sent from Berlin to Bremen and later was given the army commendation medal. One of Puhl's officers was overheard saying that he wished Puhl had been from West Kentucky rather than Bremerhaven. (The Puhl saga had an unfortunate ending the following year when Puhl was court martialed for sexual misconduct and sentenced to five years hard labor.)

Ian Berry/Magnum Photos

A simple wooden cross, a wreath of barbed wire. A photograph of a young man, murdered. The inscription on the rock reads, "For the unknown refugee."

On June 26, 1963, President John F. Kennedy paid a visit to Berlin as part of his four-day trip to West Germany. From the balcony of the Schoeneberg City Hall, Kennedy expressed his solidarity with the Berliners in words that would become famous the world over.

Two thousand years ago, the proudest boast was 'cives Romanus sum' (I am a Roman citizen). Today in the world of freedom, the proudest boast is 'Ich bin ein Berliner. . . .'

There are many people in the world who really don't understand, or say they don't, what is the great issue between the free world and the communist world. Let them come to Berlin. There are some who say that communism is the wave of the future. There are some in Europe and elsewhere who say, 'We can work with the communists.' Let them come to Berlin. And there are even a few who say it is true that communism is an evil system, but it permits us to make economic progress. Let them come to Berlin.

Freedom has many difficulties and democracy is not perfect. But we never had to put up a wall to keep our people in, to prevent them from leaving us.

The crowd went wild at the conclusion of Kennedy's speech. "All free men, wherever they live, are citizens of Berlin, and, therefore, as a free man, I take pride in the words *'Ich bin ein Berliner.'*"

The background of the speech is intriguing. Robert Lochner, who had become the head of RIAS, was chosen to be President Kennedy's interpreter on his visit to Germany. He recalls:

A week before the trip, I was called to the White House and Mc-George Bundy, the president's security advisor, asked me to prepare a few simple phrases in German, which I did in the White House on a typewriter with large letters. He took me into the Oval Office, and I handed one copy to the president and slowly spoke out the first sentence and asked him to repeat it. It was awful.

As Kennedy looked up, he must have seen my rather distressed face, so he said, 'Not very good, was it?' What do you say to a president under those circumstances? All I could think of was to blurt out, 'Well, it was at least better than your brother Bobby,' because he had just been to Berlin and had tried several phrases in German and had completely mangled them. Fortunately, the president took it with good humor and laughed and turned to McGeorge Bundy and said, 'Let's leave the foreign languages to the distaff side.' Of course, everybody knew Mrs. Kennedy spoke fluent French.

In fact, Kennedy may not have intended to say even a short sentence in German in Berlin. In none of the speeches given on the first part of his trip, in Bonn and Cologne and Frankfurt, did he utter a word of German.

German Information Center

President John F. Kennedy passing a review of American troops on Clayallee during his historic visit to Berlin on June 26, 1963.

German Information Center

The crowd went wild at the end of Kennedy's speech. "All free men, wherever they live, are citizens of Berlin, and, therefore, as a free man, I take pride in the words, 'Ich bin ein Berliner.'

AP/Wide World Photos

An unforgettable moment in the long history of the German capital: JFK on the balcony of the Schoeneberg Town Hall. The crowd was estimated to be more than a quarter of a million strong.

After the triumphant trip around the city of Berlin, which outdid those of Cologne and Frankfurt, Kennedy took heart.

As we walked up the stairs of the City Hall towards Willy Brandt's office, the president called me over and said, 'I want you to write out on a slip of paper for me "I am a Berliner" in German.' He tried it a few times. In other words, it was not in the script in German. My own personal theory is that he was so impressed by this reception of the Berliners that he decided to strengthen it by saying it in German.

The suggestion that the German phrase was added in the last minute has support. After the speech, the president and his entourage were again in Mayor Willy Brandt's office for a while. Here Lochner overheard McGeorge Bundy voice some concern over the speech, suggesting, respectfully to be sure, 'Mr. President, I think you went too far.' I could only interpret that as meaning that McGeorge Bundy had immediately recognized that by saying it in German, it became that much more provocative and indeed, I would argue, the phrase would not have gone around the world, if he had said it in English."

The speech certainly won Kennedy the hearts of the Berliners. When the president was assassinated a few months later, recalls James Atwood, the Berliners lit candles in their windows. In front of City Hall, where Kennedy had given his speech, some hundred thousand people quietly gathered, holding candles.

The next day, a West Berlin citizen I hardly even knew came to my house with his wife, in his coat and tie and a big bouquet of flowers, and knocked on my door at six o'clock in the evening. He said, 'Major Atwood, excuse me for disturbing you,' and he started crying. 'You are the only American I know and I would like to express my sorrow at the loss of your president.' This man was standing there crying, giving me, the only American he knew, a bouquet of flowers. I have never forgotten that.

German Information Center

Nobody had ordered them to come . . . Close to a hundred thousand mourning citizens, Mayor Willy Brandt (on top step) among them, gathered in front of the Schoeneberg Town Hall hours after the news of John F. Kennedy's assassination had reached the town.

∎ PROVOCATIONS CONTINUE ∎

Over the protest of the three western military commanders in Berlin, the East German government introduced conscription into the *Volksarmee* for East Berliners in 1962, in direct violation of the Four Powers Agreement and Berlin's status as a nonmilitarized city. The year after, the East Germans held their first military parade in East Berlin on the first of May.

And the East German chicaneries continued. On the access roads to Berlin, traffic was slowed to a stand-still by red traffic lights, which would create mile-long queues. General John Hay, U.S. commander of the Berlin Brigade from 1964 to 1966, recalls how aggravating the harassment could be at the time. "The East Germans were always trying to figure out ways to make it difficult for us, to harass us. They certainly accomplished that, but we tried to give them back in kind. You'd get so damned mad that you had to search for things to annoy them. The frustrating bit was of course that one had to be exceedingly careful in response."

Exercising allied rights on the surface access routes remained one of the Brigade's most important missions. Convoys would sometimes be stuck for hours, which meant that soldiers, who could not leave their vehicles, would have to use a bottle to relieve themselves. Patrols would be stopped and accused of speeding.

AP/Wide World Photos

Soviet armored personnel vehicles block U.S. Army
convoys at Babelsberg checkpoint, October 12, 1963.

Soviet fighter jets roar over the Congress Hall in West Berlin.

Ullstein

The East Germans would even stage phony accidents for public consumption, such as having motorcycle riders come up beside an American patrol and slide the bike down and sideways in a most dramatic fashion. Television cameras would be on the ready, prepared to film the "accident." The Jeep never actually hit the bike, but that was not evident from the pictures. There would even be later reports from the hospital about the injured rider.

"The ambassador got to wondering, even though I would tell him that this was all trumped up," says Hay. "You do that often enough, and he'd get to wondering whether I was letting these patrols run wild. I put instrumentation on the vehicles so that the speed was automatically recorded at all times, so that I could prove we weren't speeding."

The Soviets had other tricks up their sleeve. They would fly in over Clay Headquarters at speeds of Mark I plus, breaking the sound barrier with a tremendous boom. Hay did not have any high-speed jets with which to retaliate, but he did make the best use he could of his helicopters. "I knew where their headquarters was. I'd send the helicopters low over their headquarters. Not that it was a threat, but it annoyed the devil out of them."

In 1965, the Soviets chose to hold air maneuvers over the Congress Hall in West Berlin, with the result that windows shattered throughout West Berlin because of the sonic booms. In early April, when the West Germans announced that they were going to hold a *Bundestag* session in the Reichstag in Berlin, the Soviets immediately protested and Khrushchev furiously issued all kinds of threats. The West Germans went ahead anyway. On April 5, word came that the Soviet army was on the move. It surrounded Berlin and cut off the roads, including the autobahn under the pretense that it was needed for their troops.

On April 6, the parliament session started, and all hell broke loose. The Soviet air force swooped down on Berlin; MiG 19s and Sukhois buzzed every plane coming into Berlin. They also buzzed the parliament session. The noise was incredible.

Jack Kohler remembers that occasion vividly. The office of the Associated Press, where he worked as a reporter, was on the corner of the Kurfuerstendamm, right across from the Kempinski hotel. Kohler saw plenty of the action. "I was sitting at my typewriter, writing the story, and I would look out the window and see these goddam Sukhoi fighters flying along the Kurfuerstendamm, with one wing hanging into the goddam road."

"The planes were coming across the city at a thousand feet or less. Then four MiG 19s came streaking across the French sector. Everybody went crazy." This chicanery lasted for three or four days until the parliament session was over. "It was an incredible provocation. The fact that nothing happened is a miracle," says Kohler.

AMERICANS IN BERLIN

For four decades, all soldiers who were assigned to Berlin were carefully screened. They had to have served in previous assignments and proven themselves to be good soldiers. Before being sent, their records were checked for marital problems, psychological problems, or difficulty handling finances, all of which could make a soldier a potential target for the intelligence agencies from the other side. Only then would they be stationed in Berlin. Some of America's most illustrious soldiers have passed through Berlin. Service in Berlin resulted in a kind of fraternity, a network through which people would stay in touch throughout their career.

H. Norman Schwarzkopf, Gulf War hero, served in Berlin from 1959 to 1961. "You did not get any eightballs in Berlin," Schwarzkopf says. "The soldiers you got in Berlin were absolutely the finest that were available. And, of course, if you did find a troublemaker, he was immediately shipped out of the area."

The reasons for this careful selection were obvious. The U.S. Army knew the Soviets were watching their every move. Thus when U.S. soldiers were practicing their fighting skills in the training areas, the Soviets often watched from a tall cherry picker on the eastern side. The U.S. Army also wanted to show the Berliners that they were sending the best and brightest soldiers. And because Berlin was so tense and in such an exposed position, the army sent only soldiers who were 100 percent reliable; there were to be no incidents with people barking at the moon or shooting guns into the air Texas-style.

Says Lt. Col. Billy Arthur, "If you were in Fort Benning, Georgia, where I had been, and a GI gets a few too many beers, and for one reason or another goes to the motor pool and takes a vehicle out, a tank or a truck, and drives it around, it is no problem in Fort Benning, Georgia. You call out the highway patrol and you capture him. In Berlin, if he does that, it is a whole different ball game. He can trigger an international incident."

Traveling to Berlin, there was no mistaking that this was an isolated island. Americans had to travel two and a half hours by car to get there, the distance from Checkpoint Alpha at Helmstedt to Checkpoint Bravo on the West Berlin–East German boundary. If the Americans arrived in Berlin in less than those two and a half hours, the Russians would harass them for having driven too fast. If they were late, they would be questioned by the Russians about what they had been doing all that time, the assumption being that they had been spying.

Norman Schwarzkopf started out in Berlin as a platoon leader, pulling assignments like guard duty at Spandau Prison and running reconnaissance patrols into East Berlin. Schwarzkopf later became the aide de camp to the commanding U.S. general in Berlin.

What made Berlin so special in his view was the sense of mission and duty. A soldier in Berlin was really on the front line.

Every day in Berlin was very exciting. We lived in such close proximity to our potential adversaries and were of course completely surrounded by them, so it was very, very easy to motivate our troops. All you had to do was take them to the border and point across it and say, 'There is a Russian soldier, and you may have to fight him tomorrow.'

This, of course, was true in spades after the Soviets erected the Wall. The Soviets prudently waited to give the go-ahead for the building of the

Burt Glinn/Magnum Photos

On chopper patrol over Berlin.

Wall until one week after Schwarzkopf left the country, as he likes to point out himself.

"There were continuous crises arising, and as each crisis would arise, your juices got flowing more and more to make sure that you were absolutely honed to the sharpest edge of readiness. You had to be, living in that environment," says Schwarzkopf. For instance, on the door to their weapons room, Schwarzkopf's reconnaissance group hung a big sign that read, RECON WEAPONS: BEST WEAPONS ROOM IN THE BATTLE GROUP, challenging any inspector to find fault with them.[1] As anybody who has served in the army will testify, that kind of dare is suicidal unless you are dead certain that you will measure up.

Stuart Alpart/U.S. Army Signal Division

*War games in the Grunewald. Handling the M60 is
Pvt. Abraham Borja while PFC John Gile, also from
2nd Battalion, 34th Infantry, is driving the jeep to a
new position.*

That kind of can-do spirit permeated all aspects of military life in
Berlin. It was a constant war of nerves with the Soviets. For duty at the
Spandau Prison, for instance, where the Nazi war criminals were held
and where guard responsibility was rotated between the four wartime
victors one month at a time, Brigadier General John Hay, Jr. recalls, "I
always selected people who were well over six feet, all of the same
height, and excellent in close order drill. I wanted always for our guard to
look better, taller, bigger, more precise than the Soviets' did, even though
there was no public there."

The psychological warfare even extended to social occasions. One year, at the annual pellet rifle and pistol competition between the generals of the Russian, British, French, and U.S. forces, which was held in the British sector, Hay won the air pistol competition. The plaque reads: "Winner First Place, International Pistol, 1.77. Brig. Gen. Hay, 26 March, 1965." The Russian general did not do too well. Afterwards, Hay used every opportunity to rub it in and remind the Russian that he lost. In fact, Hay still derives satisfaction from the memory. While this may sound childish to some, it served a purpose in Berlin. Never appear weak to a superior adversary.

A strict principle of tit for tat applied across the board, according to Col. Roy Murray. Whenever the Russians did something the allied command did not like, the Allies would retaliate in kind. "If the Russians held one of our men for forty minutes, we always waited for the next Russian of some rank. The MPs would pull his car over to a side road, and they would sit there with him for the next forty minutes, equal to the time our man had been kept in East Berlin. Then they would let him go."

Everybody stationed in the city understood that the Berlin Brigade was a tripwire more than a defense force and that if, in fact, war was to break out, they would either be cut off or overrun. "I don't think there were any illusions among the people there that you probably would not get out," says Billy Arthur. "We all knew that, but that is part of being a soldier. The families knew that, too, and you hoped that the evacuation plans would work, that you would have warning in advance so your dependents could be evacuated. But I am not sure that any of us were very confident of those plans."

City combat, of course, favors the defenders. The aim of the western allied defense was to make an assault so difficult that the Soviets would think twice about fighting a second battle for Berlin, and that they would choose to bypass the city. Meanwhile, hopefully, a favorable outcome could be obtained elsewhere.

"I have often been asked if there was ever such a thing as an offensive

U.S. Army

The 759 MP horse platoon, the only mounted military police platoon in the entire U.S. Army, was stationed in Berlin. It was trained for riot patrol and guarding the wooded sections of the border between the American and Soviet sectors. From left: Cpl. Don Teachout, PFC Jack Green, PFC Ernest Murphy, and Sgt. Leonard Knapp.

Rene Burri/Magnum Photos

Control point near Checkpoint Charlie on Friedrich-strasse, August 1961.

operational plan," says Teddy Mohr, who was chief of personnel security at Clayallee.

 There was not. How do I know? I was the custodian of all of the classified documents on Berlin. I knew there had never been one. Bear in mind that within the twenty-mile ring around Berlin, there were over a hundred thousand communist troops. With this garrison of perhaps five to six thousand American soldiers, the British and French having perhaps three to four thousand together, there was really nothing that many of us felt we could do. If they had wanted to destroy us, it would have been no problem.

According to Mohr, one of the scenarios that was advanced, and in fact was a cause of some concern, was that the East German army, the *Nationale Volksarmee* (NVA), would board the U-Bahn train in civilian clothes, converge at various key points to put on their uniforms, and, voilà, proclaim that West Berlin was now occupied. That is why the Americans had constant watches on all subways. In fact, all transportation was closely watched by the Allies. The mission of the scout platoons was to get information on anything that looked like a troop build-up or deposits of ammunition or supplies, or what have you.

Perhaps the detail most illustrative of Berlin's precarious military state is afforded by the British. The British had issued each soldier a survival kit, much like those issued to British airmen during World War II. It was a sealed, waterproof pocket containing a silk scarf on the one side of which was a map of Berlin and its immediate environs, useful for trying to get out of the city. On the other side of the scarf was a map of Germany and its neighboring countries. The pocket also contained a document identifying the holder as a British soldier; it stated that the British government would be grateful to whomever would be willing to help. This message was printed in German and in the languages of the countries adjacent to Germany. The pocket also contained a button compass and, recalls British historian and former commandant of Spandau Prison Lt. Col. Tony Le Tissier, "There was a tiny metal file to saw your way out of prison."

▌ THE STRESS FACTOR ▌

For the individual American soldier, the level of stress could be severe. At Thanksgiving 1961, First Lieutenant Norbert D. Grabowski found himself in the middle of an episode that had all the ingredients of an international incident.

Every day, duty trains operated between Berlin and West Germany. There were two daily departures, one bound for Frankfurt and one for Bremerhaven. These were passenger trains, designed to accommodate official travel and other needs of the U.S. forces and their dependents. Usually, there were a number of passenger cars, a baggage car, and sometimes one or two freight cars. One of the passenger cars was always used as the "command car" for the crew. There was the officer in charge, a noncommissioned officer, a radio operator, an interpreter who was fluent in Russian and German, and a number of military police. An East German conductor was also on board, since the train traveled over East German rail lines. Inside the train, however, he was restricted to the command car. The day before Thanksgiving, Grabowski was the commanding officer on the duty train.

The train's route started at Berlin Lichterfelde, where the passengers were processed, the train secured, and the East German conductor brought on board. From there it went through Potsdam and Magdeburg to Marienborn, where the train routinely underwent inspection by the Russian military. The train didn't stop until Helmstedt six hours later, the first West German station on the route. Most of the time, the crew was in contact with headquarters over the radio.

Working with the Russians could be a dreadful pain, Grabowski recalls. "We were constantly delayed or harassed." Document discrepancies were a favorite point of complaint for the Russians.

They would take a flag order for a First Lieutenant Jones. They would find John C. Jones on the flag order and J. C. Jones on his identity card. This minor discrepancy became a violation of international agreements. All kinds of hell was raised, approval from headquarters had to be sought, and the train would be delayed for one, two, or three hours.

There were unwritten rules in working with these guys. You always had to have cigarettes with you because you exchanged cigarettes. You got these stinky old Papyrossa from them, and they got good Cool or Camels. On big holidays, they would bring a bottle of cheap vodka, and you would bring a bottle of booze and we would switch.

Following the building of the Wall, East Germans tried anything to escape, which included trying to board the duty train. A lot of construction work along the rail lines slowed the train's speed, making it possible to jump aboard. Those who managed to break a window could clamber inside. At Marienborn, the Russians would invariably inquire about the broken windows, and the train commander would produce the so-called "duty rock," which he carried expressly for this purpose, blaming the broken window on hooligans. Rampant hooliganism outside Magdeburg got a lot of blame in those days.

On the day before Thanksgiving, 1961, an East German in his mid- to late-twenties jumped on the train outside of Potsdam. Realizing that the doors were locked, he bashed in the window with his bag. "The problem was that the dumb bastard picked the command car," says Grabowski, "and as soon as the glass broke, the East German conductor jumped out into the walkway and saw him come through the window. I grabbed him, threw him into a corner and put a couple of MPs on him. I talked a little to him. He wanted to go to the West, and this was his way to do it."

Grabowski immediately sent a coded message to Berlin by radio indicating that an East German was on board. According to the policy that had been worked out by the U.S. command, the train commander would neither confirm nor deny the presence of an East German on the train, but would continue to insist on right of passage. Should any such individual have boarded the train, the officer was to say, the person would have had to do so by force and therefore he belonged under the jurisdiction of the military police.

Grabowski spent an hour trying to talk the conductor into not turning the East German in, as he would face a long prison sentence. When they got to Marienborn, however, it became clear that Grabowski's efforts had not been successful. The Russians said they had gotten word that there was a criminal on board—a rapist, murderer, and mugger—and asked to have him turned over. Grabowski gave them the standard line. Foreseeing trouble, Grabowski appointed a senior officer to take over in case something happened to him and appointed captains and majors to be car commanders as well. "Here I was, a lousy first lieutenant!" he says. "The passengers thought it was the greatest thing in the world. They were now part of the Cold War!"

After a half hour, a Russian major arrived. He insisted that the East German was wanted in seven countries, no less. But Grabowski stuck to his instructions. Realizing that the Russians were likely to get serious, Grabowski placed a soldier by every hand brake on every car and told them to look out the window. If Grabowski raised his arm, they were to work the hand brakes.

Sure enough. Before long, a Russian lieutenant colonel came up and stated that because of Grabowski's intransigence, they were going to have to move his train to a siding.

"I raised my hand, and every soldier turned their hand brake like crazy. I told the officer that I had just locked the train and that he did not have enough motor power within one hundred fifty miles to move it. The brakes were mechanical hand brakes that you could unlock only from the inside, unless you wanted to dismantle the undercarriage of the train." And the only way Grabowski would unlock them was if the Russian would give his word of honor as an officer that the train could continue to pass.

The situation became more tense by the minute. Grabowski's train was blocking the Moscow-Paris express, which had to be rerouted. Grabowski received a tongue-lashing by a Russian colonel and was told that the

Russian district commander would come and see him. He still refused to leave his train. When the Russians threatened to take away the train's engine, Grabowski let them know that the press would be very interested to hear how the Russians had removed the engine, and therefore the heat, from a train full of women and children in the middle of November. That gave the Russians second thoughts. Then Grabowski decided to engage in a bit of psychological warfare of his own. "I started breaking out the C rations and the water and told the passengers to use the toilets as much as possible. I wanted to stink up Marienborn. Those trains dropped it right on the tracks. It may be uncomfortable for us, but it will also be uncomfortable for them."

It was a noble stand, but finally a message came through from the U.S. headquarters in Berlin, informing Grabowski that Colonel Ernest Von Pawel, head of the U.S. military mission in Potsdam, was on route to Marienborn. When Von Pawel arrived, he told Grabowski that he had to turn over the man to the Russians. Grabowski refused, since he had not received orders to that effect from his headquarters in Berlin, but finally, he was forced to compromise: Von Pawel took custody of the man and then turned him over to the Soviets. The man was later sentenced to a long jail term.

Grabowski later received a commendation for his courage. He had done as much as could be demanded of any officer. But ultimately, he was up against forces bigger than himself.

▌ DER JOINT IS JUMPING ▌

As American servicemen discovered over the years, Berlin is more than the oppressive city portrayed in Cold-War fiction. Berlin was so attractive to Americans, despite its precarious location, in part because it is an extremely varied city dotted with beautiful parks and lakes. In fact, you can forget you are in a city. Thirty percent of the land surface in West

Berlin is trees and water. On arrival, Americans were astonished by how pastoral it could be.

"It has always been known as the best-kept secret of the U.S. Army," comments Colonel Stuart Herrington, who was stationed in Berlin in the 1960s and again in the 1980s, "It's a wonderful city with first-class facilities and a friendly population. That's separate from the usual image of Berlin as some asphalt jungle surrounded by an ugly wall."

In Berlin, city and country, military and civilians came together in a fashion most unusual for Americans, who were accustomed to bases and training areas located far from major population centers. This could have unexpected consequences. William Bentz recalls his first maneuver in the Grunewald forest as a rifle platoon leader with forty soldiers under him. "I had my platoon all assembled in a wood line. The edge of the wood line was going to be the line of departure. I got up and gave one of these infantry 'follow me' speeches and almost got run down by a German who was riding on this bicycle path."

Wannsee was the U.S. Army's recreational area. A house that was said to have belonged to Joseph Goebbels had been requisitioned for the pur-

U.S. Air Force

A Christmas party organized by American soldiers for orphans, 1964. This photograph is one of thousands that document the friendship formed between the "Amis" and the Berliners.

pose. (In Berlin, requisitioned houses always seemed to have belonged to either Joachim von Ribbentrop or Joseph Goebbels.) Available were swimming, paddle boats, sailboats, and hunting, including plenty of opportunities for duck hunting.

One of those who enjoyed the duck hunting was General Clay. One morning, during Clay's second stint in Berlin, when Major James Atwood had finished his daily briefing with the general, a small duck whistle fell out of his attaché case with an embarrassingly loud quack. Apologetically, Atwood caught the errant bird call, noting that the general had probably never seen one of these devices. On the contrary, said Clay, "I use them myself all the time." Atwood then proceeded to ask if the general would be interested in a little duck hunting on the Wannsee. "Certainly," Clay answered. "And when would it suit the General?" "How about tomorrow morning?"

The following morning, the young major arrived at the general's quarters in full hunting gear and was careful not to rattle the fine Meissen china cups over breakfast. They then drove out to Wannsee and got into a boat. Atwood had loaned the general his Browning semiautomatic 12-gauge shotgun. Suddenly, a brace of six mallards rose from the reeds. The general lined up the rifle, and "pow" went the first shot. The leading mallard dropped. "Pow, pow" rang the next two. The second and third birds dropped. "You take the last three, Major," Clay said, handing Atwood the gun. If there were any young officers who had misgivings about this old guy who had been called back into duty (and there were certainly those who did), their doubts were quickly dispelled by little episodes like this.

For the culturally inclined, Berlin was a treat as well. The city has more museums than either New York or Moscow, one reason being that the collections were split between East and West Berlin, so there were two sets of museums for almost any subject or period—two Islamic museums, two Egyptian museums, two National Galleries, two collections of copper engravings, etc. The best known congregation of museums, of course, was on Museum Island, between the arms of the Spree River. American officers would make a point of frequenting the museums there, as well as East Berlin's many theaters, not just for the enjoyment of it, but also because it gave them an occasion to exercise their right to move freely about East Berlin.

For young officers who came to Berlin in the 1960s, Berlin was something special. It reflected an earlier army, an army that a lot of the young officers had not seen before. There were very many formal occasions. People had to dress in their mess blues and their dress blues. There were receptions and balls. All the occupation powers had them. Even the Russians showed up at the Fourth of July receptions. On top of this, there were eleven consulates.

"I was dating my wife at the time, and the first time I took her to one of those receptions, it was at the Funkturm, the old Radiotower," Norbert Grabowski recalls. "My wife said, 'My God, it looks like something out of Vienna in the early 1800s.' The French, of course, were in their resplendent uniforms, the British came in all their different regimental uniforms, and the diplomats sported cummerbunds and medals on their sashes."

Colonel Roy Murray, chief of staff in the 1960s, found himself thrust into the middle of the social whirl. In fact, his job included attending all the official functions. "Really it got to the point where I never had time to take our two sons out anywhere. We were out almost every night. Some nights, my driver and I sat down and mapped where we were going to the cocktail parties. Finally, the general said I did not have to accept invitations for Sunday."

Formalities and customs were adhered to with great precision. The commanding officer received a new arrival and his lady formally at his house shortly after they arrived. This was done in dress uniform. At the officers club, when an officer left, he posted his card on the bulletin board as the proper way of saying good-bye.

The officers club, Harnack House in Dahlem about three blocks from the old headquarters, was the center of an officer's social life. It was a grand old building formerly belonging to the Max Planck Institute, spacious but still intimate, wood-paneled with high ceilings. It also had an elegant garden behind the house, where the officers would have parties and receptions. The club had a superb professional German staff, good food, and regular entertainment. There was a saying: If you wanted to meet somebody who was stationed in Berlin, you didn't have to look far. All you had to do was spend two or three nights in the officers club and you'd run into him. In general, when people went out in Berlin, they either started in the officers club or ended there.

One table was not marked, but everybody knew it was reserved for the commanding general. He would show up two or three times a week.

What is an officers club without a legendary bartender? At Harnack House, Grabowski, who for a while was the officer in charge of accounts at the bar, recalls the bartender's name was Luxa. He spoke seven or eight languages, including Serbo-Croatian, being from some unspecified part of the Balkans. He had an astonishing command of English in a stilted sort of way, and charmed the ladies with old-world Austrian flourishes, such as kissing them on the hand.

The manager of the Hilton hotel used to love to watch Luxa at work, threatening to steal him from the club. But when the Hilton offered Luxa a job that would have paid him substantially more than he was paid at Harnack House, Luxa turned down the offer. That seemed suspicious to Grabowski. Why would anyone turn down an offer like that? "I decided that Luxa must be a spy."

"I went to my intelligence friends and told them the story. They laughed and said they had checked Luxa eighteen different ways. In fact, many years before, Luxa had been a bartender in the Russian officers club in Vienna. They had checked him out and were convinced he was not in espionage."

Grabowski reasoned that if Luxa wasn't a spy, he must be a thief, who was stealing from the officers club, and he decided to catch him in the act. The bar at Harnack House was subterranean with long, narrow windows, the upper third of which were above ground. Grabowski planned to watch Luxa secretly and told him to go ahead and close up the bar for the night.

Then Grabowski raced out into the yard behind the house. Before leaving, he had opened one curtain just a tiny bit so he could watch the bar. But he could not see Luxa doing anything wrong. He locked up all the liquors, and did not put anything into a bag or his coat pockets. He put all the money into the proper cash bags. This went on for three nights and left Grabowski none the wiser.

"I came in one late afternoon," he recalls.

 *Luxa was setting up the bar and he says to me, 'Lieutenant, tell me, how old are you?' I say, 'I am twenty-three years old.' And he says in his marvelous central European accent, 'You know, I have been bartender longer than you are alive. You know I am very good bartender.' 'Luxa, you are the best.' 'You know I am so good that if I wanted to steal from you, you could never catch me.' I say, 'I can believe that.' And he says, 'Then why do you lie out in garden every night watching me?'*

Berlin had a way of teaching young lieutenants a lesson in life.

Most of the distinguished visitors who came to Berlin wound up, like everyone else, at the officers club. After the Wall, every congressman and senator who came to Europe and every movie star who wanted to see the Berlin Wall paid a visit to the club, among them Jimmy Stewart and his wife. One evening, Rock Hudson showed up and the waitresses all swooned. That was when Hudson was still considered a ladies' man. "Old Rock cut a swath in there," says Grabowski, "it was unbelievable. Those waitresses would just not look at any of us mortal men for days to come. It took them days to regain their equilibrium. Elke Sommer used to grace the place with her beauty and her throaty laughter. Even Willy Brandt sucked up a few cognacs in the Harnack House Bar."

Filmmaker Billy Wilder chose an interesting time to shoot his movie *One Two Three* starring James Cagney. He had in fact chosen the week the Wall went up and had been planning to shoot near Brandenburg Gate. AFN reporter Dick Rosse drove Cagney down to look at the barriers. Cagney's comment: "Get me back to the hotel. They got guns."[2] The film was finished in Munich. The film was a flop, but Billy Wilder redeemed himself later by coming up with one of the great lines about the city of Berlin. He remarked of a piece of music he found particularly offensive that it was so bad it must have been written by Irving East Berlin.

Harnack House was also frequented by the British officers, the French, and even a number of Russians. The Russians were intelligence officers and diplomats who had free access to West Berlin and could move around as they pleased. "Midnight in Moscow" was an enduring musical request from the Russians, who would hit the dance floor with arms and legs flying.

Before the Wall went up, the Russian commandant and his staff would attend the Armed Forces Day celebrations at Harnack House. The Russians all spoke German and none of them would admit to speaking English. "That was all, of course, a bloody lie," says Grabowski. "Because as you were speaking to them in German, if there was a conversation going on behind them in English, their ears literally turned backwards to try to catch the conversation."

Berlin is famous for its cafes, which were perfect for whiling away a Sunday afternoon. Before the city became divided, Cafe Kranzler was a famous cafe on the Kurfuerstendamm, where all the official spies used to meet every Sunday. You could go to Cafe Kranzler and have your coffee and *Schwarzwaelder Torte* and meet the spies. Someone familiar with the scene could look around and pick them out easily. "Over there are attachés from the Polish embassy, over there are the Russians, and the two guys in the corner in the pork pie hats are CIA."

These people were not hiding it, recalls Grabowski.

They were legitimate spies, doing their job. The waiters loved it. There were waiters at the Cafe Kranzler who knew every one of these people. 'Look, over there is Bastievev, he has not been here in twelve years. Colonel Bastievev, where have you been?' 'You are mistaken. My name is Voroshilov.' When the Wall went up, the U.S. side realized they had been overly dependent on their intelligence on the Eastern countries out of Berlin. These sources dried up real quickly.

The place to dine out in Berlin, most officers agree, was the Maison de France. There was also a club in the Napoleon Barracks and one at

Wannsee called the Pavilion Du Lac, which served seven-course meals with plenty of wine at most reasonable prices.

Another popular restaurant, also at Wannsee, was called Die gruene Laterne (The Green Lantern). Invariably, the troops renamed it "The Green Latrine." "They used to serve a marvelous steak with all the trimmings and a bottle of Beaujolais for the equivalent of about $2.50." One day Grabowski opened the *Berliner Tagesspiegel* and read that the owner had been arrested for selling horse meat. In Germany, as in other countries in Europe, it is not illegal to sell horse meat, but you have to advertise that that is what you are serving. Americans normally do not like the idea of eating horses, so this caused a certain amount of consternation. The owner went to jail for three months and opened his restaurant again. This time, he put *Pferdefleisch* or horse meat on the menu for all to see. "The funny thing, most of us went right back," says Grabowski.

Berlin has an exciting, 'round-the-clock night life with more bars, *Eckkneipen*, and nightclubs than Las Vegas and about the same opening hours. At the *Badewanne*, the Bathtub, one could hear the best jazz in Europe. When in Berlin on a concert tour, Louis Armstrong would sneak out and head for the *Badewanne*, lick his trumpet, and blow the place up.

Another famous jazz name, Ella Fitzgerald, visited the city in 1960, giving a memorable performance in the Deutschlandhalle. When doing "Mac the Knife," she forgot the lyrics, but "Ella and her Fellas" scatted and improvised their way through the tune to the delight of her audience of twenty thousand. This time it was not hunger that got the Berliners to get up from their seats. It was joy. In "The Lady Is a Tramp," she managed to sneak in a reference to the sumptuous Kempinski Hotel.

As for the bars, the Resi bar was a giant place with a water show on the stage. It also, most famously, had pneumatic tubes and telephones on each table. If a young lady caught your fancy, you either sent her a message through the pneumatic tube or you called her on the phone. It added an element of intrigue to the evening, being able to call a stranger at another table, wave across the room, and arrange to meet on the dance floor.

Recalls Norman Schwarzkopf:

> *I used to have a lot of fun at the Resi bar. Sometimes I would be out with my general, and I would have to be wearing my dress blue uniform with my gold aiguillette hanging all over. The party would end early and a bunch of us would take off and go down to the Resi bar. I would sit there, and you would get a telephone call from someone who would ask, 'What is that uniform you are wearing?' I used to tell them I was in the Russian air force because it had a dark blue uniform. I had a lot of fun with things like that.*

For a young officer, one of Berlin's most attractive characteristics was the disproportionate number of women. Says Schwarzkopf, "I was a bachelor when I was there. As a result of the relocation policies that were in effect at that time many men that came across from the East were immediately relocated to West Germany some place, but many women were not. As a result, the ratio of women to men was considerably in our favor as men."

For the more adventurous, a nightclub called Cherchez la Femme offered a different kind of entertainment, more in line with the Berlin known from the movie *Cabaret*. The entertainment was female impersonators and they were a daring group. One highly popular singer was called Ricky Rene; he/she used to convert American songs like "Purple People Eater" into German and sported a trademark outfit of a big blonde wig, brassiere, and G-string with a question mark in front. At the shocking conclusion of her number, the crowd would go wild, while all good men would be appalled. As could be expected, the place was full of Brits who have a long and naughty tradition of drag acts.

Once a month, Roy Murray's wife Donna put on parties just for the Americans. "We wanted to let our hair down, we did not need anybody else there to help us," she says. For one, a Shipwreck Party, the invitations were delivered in bottles, and the living room was decorated with stuff the engineers had dredged up from the Wannsee and waterlogged crates. The guests came dressed as if they had just been shipwrecked on an island. "One couple even doused themselves with our garden hose before they came in the door." Donna Murray also put on a Forty-Niner party for which the German police helpfully provided confiscated gambling equipment, loaning it to the Americans for the weekend. She put on a Back-to-School Party, for which the invitations were written on small slates, cafeteria equipment was borrowed from the Berliner school system, and everybody came dressed as a schoolchild. "The purpose of these parties was to add a little comic relief to what was really a very formal situation because of where we were and what we were doing. We needed to just totally unwind and relax," says Donna Murray. "After the Wall went up, we needed even a little more of that."

The Murrays—and many other Americans who served in Berlin over the years—consider it the best place they had ever been stationed. Indeed a great many servicemen ended up going back to Berlin to live as civilians. "We have moved thirty-four times, compliments of the United States Army, and I always looked forward to going to the next place, because it was an adventure. Berlin is the only place I ever cried leaving," says Donna Murray.

She recalls the day they received her husband's transfer orders to Fort Watjuka, in Arizona, where her husband was going to take over as director of the Combat Surveillance School. "Fort who?" was her first reaction. "When I got there, I thought I had been dropped into the depths of hell. The contrast was phenomenal, from formal clothes to blue jeans and boots." The ability to adapt is, of course, characteristic of an army wife, but the good-bye to Berlin was nonetheless a teary affair.

 At the train station in Berlin, the French and the British, the legation people, and the civilian Germans who had become our friends all came down to the station. As we left, the MP cars and the Berlin police cars did their dadada siren all the way to the city limits. Each time I heard one, I cried some more. We had to move to another compartment. I flooded the first one.

AFN

No other German city took to the Americans the way Berlin did. Other German cities certainly had much bigger American garrisons, Frankfurt and Munich, for example; but somehow Berliners came to have a special affinity for American ways, maybe because here the contrast in spirit between East and West was stark as nowhere else in Germany.

And nothing was as important as radio in spreading American influence. The American Forces Network may have been designed for the U.S. troops, but the Berliners also tuned in from day one. "The network was established to provide a morale boost for the Americans. If it had a beneficial influence on others who were listening, especially friends of ours, that was great, too," says Dick Rosse who worked as a news correspondent for AFN in Berlin in the early 1960s.

The station's first manager, Lieutenant Mel Dunkelman, arrived from Paris in his jeep with a trailer full of records. In Berlin, the AFN first went on the air on August 4, 1945, playing George Gershwin's "Rhapsody in Blue," making a point of choosing a piece written by a Jewish composer.[1]

"It was a very basic operation," recalls Mark White, who had come from Patton's headquarters in Munich to witness the station's first months of operation, and who would go on to become the AFN's legendary director for three decades. The "station" first broadcast from an improvised hut on the back of a truck parked in a garden on Podbielskiallee in Dahlem. "The antenna we used was a piece of wire strung between two trees," recalls White. It then moved into permanent quarters in a villa, number 28, which incidentally was said to have belonged to Joachim von Ribbentrop. The villa was chosen because of its massive iron shutters, allegedly installed to protect the former owner's extensive art collection.

In the early days, the big bands ruled the airwaves. And what music: Glenn Miller and the Dorsey brothers, Benny Goodman and the brash sound of Charlie Barnett's "Skyliner." The Berliners would hear Harry James, bursting into a cascade of glitter notes in "Trumpet Blues and Cantabile," and the great Gene Krupa hunched over his drums flailing away like some demented dwarf. They would hear the immortal Johnny Guanieri of Artie Shaw's Grammercy Five, tinkling away on his harpsi-

Mario Mach

Shirley MacLaine is welcomed by AFN's Mark White (l) and Captain Jack Maloney. According to White, the AFN "was the sound of freedom."

chord so delicately that the sound would only just reach the second floor of a doll's house.

"AFN was a new spirit. It was happy music. It gave the Berliners hope," says Mark White. "It was the sound of freedom."

For a people who had been isolated and force-fed the operatic inanities of Franz Lehar, the new titles indeed had their own strange poetry: "When Buddha Smiles," "East of the Sun," "Serenade to a Savage," and everything written by Harold Arlen and Johnny Mercer about honey-tongued, two-timing women who leave you to sing the "Blues in the Night." From Miller you could even learn some of the immutable laws of nature, as in "Must Be Jelly, 'cause Jam Don't Shake Like That." All of it was, of course, thoroughly *entartet*, perverted, as the Nazi censors used to put it, and the young people of Berlin loved it.

At the beginning of the airlift, the AFN was on the air eighteen hours a day. Soon, the Air Force put in a special request to Washington for AFN Berlin to stay on the air twenty-four hours a day, so that the pilots flying between midnight and 6:00 A.M. would have something to listen to. The wish was immediately granted. During the airlift, the pilots also used AFN as a radio beacon.

AFN was perceived by the Berliners as a guarantee of continued U.S. presence in Berlin. Recalls White, "If we went off the air for more than five minutes, the switchboard would light up like a Christmas tree, and the Berliners would call in and ask what was happening with AFN, if the Americans were leaving. We were careful to avoid holes if AFN was on the air."

The music and the U.S. soldiers became fused in the minds of young Berliners. "When the Americans came, they were in uniform, but under the uniform, they were civilians. They were not military people at heart. This was quite different from what had been the norm for a hundred years in Berlin, where a civilian was first and foremost a soldier. The American soldiers brought a new feeling to us. It impressed me deeply," says Sigurd Hildenbach, who was born in 1931 and was a RIAS radio producer for thirty-two years. When the new German army, the Bundeswehr, was formed in 1956, the slogan was "citizens in uniform."

The big band era lasted until the mid-1950s, then came the quartets like Four Lads, Four Freshmen, and Four Aces and other exponents of doo-wop. They were followed by the early rockers, Elvis Presley, Buddy Holly, Bill Haley and the Comets, Chubby Checker, "Twisting the Night Away," not to forget Connie Francis and her immortal slow tune, "Where the Boys Are."

Many a Berliner owes his English to listening to AFN Berlin. Rather than the prissy British English accents dominant elsewhere on the European continent, in Berlin you often hear an unrepentant American twang, courtesy of the AFN. The station would also teach some pretty creative grammar, as in "I Ain't Never Done Nothing to Nobody No Time."

"We did our homework in the afternoon listening to Frolic at Five," says Hildenbach. "We loved George Hudak, the disk jockey. He was celebrated like a king. I became a member of the AFN jazz club, which was founded by George Kennedy, the actor. I still have my membership card."

"We learned typically American English which was different from what we learned at school," says Hildenbach. "We liked it more than Oxford English, which was too stiff. American English was easier, more colloquial, and friendlier, no offense to the British. It was just a new way of feeling, a new way of life."

Again, during the dark days after the building of the Wall, AFN radio provided a lifeline to the outside world, making Berliners feel less claustrophobic, reminding them that there were other things in life than East German leader Walter Ulbricht. In fact, when you listened to a lazy Stan Getz bossa nova, what was Walter Ulbricht other than an uncool little squirt with an uncool little goatee and an uncool squeaky little voice?

Says Rosse, "I'm convinced that our being on the air during those especially difficult times from 1961 to 1963, was beneficial, not only for the morale of the U.S. people, but for the Berliners as well. It was another example of our 'being there.' Every little gesture was important to them at the time."

In fact, even after the Wall had gone up, AFN continued to get requests from East Germany and from East Berlin, remembers Rosse. On one occasion, a stone was tossed over the Wall by an East Berliner with a request tied to it, for a song to be played on AFN.

The East German authorities were of course aware of the pernicious influence of AFN. In an attempt to counter its impact, for a while they aired their own competing radio program, "Radio Freies Deutschland," directed at American soldiers. It used pirated copies of American hits and interspersed them with heavy doses of propaganda, mostly peddling the rationale for building the Wall and stressing the immediate and pressing necessity of signing a separate peace treaty with the East Germans.

"Radio Freies Deutschland" would even address itself to individual American soldiers, whose names were obviously pulled off AFN. To be among the select few was exciting. "I was always disappointed that my name was never mentioned, because I was on the air a lot in those days," muses Rosse. Predictably, the East German attempt to compete with AFN was not successful. Somehow, the notion of Walter Ulbricht or Erich Honecker in the disk jockeying business did not quite work.[2]

THE 1970s AND 1980s

The western reaction to the Berlin Wall, when it finally came, reassured the Berliners. Nonetheless, the city had clearly suffered a nasty blow. The defense of West Berlin was not solely a military issue; there was a city to be kept alive, and much industry had fled the city after the Wall crisis. The composition of the work force was also not ideal; one quarter of the population was sixty-five and older. Steps were taken in Bonn to shore up the city through major tax relief to lure firms back to Berlin.

For Willy Brandt it was a turning point as well. Historians have dated the birth of Brandt's famed Eastern Policy, the *Ostpolitik*, to August 1961, when he failed to get the response from the West he had expected to the Berlin Wall—that American forces would tear it down. Brandt realized that the East Germans would not be helped in a direct way by force and that the Americans were not going to take risks for the sake of maintaining the unity of Berlin.

Accordingly, Brandt reached the conclusion that the only way to deal with the division of Berlin, and to lessen its impact, was through diplomacy and constant contacts. He wanted as much as possible to normalize the Federal Republic's relations with the East Bloc, including the Soviet Union.

In 1963, Egon Bahr, who had become Willy Brandt's close associate, launched the policy of *Kleine Schritte*, small steps, to improve relations between the two Berlins. Recalls Bahr, "When the Wall went up, we realized that nobody was able to help us, neither the Americans, nor the French, nor the British, nor the Bonn government. We could either resign ourselves to it or we could, based on our own possibilities, start to make some holes in the Wall," says Bahr.

The first agreement allowing Berliners to visit relatives in the eastern sector from Christmas to New Year was reached in December 1963. Three more such arrangements were to follow. When Brandt became foreign minister in 1966 and chancellor three years later, these first steps developed into a much broader concept of *Ostpolitik*, the rapprochement between West Germany and its eastern neighbors.

The Federal Republic had until then avoided any kind of government-level contact with the East Germans, as this would constitute an acknowledgment of Germany's de facto division into two states. Furthermore, the West German government had regarded other nations' establishment of ties with the East Germans as constituting "an unfriendly act." Giving up this policy, Chancellor Willy Brandt himself conducted two meetings with East German Prime Minister Willi Stoph.

A series of international agreements followed. In August 1970, Germany and the Soviet Union concluded the Moscow Treaty, in which they renounced the use of force to settle political disputes and declared Europe's borders inviolable. (The German side, in a special letter, did make clear that this did not preclude German self-determination to reunify.)

Subsequently, in December 1970, Brandt signed the Warsaw Treaty with the Poles, declaring the Oder-Neisse River the western border of Poland. Up until this point, the German side had insisted that the border question had to wait until a peace agreement was signed with Germany as a whole. In a famous gesture of atonement, Brandt fell to his knees in front of the Polish memorial to the dead of the Jewish ghetto.[1]

As for the status of Berlin, a number of key issues were addressed in the Four Powers Agreement on Berlin, which took effect on June 3, 1972. It did not solve all of Berlin's problems, but the Soviets no longer contested the western powers' right of presence in the city, and they accepted the city's ties with the Federal Republic of Germany. After nearly two decades of Cold-War hostilities, West and East Germany established diplomatic ties in a treaty that committed the two Germanys to good neighborly relations, paving the way for international recognition of the GDR and the membership for both Germanys in the United Nations.

A practical agreement on facilitating traffic between West Germany and Berlin was reached, the so-called Transit Agreement. For the first time since the end of World War II, there now existed an undisputed legal foundation for unimpeded allied traffic to and from Berlin. West Berliners were allowed to visit relatives in East Berlin and East Germany, as well.

A fierce opponent of the agreement had been Walter Ulbricht. In May 1971 he was removed by the Soviets and replaced by Erich Honecker, the thin-lipped bureaucrat who had been in charge of the construction of the Wall. Up to the very end, Ulbricht was still making speeches exhorting West German workers to look to East Germany as a model and throw off capitalism. Actually, Ulbricht's most pressing fear, as head of the GDR, was that he would be squeezed between Moscow and Bonn. When Moscow started moving towards Bonn in the Brandt years, he became very nervous. Fearing that contacts with West Germany would lure more people to the West, he tried to block the Four Powers Agreement on Berlin.

"There was not a great deal of difference in philosophy between Ulbricht and Honecker. But Honecker was a younger man and in some ways perhaps more pragmatic," says Helmut Sonnenfeldt who was an advisor to Henry Kissinger at the time.

A July 1970 discussion between Erich Honecker and Soviet leader Leonid Brezhnev had revealed some of the Soviet concerns and irritations.[2] "There is a certain superiority of [the East Germans] with regard to the other socialist countries, your experiences, methods of leadership, etc. This is also directed at us. This also upsets us and this must be changed," Brezhnev huffed. "I know myself how Walter deals with these questions—from my own experience. . . . But it actually is not he who does anything—in reality—we are there—our power—we account for the concrete situation. It is this way in many areas. So the superiority of the GDR must be eliminated." That the Soviets expected a different tone from Honecker is clear. Honecker heeded the warning to a point, but it is ironic that two decades later Mikhail Gorbachev would find him just as intractable as Khrushchev and Brezhnev had found Ulbricht.

The Soviet reasons for encouraging *Ostpolitik* were simple: There was the advantage that the West Germans would pay the Soviets for influencing the East Germans to be less draconian in the way they handled the division, and the West Germans could even be persuaded to subsidize the East Germans to some extent. And, of course, the Soviets saw this as a chance to wean West Germany away from NATO.

Washington, on the other hand, expressed reservations about Germany's *Ostpolitik*. It was feared that the Soviets would in fact succeed in splitting off the Germans from the NATO alliance through promises of greater contacts between the two Germanys, turning West Germany more towards neutrality. At the time, Henry Kissinger remarked that he dreaded the moment "when no German chancellor can afford the hostility of the Soviet Union."

"This caused a certain amount of uneasiness because some of the vocabulary sounded like Germany getting back, in a very modest way, into its old position of maneuvering between East and West. There was a feeling that this might gain momentum, whatever the intentions of Brandt were," says Helmut Sonnenfeldt. Those with a sense of history recalled the Prussian-Russian military pact of the Napoleonic Wars and the Treaty of Rapallo between the U.S.S.R. and Germany in 1922. There had been the Red Army's relationship with the Reichswehr in the 1930s and, of course, the Molotov-Ribbentrop Pact of 1939, which paved the way for World War II.

While Washington was looking at the bigger strategic picture, the Bonn government tended to see the relationship with East Germany in more immediate, human terms. Alexander Longolius, a long-time Social Democratic member of the Berlin parliament, lays out the Social Democratic position. "The Soviets had seventeen million German hostages. If your wife is being held by a kidnapper, then you are willing to talk to that person and discuss conditions. That was exactly our position. We did not like it; we would have liked to be as independent as the United States, who has never found itself in that kind of situation. But we had to."

However, notes Sonnenfeldt, as President Richard Nixon himself began to get interested in better relations with the Soviets, and the period of détente began, it became harder for Washington to disapprove of the German policy; it would have been difficult to claim an American prerogative in dealing with the Soviets. Furthermore, whatever domestic criticism it might have excited, Brandt's *Ostpolitik* became institutionalized in the course of the 1970s, and the basic outline was followed by the conservative governments of the 1980s.

There were few major incidents relating to the status of Berlin after the signing of the Four Powers Agreement of 1972. For the first time in postwar history, the situation in Berlin approached "business as usual." Says Juergen Graf, who had become editor-in-chief of RIAS, "The big confrontation was kind of over. For a journalist who was so much involved from 1945 to 1963 after the Kennedy visit, it was in a way boring. It was routine. The questions now debated were of the type whether women over 65 can cross over now or in two years."

∎ TERRORISM ∎

In a different sense, however, the 1970s was also a period of upheaval in Germany. Radical political groups like the Baader-Meinhof gang were engaged in urban terrorism across the nation. Because of its special status, which made its citizens exempt from the draft, Berlin attracted a considerable number of left-wing, pacifist youth from West Germany.

Berlin has always been a kind of weather vane, the first place to experience political movements and fashions that would hit West Germany later. It was here the student rebellion grew first.

The U.S. engagement in Vietnam was especially unpopular. Says Lieutenant Colonel Billy Arthur,

Before the Vietnam War ended, Americans had become targets all over the world. But particularly in Berlin, the reaction was at a high pitch. It was very clear that you were an American, and that you were always visible. That was what you were supposed to be. On the one hand, the Americans had to show the flag as the defenders of Berlin in the Cold War. On the other hand, that made you the perfect target for anti-Vietnam sentiment and anti-Vietnam demonstrations. You couldn't go in some hole and hide.

Bomb threats against American facilities and schools became frequent.

You never knew whether it was to be a real bomb or not," says Billy Arthur. *"I can remember being in Harnack House one Sunday morning when the bomb squad was called in because some guy had left his briefcase in the coat room, and it was still there when some of the workers got there the next morning. So they took the thing out and blew up the briefcase of a guy who left it after work to have a couple of drinks.*

In the 1980s, hostility against the American presence intensified over the question of land-based missiles in Europe. In 1978, because of the Soviet installation of medium-range SS-20 missiles in Warsaw Pact countries, NATO saw itself forced to undertake its own modernization of its nuclear defense. In 1979, in the so-called "double-track decision," NATO proclaimed that it would install 108 Pershing II missiles and 464 cruise missiles, but offered to negotiate a reduction in numbers or their complete elimination if the Soviets would cut the number of their own missiles. Which of course the Soviets showed no inclination to do.

The Soviets were on the march. In December 1979 they invaded Afghanistan, and the international climate darkened. Thus at the beginning of the 1980s, German Chancellor Helmut Schmidt, who had succeeded Brandt in 1974, lost his customary cool and talked darkly about an unstoppable slide towards war, similar to the situation that precipitated World War I.

Ronald Reagan was now president of the United States, and the German left-wing media portrayed him as a cowboy, talking in what they considered highly irresponsible fashion about the Soviet Union as the "Evil Empire." In fact, when Ronald Reagan first visited Berlin in 1982, there were no public appearances scheduled, only a private affair for specially invited guests at the Charlottenburg Castle because of concerns over public disturbances. While twenty years before the Soviet Union had been universally recognized as the chief cause of tension in Europe, the tendency now was increasingly to downplay the ideological differences between East and West and to see the Soviet Union as just another superpower, cautious and sensible as opposed to those volatile and unpredictable Americans.

The stirrings of the popular opposition forces within Poland had created further international tensions. Chancellor Schmidt was visiting East Germany in December 1981 when martial law was imposed by Poland's communist government. The following morning, a highly distressed Schmidt announced to journalists that Erich Honecker was just as shocked as he was by the developments, giving the unfortunate impression that both Germanys had a common interest in seeing the unrest in Poland put down in the name of stability and business as usual.

Given the history of the Social Democratic Party in German politics, its opposition to the Nazis and its resistance to the communist takeover attempt after World War II, the SPD found itself in an awkward position when it came to deciding what they thought about events in Poland. Says Egon Bahr,

We had our own experience in 1953. We had the experience of Hungary and Poland. We had the experience of Czechoslovakia. We had the opinion, if the proud Poles are overdoing it, the Soviets will intervene, and the result would be that we would cry, but we would do nothing. And we should not play heroes at the shoulders of the Poles. This was our attitude. I have to confess that I underestimated the Poles. They knew better than we. But undoubtedly, the fear of an additional intervention of the Soviets against the Poles was shared in all other capitals, too.

In 1982, the government of Chancellor Schmidt collapsed and was replaced by that of CDU leader Helmut Kohl. By 1983, the time had come to install the missiles. Leonid Brezhnev threatened to create "walls of fire," if the decision was implemented. The popular German opposition to the decision was fierce. Particularly, the Green movement leapt into action.

The highly emotional nature of the Greens stood in strange contrast with the sedate prosperity of West German society in general. A product of the student movement and the peace movement in the 1970s, the Greens appealed to the young and the disaffected, to students, pacifists, ecologists, and Christian activists. Its leader during this period was Petra Kelly, who had an American stepfather and had been educated in the United States. With Joan-of-Arc–like intensity, she denounced what she saw as world-wide American aggression, suggesting at one point that the nuclear codes be encased in the heart of a child, which President Ronald Reagan would have to rip open to begin a nuclear war.

In an open letter to Mayor Eberhard Diepgen of Berlin in 1985, Kelly protested vigorously the military "occupation" of Berlin and the way it deprived the West Berliners of their democratic rights. "Do the Berliners, of all people, not have the right to decide if and how they are to be defended in the case of war?" Kelly demanded. Her idea of defending Berlin, of course, was to declare the city a nuclear-free zone.

For Americans stationed in Berlin, terrorism remained a serious concern, Colonel Stuart Herrington recalls. "There was so much preoccupation with terrorism that it began to genuinely impact and hurt one's ability to enjoy the beauties of the city." Terrorists blew up the French

Cultural House, the Maison de France on Kurfuerstendamm, right after Herrington arrived in 1983. By the time Herrington was getting ready to leave in 1986, the Libyans had bombed the La Belle discotheque, a popular hangout for U.S. servicemen. Two people were killed in the bombing, one an American serviceman, and more than two hundred were injured, fifty of them Americans. U.S. intelligence had determined that the Libyan People's Bureau in East Berlin had planned the operation, and the Reagan administration was getting ready to retaliate by bombing Tripoli.

In Berlin, security precautions had to be taken. Recalls Herrington, "They put fences around the PX, and they closed the outpost film theater on one Saturday morning because there was a report that terrorists were going to drive a truckful of explosives into this theater full of American kiddies watching the Saturday matinee. You had to open your trunk and the hood of your car just to get into the PX parking lot."

Rik DeLisle, who today is program director at UKW 94.3 in Berlin, remembers several bomb threats. In 1978, he arrived in Berlin as a sergeant of the air force assigned to Allied Forces Network. DeLisle was the host of the program "Old Gold Retold," an oldies request program, which ran every night for two hours. "One night when I was broadcasting somebody called me about ten minutes into the program and said in broken English, 'There is a bomb in your house.'" DeLisle did not know whether that referred to his quarters in Zehlendorf or to the broadcasting house in Saargemuender Strasse. He immediately called Frankfurt to have the American station there take over the show, then he called the bomb demolition squad and got out of the building. He was the only one there at the time. The demolition truck came, and then the fire truck and the police car. The demolition squad was decked out in their heavy vests and helmets.

"OK, let's go back in and have a look," they told DeLisle. "'You are crazy, that's your job. My job is to make the radio work. Your job is to find the bomb.' 'But Sergeant DeLisle, we do not know what's in there and you do. We are not going to take apart everything we see with a wire on it. Somebody has to show us.'"

A few minutes later DeLisle's boss Major Fowler, program director of

AFN, Berlin, showed up. "Boss, they are crazy," DeLisle protested. "They want me to go in there." Major Fowler just shrugged his shoulders. "It's a tough life when you are a soldier," he told his broadcaster.

We both went in and started looking around. We did not find any bomb in the quarters. We could not find anything in the studio. And then we had to go into the basement, where we opened up the door to this room where the technicians had been storing their gear for the last thirty years. Everything in the room looked like a bomb! Everything had wires coming out of it. We ended up going through looking at anything that did not have dust on it which was suspect.

Fortunately, it turned out, there was no bomb. But the next time, in the early 1980s, the phone threat against AFN was for real.

We all filed out of the radio-television station, disc jockeys, announcers, technicians, and secretaries. We went all through the station when it dawned on somebody that maybe they meant the transmitter. The transmitter was in the Pacelliallee near a soccer field. The people responsible for cutting the grass always left it uncut around the transmitter, so the grass was four feet high. And there was the bomb. Somebody had crawled unobserved through the grass and attached a bomb to the AFN transmitter.

It was removed safely by the bomb squad.

Despite the fierce domestic resistance, Chancellor Kohl went ahead with the installation of the American missiles. The threatened "ice age" that the antinuclear movement had warned so direly against failed to materialize. Instead, the Soviets finally declared themselves ready to negotiate, which led to the signing of the 1987 agreement eliminating land-based intermediate-range nuclear weapons in Europe.

The American government, however, remained worried about the safety of its troops in Berlin. If states like Iran, Iraq, or Libya set up terrorist centers in their embassies in East Berlin, they had fairly easy access to West Berlin because the West German government did not want to put up a wall on its own side. Recalls Longolius, "The Americans were concerned with the border regime becoming more liberal, that there would not be enough safeguards against terrorists coming in. They had a point very definitely." One solution was to let guards travel in civilian clothes on the S-Bahn from the border stations. "When they saw somebody they did not trust, they would travel with that person and grab them well inside West Berlin to demonstrate that this was not a border incident but something that happened in West Berlin."

While the legal issues surrounding the status of Berlin had been resolved in 1971, a low level of friction between the governments remained constant. The East German government, of course, saw its own advantage in pressing the issue of terrorism. Its salami tactics were designed to slice away little pieces of existing agreements with symbolic actions that the West would be either too lazy or too inattentive to respond to. The idea was to alter the center of gravity in the treaty. The continuing infringements included hampering auto traffic, increasing the amount of money visitors would have to change when they entered East Berlin, and interfering with the allied air corridors.

One such instance was the announcement made by East Germany in May 1986 that all foreign diplomats entering or exiting East Berlin would be required to show passports rather than the customary red identity cards. This measure, so it was claimed, was designed to accommodate western security fears in the wake of the April 5, 1986, disco bombing.

The passport issue cut to the core of the city's status. Compliance with East Germany's demand would have amounted to a recognition of the Berlin Wall as an international border, rather than a demarcation line between sectors. And on questions concerning Berlin, the western powers would deal only with the Soviet Union, not the East German government.

The measure was seen as part of a plan by East Germany to use the issue of terrorism to change the status of Berlin. U.S. Secretary of State George Schulz accused the East German action of "piggybacking on our legitimate concern about the movements of Libyans and terrorists from East Berlin and East Germany to the West." When the western powers asserted this opposition, the East Germans dropped the demand.

In other words, even when things looked most normal, vigilance had to be constant. The danger was, as one diplomat pointed out at the time, that the allied position in Berlin was based on a whole series of circumstances, understandings, practices, and precedents that came out of the Potsdam Agreement at the end of World War II and of the Four Powers Agreement of 1972. And it was on the integrity of the whole fabric of agreements that the western position in the city ultimately rested. Pulling out one or two provisions at the time would have the same effect as pulling a thread from a sweater. The impact might not be immediately noticeable, but if you persist, the whole sweater becomes unraveled.

One of the few incidents that occurred between the superpowers in Berlin that concerned the Berlin Brigade was the killing of Major Arthur D. Nicholson, Jr., in 1985. Major Nicholson was a military liaison officer with the U.S. mission in Potsdam. According to the agreement of 1947, which established missions for each occupying power (each with a staff of fourteen) in the others' zones, personnel from the missions had the right to move freely over territory in East and West Germany for the sake of observation, excepting military installations. Major Nicholson was in an authorized spot when he was shot by a Soviet guard without warning and then allowed to bleed to death.

The sergeant who accompanied Major Nicholson was kept at gunpoint inside his car and prevented from coming to the major's aid, a kind of tragic parallel to the death of Peter Fechter at the Wall. What caused the Soviet behavior? Says Colonel Stephen Bowman, who is in charge of the U.S. Military Archives in Carlisle Barracks, Pennsylvania, "It was a mistake. A young Soviet soldier saw an American officer in the training area, panicked, and shot him." The incident, which could have had a major impact on U.S.–Soviet relations, was settled quietly by diplomats.

10

SPANDAU PRISON

Throughout the Cold War, through the Berlin blockade, through the air-lift, the Berlin crisis of 1961, the Cuban missile crisis, through détente, one thing remained unchanged in Berlin: Spandau Prison. Apart from the Berlin Air Safety Center, the forbidding fortress in the middle of the city was the only place where Americans, British, French, and Russians continued to work together. It was here they kept watch over the Nazi war criminals for forty years. "While summits were being held to prevent a Third World War, we were busy arguing about Rudolf Hess's new dentures or Baldur von Schirach's knee bandage," writes Eugene K. Bird, who served as a guard officer in the early days and later came back as the American director of Spandau from 1964–72, in his book, *The Loneliest Man in the World*.

Located in the British sector, Spandau was a fitting place to incarcerate the seven top Nazis, who had been sentenced at the Nuremberg trials. As a garrison, Spandau predated the city of Berlin itself, going back to the thirteenth century. However, the massive red-brick building that American soldiers came to know was built in the 1870s. Allegedly, French prisoners from the Franco-German war of 1870–71 helped carry the bricks. During World War II, the Nazis reserved Spandau as a prison for political prisoners en route to the concentration camps and as a place of execution. It had 132 single cells, five punishment cells, ten larger cells, and a guillotine.[1] There were also facilities for hanging up to eight people at a time. When the war ended, it held six hundred prisoners.

Of the twenty-two war criminals who were tried at Nuremberg in 1947, twelve were sentenced to death and seven received sentences from ten years to life in prison. After the Nuremberg trials, Spandau's sole occupants were the seven prisoners: Baldur von Schirach, leader of the Nazi Youth (twenty years); Karl Doenitz, commander-in-chief of the German Navy (ten years); Konstantin von Neurath, Reichprotector of Bohemia (fifteen years); Erich Raeder, admiral of the Navy (life); Albert Speer, Hitler's architect and armaments minister (twenty years); Walter Funk, president of the Reichsbank (life); and Rudolf Hess, Hitler's deputy who flew to Scotland in a Messerschmitt in 1941 on a self-imposed mission to make peace with the British (life).[2]

There was no way these prisoners were going to escape. The prison was surrounded by six concrete guard towers as well as a ten-foot barbed-wire fence and an electrical fence carrying four thousand volts. The military guard contingent was responsible for the outer perimeter of the wall.

As a second lieutenant, Charles Toftoy was a guard at Spandau from 1959–61. He recalls marching his troops through the huge Spandau gate to relieve the Russian contingency during the change of the guard. "Everything had to be perfect to a gnat's eye. I had to halt them right on the exact spot because when you turned to face the Russians, you had to be perfectly lined up with them. And of course, you had not seen them ahead of time, so you had to practice these distances. I had to really drill the soldiers so that the distance was exactly right."

It was with good reason the drill at Spandau was considered something special. "I had generals observing me, not captains or colonels. [They were] like the owners of a football team in a little box, watching their team perform," Toftoy recalls. The two guard teams would halt, present arms, the Russian officer would salute Toftoy and he the Russian officer, whereupon the Russians would leave through the gate.

Occasional threats against the prisoners, to capture or kidnap any one of them, meant that security was extremely tight. The scenarios included various James-Bond plots, including attempts to skydive into the prison.

U.S. Army

Changing of the guard with a handshake. Soviet and U.S. contingents in front of Spandau Prison, where German war criminals were housed.

"Though guard duty can be kind of boring, to have one of those men taken from under your wing would be pretty embarrassing, not to mention a lot of other things," he says.

To test his troops, Toftoy would set his alarm clock at different times of the night. "I used to wake up like 2:30 in the morning and then sneak around and throw pebbles on different locations to make sure the guards were awake. If the guard at the tower said, 'Halt,' I knew he was awake. They never knew when to expect me. I think the troops thought I may have been a little nuts, but there was a reason."

The actual guarding of the cells and the care and the physical contact with the prisoners was done by permanent warders and the governors.

There were four prison governors, one from each of the four occupying powers. They were the key keepers. Each governor had a team of fifteen warders who were on duty twenty-four hours a day. The French were responsible for the finances, the British for the upkeep of the buildings, the Americans for the medical care and the cell block maintenance, and the Russians for hiring people.

Though the cooperation in Spandau continued through thick and thin, it was a strained affair much of the time, as might be expected. The main disagreement between the allied powers centered on the treatment of the prisoners. The western powers often favored a more lenient treatment on humanitarian grounds, which the Soviets fiercely resisted, arguing that there are some crimes for which the statute of limitations never runs out. After all, the Russians had lost over twenty million people in the war.

"Some of our meetings lasted three minutes, some lasted three days," says Bird. "Just talking about simple things like what can a prisoner receive from his family as a gift. Censoring was another bone of contention. The Russians insisted that they not be able to read or write about anything concerning World War I and World War II, their health, or Spandau Prison itself." After lengthy discussions, they decided on one newspaper from the GDR, a communist newspaper, and one from each of the allied zones.

As to letters, one every four weeks was the agreed limit, just from family members, and no longer than two thousand words. There were debates over amenities such as refrigerators and transistor radios. According to Bird, Hess liked the Beatles, because of the beat.

Diet was another touchy subject. In the beginning, there were various types of rations; the worst of the menus was the category-three ration, which was actually a starvation diet and would in time have caused some deaths from malnutrition. The Americans refused to starve the prisoners, insisting that their punishment should be only what was ordered by the court, which did not include death from starvation. "When we took over from the Russians," Bird recalls, "the general ordered that you take that food in with bayonets if you have to. And that is exactly what happened. We said this is our month, and we are going to take this food in whether you want or not and we won our case." Since the prison was located in a western sector, western standards would apply.

The prisoners were to be addressed only by number, which were written on the back of their prison uniforms and across their trouser knees. Rudolf Hess was "Number Seven" to the warders for the forty years he resided in the prison. The guards were not allowed to talk to or shake hands with the prisoners. In fact by writing his book on Hess, which was published in 1974, Bird broke rules by interviewing and photographing Hess. However, Bird claimed his first amendment rights and cited in his defense a memorandum authored by General Eisenhower when he was Commander-in-Chief of the Allied Forces in Europe, in which he said that every officer or person in position of authority had an obligation to record matters of historical interest.

Though never in direct contact with the prisoners, there was one time when the soldiers on guard duty could actually observe them. That was when, every four hours, there was a change of guards in the towers. In the back of the prison was a garden area where the prisoners were allowed to come out, officially only one hour a day, but depending on who was on duty, they stayed longer, on average two hours. It happened quite often that the prisoners were out in the yard during the changing of the guard.

Since no one could prevent observation, the guards got at least an impression of their charges. Hess, the deputy Fuehrer, looked sinister with deeply sunken eyes and bushy eyebrows. He spent a lot of time sitting on a stone bench, immobile, and staring straight ahead. When Hess arrived at Spandau, it had been quite a different story; he clearly believed he was destined to become the leader of the new Germany and had written long press releases for the grand occasion when he would take over Germany and negotiate with the Allies. Hess was also known for being difficult, forever complaining that his food was being poisoned and howling in his cell at night from supposed stomach problems. He also refused to see his family for twenty-two years.

Speer was busy using his architectural talents to create a kitchen garden. He had a little wheelbarrow, in which he loaded rocks and moved them from one side of the garden to the other. It looked crazy, but he got a lot of exercise out of it. He was also on an imaginary walking tour of the world, traversing whole continents by averaging some seventeen kilometers a day. Baldur von Schirach also had a little garden which he tended.

The unofficial language of Spandau Prison, through which everyone communicated, warders and prisoners, was German. The French took a certain Gallic pride in not speaking English, and the Soviets, though many undoubtedly spoke English very well, were not allowed to admit that they knew English. They were trained to listen to see what they could pick up.

With the change in the military guard, the kitchen changed as well. Like the prisoners, the permanent warders, some of them there for a number of years, were subjected to French food one month, the next month British food, then American food, and then Russian food.

Lieutenant Colonel Tony Le Tissier took up his post in October 1981 as British governor. By then, only Rudolf Hess was left. Von Neurath, Raeder, and Funk had been released in 1954, 1955, and 1957 respectively because of poor health. Doenitz served out his entire sentence and was released in 1956, and in 1966 the turn came to Speer and von Schirach. Several attempts to have Hess released on humanitarian grounds had failed, everytime running into stiff Soviet opposition. The Soviets argued convincingly that Hess was the last living symbol of the Nazi Party and that he had in fact been a most important member of that party. Furthermore, they argued, the only reason he had flown to Britain was in the hope of creating a situation where Germany could attack the Soviet Union without worrying about Britain. Besides, conditions in Spandau were better than those of the majority of Russian prisons. This was no doubt true.

"Hess's favorite place was in the garden," says Le Tissier. "He would tell the warder in attendance that he wanted to go into the garden. He would take up to an hour to get dressed to go into the garden." Throughout his imprisonment, however, Hess refused to do any kind of menial work in the garden, which he considered beneath his dignity. His dignity did allow him to feed the birds, though.

Hess dressing himself for these excursions was quite a sight. "He would dress up in the most elaborate fashion, protecting himself from any eventuality from the weather. In winter, in particular, he wore a baraclava helmet under a hat with a scarf around his neck. He wore a coat that came down to his ankles and he wore moonboots," says Le Tissier.

At one point, Hess decided that his loden greatcoat, which came all the way down to his ankles, needed to be replaced. It was impossible to find anything like it, but he had seen one of the Russian warders wear a sort of padded jacket, and he thought he would like one, too. The problem was that none of them were built to his specifications. In the end, the British military tailor tacked a skirt onto the chosen garment, and Hess had himself a padded Russian kapok jacket that came all the way down the ground.

The Spandau operation, of course, came to a rather unexpected end on August 17, 1987, when Rudolf Hess committed suicide at the age of 93. He had spent that day in the garden. On this occasion he wore a raincoat and a sombrero. The sentry on duty that day was particularly curious because he had never seen Hess before. He saw Hess walking slowly down the garden, occasionally stopping and looking around, as though saying good-bye.

The warder on duty went ahead to unlock a small cabin in the garden, which Hess used in bad weather. Hess went in and closed the door after him. After two minutes, the warder came back and found that Hess had committed suicide by hanging himself from one of the four reading lamps in the cabin. "He had tied a single, one-over loop on an extension cord, stuck his head in it, and slid down the wall with his feet out in front," says Le Tissier. "If you do that with a cable, although the knot moves, the cord remains absolutely straight and tightens. That and a weak heart was sufficient to kill him."

When the warder came back, he discovered Hess on the floor, apparently still alive. The warder slipped off the noose, put Hess's head on a folded blanket, loosened his clothing, ran to the back of the building where there was an old field telephone, and blew the alarm. The gate warder flashed the word "paradox" to the hospital, the prearranged code word to the hospital to send an ambulance straight away. All attempts to resuscitate the prisoner, however, were futile.[3]

Conspiracy theories started circulating immediately that Hess had been murdered. "This is clearly nonsense," says Le Tissier. "The guard company was American. They all knew each other and there were no strangers in that place. Allegations that the British SAS had gotten in were also nonsense; they would have been recognized as strangers."

The Four Powers Agreement gave precise instructions what to do when Hess died. Strangely enough, these contingency plans included no reference to potential suicide, despite the fact that Hess had tried committing suicide twenty years previously when he had broken his glasses and tried to cut his wrists with the shards. The prepared press statement did not cover this contingency, and when it was given it aroused suspicion. *60 Minutes* and the BBC started the speculation. One question was, why was there no v-mark on Hess's neck from the cord? Eventually, the speculation subsided when the suicide note was read.

Why did Hess commit suicide at the age of ninety-three? Why bother after forty years? "In this case the reason was quite simple," say Le Tissier. "He was a very proud man and he had become incontinent. This was something he could not tolerate. He hid it from the doctors. He tried various experiments to try to check it, but it did not work. On one occasion, he tried eating four hard-boiled eggs in succession, which only gave him heart palpitations, and he had to be brought to the hospital."

After Hess's suicide in 1987, Spandau Prison was razed and the rubble carefully buried in an undisclosed location. The purpose was to prevent the old prison from becoming a kind of shrine to the Nazi leaders.

With Hess's death ended one of the more bizarre chapters in Berlin history. What replaced the prison could not be more mundane: a British shopping center.[4]

THE FALL OF THE WALL

In the fall of 1989, the events that had begun in Poland in the early 1980s reached a culmination. The Soviet Union had seen a turnover of old men in the leadership position, and in 1985 Mikhail Gorbachev had come along with his policies of Perestroika and Glasnost. The rest of the world was as unprepared as Gorbachev at the dramatic speed with which the East Bloc unraveled when exposed to "openness" and "reform."

In Poland, a stubborn shipyard electrician by the name of Lech Walesa led his coworkers in strikes against the "workers' state" and forced the government of General Wojciech Jaruzelski into negotiations and semi-free elections. In Hungary, the government developed a mind of its own, giving up its constitutional monopoly on power, and in May 1989 it removed the barbed-wire along the Austrian-Hungarian border.

When Mikhail Gorbachev came to East Berlin to celebrate the fortieth anniversary of the German Democratic Republic on October 7, 1989, he sternly admonished East German leader Erich Honecker that it was time for change. "Life punishes those who come too late," Gorbachev scolded Honecker. He was right. East Germany's grand anniversary parade would turn out to be the funeral procession of the communist regime as well.

Hoping that the Eastern European regimes would opt to reform themselves, as he was trying to reform the Soviet Union, Gorbachev asserted that they could no longer count on the power of the Soviet Union to shore them up. He expressly excluded "the possibility of the use of force or threat of force, above all military force, by one alliance against another, within alliances, or anywhere else." If sincerely meant, this would be the death of the so-called Brezhnev doctrine, enunciated by Soviet leader Leonid Brezhnev as Warsaw Pact troops squashed the Prague spring in 1968, the doctrine by which the Soviets reserved themselves the right to interfere in other countries if the Communists' monopoly on power was threatened.

Erich Honecker would have none of this reform nonsense. He was busy stating that while Perestroika and Glasnost might well be needed in the Soviet Union, they were irrelevant to East Germany, which had achieved socialist perfection long ago. Honecker warned prophetically that "socialism and capitalism are no more compatible than fire and water." The official media like *Neues Deutschland* treated the Soviet leader as a dangerous radical and edited Gorbachev's speeches heavily, sometimes ignoring them altogether.

In reality, East Germany was far from perfection, in a communist sense or any other sense. Throughout the 1980s, East Germany was cited by many experts—including in the West—as the tenth strongest economy in the world. But to people who had a chance to look at the country closely, that claim always seemed suspicious. During an excursion into East Berlin, Col. Dieter Satz, commander of Tempelhof Airport, and a few of his fellow officers fell to discussing the state of the city. If each were given a city block, how would they start to fix it up? Says Satz,

It was a fairly lively discussion, and finally we all agreed, you would have to start at renewing the sewers and work from there on up. Nothing else was really salvageable. Once you got off Karl-Marx-Allee and got into the back streets, you could see the wood was decayed, and you knew the electrical and telecommunications support was certainly not adequate. All in all, one could compare parts of East Berlin and parts of Potsdam with Alexandria, Egypt. The only difference being that the climate is considerably kinder in Alexandria, Egypt.

By the fall of 1989, the East German regime could no longer hold out against the will of its own people. Vacationing East Germans in Hungary, which officially had absolved itself from its promise to turn political refugees back to East Germany, started crossing the border into Austria in growing numbers. It was a repeat of the mass exodus of 1961, which led to the building of the Wall. In a period of three weeks, some forty thousand East Germans escaped through this route.

Thousands of other East Germans invaded the West German embassy in Prague, demanding permission to go West. Specially sealed trains took them through East Germany to freedom in West Germany. In October, mass demonstrations developed in the major East German cities like Leipzig and Dresden, with citizens demanding freedom and democracy.

Erich Honecker was not prepared to give them that. At the fortieth anniversary celebrations, he had railed bitterly against "a wanton, internationally coordinated defamation of the GDR, designed to sow doubt about the vitality and advantages of socialism." Previously, during the summer of 1989, he had sent politburo member Egon Krenz to Peking to express the East German government's admiration of the Chinese use of power against the student revolt in Tiananmen Square.

What made reform particularly difficult to contemplate in East Germany was the fact that the GDR was more a political construct than a nation, the result of Germany's division after World War II. When the Eastern European states, like Hungary and Poland, were allowed to become more like Western European states, when the Communists were no longer in control, there continued to be countries called Poland and Hungary. In East Germany, on the other hand, the Communist Party's monopoly on power was the sole reason for the existence of two Germanys. As Krenz pointed out, "Without the Communist Party, there is no German Democratic Republic." This simple fact explains the regime's reaction, often bordering on panic, to reforms in other Warsaw Pact nations. Reform in any meaningful sense would undermine the entire East German power structure.

Preparations for a forceful resolution to the outburst of independent-mindedness among the East Germans were extensive. In Leipzig, extra hotel beds had been set up in the city's hospitals and extra supplies of blood plasma had been brought in.

However, without the support from the Soviets, a Tiananmen Square solution became impossible. In the end, local commanders, lacking any clear orders from East Berlin, gave in to the demonstrators' demand for peaceful dialogue. On October 18, the SED Central Committee accepted Honecker's request for retirement "due to health reasons," which is East German for being forced out, and Egon Krenz was elected general secretary in his stead. Known as the man with the "phoniest smile in the GDR," Krenz was clearly only a transitional figure.

One of the few people who believed East Germany would crumble was Vernon Walters, troubleshooter for successive U.S. presidents and ambassador to the Federal Republic of Germany from 1989 to 1991. At a press conference shortly after his arrival, he had predicted the fall of the Wall and German unification, and in private conversations with German politicians, he said he believed it would even happen while he was ambassador. With the Soviet withdrawal from Afghanistan, it was clear to Walters that a decision had been made at the highest level in the Soviet Union that the Brezhnev doctrine was no longer operational.

However, as many western experts saw it, it was one thing to pull out of Afghanistan, which was situated on the fringes of the Soviet empire, but it was something else to give up the very center of Soviet power in Europe. At the time, Walters' remarks led to a good deal of head shaking, both in Bonn and in Washington. In fact, Walters' boss, Secretary of State James Baker, feared that such comments might undercut Gorbachev's shaky position at home, and hastened to describe the U.S. ambassador as a generally well-informed man, but in this case speaking entirely for himself, not for the State Department.

"I probably would have resigned had I not received a private message from President Bush telling me I had his full confidence," says Walters. The only people in Bonn who took Walters seriously were Chancellor Kohl and his close associate Wolfgang Schaeuble. The reason Walters had no qualms about openly stating his opinion was that he regarded

Gorbachev as doomed anyway, having set forces in motion that were beyond his control.

In November 1989, the focus of East German unrest shifted to Berlin. For weeks, the East German regime had been under pressure to liberalize. The regime had been faced with massive demonstrations, mostly nonvio lent, escalating from fifty thousand to one hundred thousand, then two hundred thousand. The final demonstration, on November 4, numbered five hundred thousand people who gathered on Alexanderplatz.

In what was clearly one of the biggest mistakes ever made by the East German regime, Guenter Schabowski, one of the party bigwigs, held a press conference on November 9. An assistant walked in and handed him a piece of paper. Schabowksi read the message aloud, which announced the decision of the East German government to make it easier to get visas, to allow more travel to the West, without any preparation. Some-body asked him when this would take effect. He looked at the paper and said, "Now, I suppose."

Schabowksi's words were taken as the decision to open the Wall. Great crowds of East Berliners converged on the checkpoints. Walking up to the guards, they demanded to know why they were still there, since the Wall was now open. The guards did not know anything, but before they could react, people just pushed right through. The only thing that could have stopped them was gunfire, and the East German soldiers were not willing to resort to force. They gave in and let the crowds through.

At the time, Major General Raymond E. Haddock, U.S. commander in Berlin, was in a meeting with executives of the Dresdener Bank at the headquarters in Clayallee, discussing the achievements of the Allies in Berlin. In the middle of the question-and-answer session, Haddock's chief of staff, Col. John Counts, whispered in his ear that something was hap-pening at the Wall. Haddock ordered him to go and check. Counts soon returned with the news that the television stations were carrying cover-age of people coming through the Wall.

Immediately, the western Allies started to confer feverishly among themselves about how to handle the situation if it came to violence. The

British cleverly sent a military band to soothe the nerves of the crowd and, of course, to monitor developments.[1]

During the course of the evening, the East German regime realized that it had made a terrible mistake. An announcement went out in the course of the evening that only people with approved visas would be allowed through after eight o'clock the following morning.

"The next morning, my wife and I were standing in Heinrich-Heine-Strasse, greeting people as they came through," says Haddock. "At eight o'clock people were still coming through, champagne was flowing, and school kids were greeting everybody. I walked up and talked to a guard. I said I understood there was going to be some change at eight o'clock, and only people who had visas were going to be able to come through. The guard said, '*Visa macht nichts*. The Wall is open. It is over.' He was as

Magnum Photos

November 1989. A peaceful revolution changes history forever. The people are on top—the Wall comes down. The flame of freedom, as President Kennedy predicted, did not die under the boot of the oppressors.

AP/Wide World Photos

An East German policeman makes a V-sign in a salute to the West through a hole in the battered Wall near Brandenburg Gate.

happy about it as were his brethren who were coming through. The guards simply refused to respond to the order."

The reaction of the young East German border guards was a cause of a good deal of concern at the U.S. headquarters in Clayallee. Immediately after the opening of the Wall, people from both sides danced on the Wall at Brandenburg Gate. But that was tolerated only for a day or so before the East Germans moved up and occupied the top of that piece of the Wall. The border guards were clearly under extreme pressure, but they all remained disciplined. U.S. commanders give credit to the East German officers for keeping their troops under control. Had they lost it, all hell could have broken loose. Says Haddock,

> *Initially, we had some concern about our own soldiers being up to trying to capture a souvenir. We were concerned that the soldiers might provoke a reaction from the East German soldiers, and therefore we ordered our soldiers to wait. They should not get up and try to chip away at the Wall until sometime later. And by and large our soldiers respected that order and stayed back.*

On Saturday, November 11, Ambassador Walters came down to take in the sight himself. He had wanted to come down there on the first night, but his staff advised him to stay in Bonn. It was yet unclear what the Russian reaction would be, which made it important to stay in close contact with the German government. General Haddock immediately took him up in a helicopter, flying along the Wall. They could see the enormous columns of vehicles and people heading for the Wall.

They crossed the area by Freedom Bridge going over to Potsdam. Haddock told Walters that Glienicker Bridge was open for the first time that morning and suggested they land and walk across the bridge. Glienicker Bridge had a special significance for Walters as a former Deputy Director of the CIA. This was where the superpowers had exchanged spies during the Cold War.

The bridge was now loaded with people and vehicles. "People grabbed our hands, saying 'Thank you. If it were not for the Americans, this would not have happened.' There were about two thousand West Berliners in their cars, waiting to take the East Germans anywhere they wanted to go. I have never seen so many grown men with tears in their eyes as I saw that day on Glienicker Bridge," says Walters.

From Glienicker Bridge, they drove on by car to Potsdamer Platz and to the Brandenburg Gate, where they witnessed East German border guards helping some of the young people up on the Wall to celebrate. Recalls Walters, "I am not a German. I fought against the German army, I was wounded by the German army, but this was an extraordinary moment. When I saw the *Grenzpolizei* helping the demonstrators on to the Wall, I thought that the long war that had gone on all my adult life since World War II was now coming to an end."

As was the case when the Wall went up twenty-eight years previously, its fall came as a surprise, at least in the sense that it was not something even the East Germans had planned. But, says Haddock, "You can't say it was a total surprise because the pressures were building in the East." Two weeks prior to November 9, Haddock had attended a *Herren Abend* in Cologne. Another guest that evening was Wolfgang Vogel, the lawyer who had been the East German middleman in the ransom of East German dissidents. On this occasion, Vogel had asked Haddock what the Americans would do if one day large numbers of East Berliners started coming through the Wall. "I thought about it a minute, then answered, 'I would hold up a large sign saying *Herzlich Willkommen.*'"

Vogel told Haddock he ought to think about it. Considering the source, he began to do just that. On return to his headquarters in Berlin, he called his staff together, military and diplomatic, and told them to consider the proposition that for whatever reason, they might suddenly be faced with large numbers of East Berliners coming across the Wall. Says Haddock,

 *Over a period of several days, we came up with a set of principles that would guide our actions, how we would react. Specifically, we felt that it was essential that everything would be done in full coordination with the elected representatives of the city and that the control of the civilian population would be in the hands of the German police. Allied soldiers would not go in the streets to try to maintain order unless there was a crisis.*

What particularly occupied the Americans was the reaction of the Russians. As Haddock had been waiting for Walters in the airport, a staff officer let him know that Russian General Boris Snetkov, commander-in-chief of the Soviet Forces in Germany, wanted to know what the Americans were doing to ensure the situation did not get out of control. This was the second time Snetkov had posed this question. The day before, Haddock had responded with a brief statement: "The U.S. military is in close and continuous contact with the elected representatives of Berlin." That was the full extent of Haddock's reply.

"What I wanted to convey to Boris Snetkov, who was looking for some military action, was that from our side, the people coming across the border did not constitute a threat that required us to take action," says Haddock. "We were working with the governing mayor and with the police, but we did not see at any time the necessity for allied soldiers to intervene. From his side, he may have seen it differently." The Russian was clearly not satisfied with the answer.

To prevent further enquiries, Haddock called the U.S. headquarters in

Heidelberg, where his superior, Gen. Crosby Saint, told Haddock to take a piece of Saint's official four-star stationary, write out the exact same reply one more time, sign it in Saint's name, and have it hand delivered to the Russians. There were no further questions from General Snetkov.

Throughout, the possibility that the East Germans might opt for a Tiananmen Square solution had to be considered. One thing was clear to the Americans: They could not take an allied military force into East Berlin in order to intervene in an internal disturbance. At most, there would have been loud protests at the United Nations, massive exposure in the press, and pressure applied to Soviet representatives wherever they were. But the old guidelines of no involvement on the eastern side still applied.

One of the contingencies to be prepared for in case the East Germans chose a violent solution was a new influx of refugees, some of whom might be casualties. Colonel Dieter Satz, as commander of Tempelhof Airport, would be one of the key people involved in handling such an eventuality.

"Tempelhof is a huge place, and you can do all sorts of things if you absolutely have to. We started looking at it from that standpoint. As far as a roof over the head is concerned, that is no problem in Berlin. If you close down the U-Bahn, you have a tremendous amount of sheltered space." As for supplies, "There were the emergency relief supplies that had been stockpiled for the possibility of a blockade available, covering everything from diapers to coal. Short of a military confrontation, there really was not a problem," says Satz.

In fact, the American forces in Berlin had already been taking in thousands of East German refugees who had escaped through Hungary to West Germany and had ended up in Berlin. For this purpose, some of the American barracks were opened. A number of U.S. soldiers had been assigned to support the refugees, running kitchens, providing clothing, running buses.

But all this contingency planning fortunately proved unnecessary. There were no East German attempts to reverse the fall of the Wall.

Throughout it all, some had been wondering why the initial statements by President George Bush on the breaching of the Wall were rather low key, and some later blamed Bush for not living up to the occasion, for being unable to find the rhetoric to match the historic moment. However, Bush's famed penchant for prudence may have been the correct response. The idea of a U.S. president dancing the Victory Polka on the Berlin Wall, even if only in a metaphorical sense, might not have been in the best interest of the Berliners. Bush may have felt that too much triumphalism would cause the Soviets to change their minds.

∎ PLANS FOR REUNIFICATION ∎

The initial idea for reunification was much more modest than what actually happened: a gradual union that would preserve a distinct East German identity through the existence of two federated states. This was the preferred solution by the opposition Social Democrats right up almost to the end. On this point, the SPD was in agreement with the East German SED, which invited them to have a common congress on the question and issue a common communiqué.

Vernon Walters warned against such a step. "I will not mix in internal German affairs, and I am not a Social Democrat, but that would be incredibly stupid. This whole thing is going to come tumbling down," was what he told Social Democratic politicians. It would be painful, Walters warned the Social Democrats, if too many letters addressed to *Lieber Genosse,* dear comrade, were found after unification.[2]

Indeed, the federal idea proved unrealistic. East Germany was like a house that has been subjected to demolition by dynamite. For a moment, the structure seems to be intact, only to come down with a gigantic crash. It quickly became clear that the East German regime could not deal with the situation.

The exodus from East Germany only became greater when the government of Hans Modrow, successor to Egon Krenz, suggested the creation of a new security service to protect East Germany from alleged Neo-Nazi

AP/Wide World Photos

Celebration of the unification of East and West Germany at the Brandenburg Gate, for three decades the symbol of division.

activity. Whole sectors of industry and hospitals stood idle and depopulated. In many areas, mail could no longer be delivered because the mailman had gone West. There was almost a touch of surrealism about the mass migration. In one small city, a whole municipal bus company decided to cross over en masse and in uniform, as if in some East German version of "The Twelve Days of Christmas," with twelve drummers drumming, eleven pipers piping, ten lords a-leaping . . .

Despite appeals from Modrow and Kohl to stay home, the East Germans left in droves. The figure for January 1990 was 73,729. At this rate, according to one demographer, by the year 2006 nobody would be left in the country, except perhaps a scraggly partridge in a polluted pear tree.

To avoid "reunification on West German soil," which would worsen West Germany's chronic housing shortage and strain its social welfare system beyond the limit, the West German government concluded that it would have to provide aid to the new East Germany. More importantly, Kohl put himself squarely at the head of the reunification process. He proclaimed his ten-point plan for the unification of Germany, trying to give some direction to a process that was threatening to get out of hand, and he decided to press on as quickly as possible.

▌ THE ALLIES' REACTION ▌

From the very beginning, the United States supported Helmut Kohl's unification efforts. The United States supported a unified Germany that was firmly embedded in the NATO alliance and the European Community (EC).

However, while the United States welcomed German unity, France and Britain were decidedly more reserved about the prospect of an early German union. At the time, one of Margaret Thatcher's cabinet ministers had to resign over the comment that the EC was "a German racket for taking over Europe," which many took to reflect the thinking of the Iron Lady herself. To Margaret Thatcher, it was felt, German unification was an unpleasant topic, preferably to be faced sometime in the next century.

In France, French President Francois Mitterand had no trouble containing his enthusiasm over unification. It was clear to him that Europe's center of gravity would invariably be pushed to the east, from Paris to Berlin, with German unification.

Most important, however, was the reaction of the Soviets, who were pushing for a neutral, nonaligned Germany. As Henry Kissinger pointed out, such a Germany would sooner or later, if history is any guide, try to protect itself against its neighbors. NATO Secretary Manfred Woerner, a former West German defense minister, put it this way, "A drifting neutral

Germany cannot be the solution. It would not even be in the enlightened self-interest of the Russians."

After much negotiation and promises of financial aid, Helmut Kohl finally obtained a commitment from Mikhail Gorbachev in 1990 to allow the Germans to settle the question of unity themselves, as well as the type of system under which they wanted to live. One of the inducements was a promise by the Kohl government to finance the resettlement and building of housing for the returning Russian troops. Unfortunately, the program has since encountered delays and bureaucratic snags at the Russian end.

▌ THE THREAT TO BERLIN ▌

So how big was the threat to Berlin, some have asked in the aftermath of the collapse of the Warsaw Pact and the Soviet withdrawal from Eastern Europe. Were the Soviets really prepared to start World War III, overrun West Berlin, and attack the Federal Republic? Was the Cold War really such a big deal? Was it not just a gigantic waste of money?

Some interesting details have emerged from East German files in the years since reunification. The Warsaw Pact preparations for war with the West were more extensive than NATO ever thought possible. "We have found that the National People's Army made every preparation necessary to conquer and occupy the West, and especially West Germany," Vice Admiral Ulrich Weisser, chief of the planning staff for the German *Bundeswehr* told *The Washington Post*.[3] The East German army was ready to "invade within hours of a political decision."

Dr. Otto Wenzel, a Berlin historian, has seen the East German war plans and written extensively on the subject. According to Wenzel, both in their scope and detail, East German war games were no mere theoretical exercises. "We know from former officers of the National People's Army that there were exact plans to invade West Berlin. Those officers will remain anonymous as they fear trouble from their former colleagues who view them as traitors."

According to Wenzel, money was ready for circulation in the occupation zone; some 4.9 billion banknotes had been printed; lists of people to be apprehended had been drawn up; 8,000 medals had even been struck for gallantry in the upcoming battle, little von Bluecher medals, named after the Prussian field marshal who came to the rescue of the Duke of Wellington at the battle of Waterloo. The medal came in three classes, gold, silver, and bronze.[4] The ammunition supplies found at East German bases for its 160,000-man army exceeded those of the 500,000-strong West German *Bundeswehr*.

The basic plan was laid down in 1985, and was updated and polished every year up to 1989, when the East German regime collapsed. The plans for the taking of Berlin were especially elaborate. Given the signal to advance, Soviet and East German units would burst through the Wall and race to secure the U.S., French, and British bases, taking over all key installations. The communist troops would enjoy a three to one advantage over the western forces, 32,000 versus 12,000.[5]

The fighting morale of the allied forces was to be undermined by leaflets dropped from the air, stating that the French and the British were defending American interests rather than their own and losing their lives for American war goals. Americans troops were to be reminded that they had never triumphed over socialist forces. The civilian population was encouraged to both active and passive resistance against a bloody and prolonged defense of the city.

To this one can add elaborate plans for establishing a new administration after the city had been conquered. Sixty-five of the eighty-five posts in the new leadership were filled in the 1985 plan. The manpower plan listed billet, rank, first and last name, and personal identification numbers. "These were real names, of actual living persons, not fictional names," Wenzel stresses.

A key objective would be the arrest and detention of individuals deemed hostile to the new regime. The Ministry of State Security had compiled extensive files on citizens of West Berlin. Detainees would include politicians, senior police officials, senior civil servants, and journalists who were known to have anti-leftist leanings. Detainees were to be brought to internment camps for immediate interrogation. The information gained from these interrogations would be used to build up a program aimed at rendering ineffective those who had gone underground.[6]

That this scenario never became reality can only be ascribed to the steadfastness of the West. Despite the periods where the western Allies looked less than impressive, despite the times when they were forced to stand by and see the Soviets impose their will on the East Berliners, the commitment to the freedom of West Berlin was strong enough to outlast the threats to its existence. For that the West Berliners can thank the allied troops who were stationed there, and their own determination to remain free.

Meanwhile the arguments go on—whether the collapse of Communism could have occurred earlier or later, or that *Ostpolitik* might have prolonged the life of the communist regime. Answers Longolius, "If you say we should have allowed the system to fall apart and collapse earlier, nobody can prove how those in power would have reacted in panic. I have a very strong sense they would have been more repressive and more aggressive against the West, blaming us for their weaknesses and the people would have suffered tremendously." This much at least is clear—the *Ostpolitik* got the East German regime hooked on hard currency infusions from West Germany.

Another argument centers on to whom the credit goes for the demise of the East Bloc, Ronald Reagan or Mikhail Gorbachev. When on June 12, 1987, Ronald Reagan visited Berlin and made his famous challenge to Gorbachev in front of the Brandenburg Gate, many called him a wild-eyed dreamer, in pursuit of an impossible goal. "There is one sign the Soviets could make that would be unmistakable, that would advance dramatically the cause of freedom and peace," he said. "General Secretary Gorbachev, if you seek peace, if you seek prosperity for the Soviet Union and Eastern Europe, if you seek liberalization, come here to this gate. Mr. Gorbachev, open this gate. Mr. Gorbachev, tear down this wall."

German Information Center

President Ronald Reagan and his wife Nancy visited Berlin on June 12, 1987, to celebrate the 750th birthday of the city. In a speech in front of the Brandenburg Gate, he challenged the Soviet leader Mikhail Gorbachev to take the Wall down. He later visited troops at Tempelhof Airport.

Ronald Reagan kept up the pressure and demonstrated that the West could and would match the Soviet Union all over the world. For his part, Mikhail Gorbachev realized that Soviet resources would inevitably fall short and that the communist world had to change.

The role the United States, Britain, France, and the Soviet Union played officially came to an end in 1990. The final treaty, the result of the so-called Two plus Four negotiations between the four World War II victors and the two Germanys on the future of Germany was signed in Moscow on September 12, 1990. It brought to a close the Allies' "rights and responsibilities in Berlin and Germany as a whole" and "all respective institutions of the four powers" as of midnight, October 3.

Colonel Stephen Bowman was the officer in charge of closing the American checkpoints Alpha at Helmstedt on the West German–East German border and Bravo at Babelsberg on the East German–West Berlin border. A brief British, French, and American ceremony was held in the afternoon of October 2, 1990.

Until the very last, the Soviet rituals were obeyed as they had been for four decades: inspections, checking of papers, examination of vehicles. Sometime after dark, on the night of October 2, 1990, the Soviet guards melted away. "There was no ceremony. They just left the guard post. They just left in the dark, sort of slipped away," says Bowman. The next day, vandals came and broke all the glass and tore up the post.

▮ PACKING UP ▮

The man in charge of packing up for the Americans was Chief of Staff Col. Alfred W. Baker, a legendary soldier who had served in Vietnam and in the Middle East. Over a three-year period in Vietnam, he earned four Purple Hearts. Baker first served in Berlin in the 1960s as a young lieutenant, and was called back to oversee the pullback of the Berlin Brigade.

The U-Haul move, completed in 1994, involved thirty-four tanks, eight large artillery pieces, and more than five hundred pieces of military rolling stock—trucks, personnel carriers, and bulldozers—eight thousand rifles, pistols, gas masks, chemical uniforms, and decontamination units. Property to the value of some 8 billion marks has had to be restored to the German government. Most of it, Baker notes with satisfaction, went back into immediate use, a classical turn-key operation.

Looking back over the decades, the Berlin Brigade worked magnificently. Baker praises the relationship it had with the population of Berlin. "We had to be able to stay here with the consent of the people. If the Berliners had not wanted us to stay, we could not have stayed."

What he is most proud of is having been part of a policy that has been successful, that worked as it was supposed to. The Marshall Plan, he believes, "was the most enlightened plan that was ever conceived at the end of a war. More than any other thing, I am proud of my government for that foresight."

As to the Russians, there is no sense of triumphalism. Says Baker, "Some of the Russians I have known for a long time. I feel sorry for them. I do not know what I would have done if after thirty years in the military, I had been told that the constitution I had sworn to defend and had been wounded for and all the things I believe in—that they are all lies. I am not sure I could have stood that."

June 18, 1994, was a real Berliner occasion. Everybody had turned out to see the last allied parade on the Strasse des 17. Juni to express their appreciation. The troops, which had been in Berlin for four and a half decades, were going home. First came the French in their crisp khaki and their kepis, the kind of headgear only a Frenchman could have designed and only a Frenchman can wear with dignity. Then came the British. Especially splendid were the Highland Grenadiers who were decked out in kilts and leopard skin. Finally came the Americans, led by a drum major who was much admired for his marching style, which had a touch of jazz and Glen Miller. A squadron of helicopters came thundering low, and finally an old vintage Dakota, a reminder of the airlift, came lumbering over the heads of the spectators.

The Russians had also wanted to be in the parade, but had been politely but firmly turned down by the German government and the western Allies. The change in Russian politics was deemed a little too new to merit inclusion. Instead, they held their own parade a few weeks later in

Thomas Hartmann/Ullstein

*The last commander-in-chief to visit his troops in
Berlin was Bill Clinton on June 11, 1994. The last
commander of the Berlin Brigade, Col. James Banks,
here riding with his guest from Washington, accepted
the president's compliment, "Thank you for a job well
done," for all the men and women in uniform who had
served in Berlin over 49 years.*

Treptow, a suburb of Berlin. But no tanks were allowed this time since
tank threads would churn up the streets. Among Berliners there is a
relief that they are gone combined with a sympathy for the uncertain
future awaiting the returning Russian soldiers in their own country.

As for the Americans, politicians may have wobbled, but soldiers were
always ready to serve. About the Berlin Brigade it can truly be said that
its mission had been completed. On July 12, at a ceremony at McNair Barracks, President Bill Clinton officially inactivated the Berlin Brigade, cas-
ing its colors. "America salutes you. Mission accomplished."

On August 15, AFN radio and TV Berlin went off the air. In his farewell
speech, the Commander of the American Forces Network, Europe, Col.

German Information Center

Farewell parade, June 18 1994. 75,000 Berliners, their mayor Eberhard Diepgen, the ambassadors of France, the United Kingdom, and the United States of America, and Generals Walter H. Yates (U.S.), David de Gonville Bromhead (U.K.), and Jean Brullard (France) paid respect to 1,950 soldiers of the three western Allies who marched down the Strasse des 17. Juni.

Robert E. Gaylord said that "this station became a friend and without a doubt one of the best ambassadors our nation ever had."

In September 1994, the western Allies pulled their last troops out of Berlin. The last Soviet soldier had left German soil on August 31, 1994, four months earlier than planned. The Soviet bases are ecological disaster zones now, full of the lethal legacy of decades of Cold War. Reflecting the acute economic scarcity still besetting Russia, in the barracks everything has been removed—electrical fixtures, faucets, even the urinals. Once again, everything removable has been carted back to Russia.

This is not the end of the connection between the United States and Berlin. Old organizations like *Luftbrueckendank*, which gives scholarships and helps widows in financial need, will continue to function. Businesses are funding exchange programs, and the Berlin parliament has started a Checkpoint Charlie Foundation, which seeks to strengthen ties between Berliners and Americans.

And many of the older defenders of the city have made their homes in Berlin. Lt. Col. Atwood lives there, as does Teddy Mohr and Melvin Lasky. Every Sunday night from 9:00 to 11:00, Mark White with his golden voice hosts a show celebrating the big band era on Radio JFK. All the old favorites can be heard here: Count Basie, Duke Ellington, Jack Teagarden, Peggy Lee, and Buddy Rich. "Welcome to another spectacular night in Berlin," intones White. He has spent his whole adult life in Berlin and would not dream of moving, except for the winter months, which he spends in Florida.

Back in some of the darkest days of Berlin, right after the Wall had gone up and businessmen were deserting the city, Willy Brandt suggested that it would be a nice symbolic gesture for Captain Jack Bennett to build a house in Berlin. When Bennett could not get a bank guarantee, Brandt said that he would get the main political parties to cosign the mortgage. And so they did.

So Captain Jack Bennett still sits in his magnificent garden in Berlin, right on the bank of the Halensee, intermittently firing an ancient cap gun (blanks, of course) at the blackbirds who steal his cherries.

Bennett took a chance on Berlin, and Berlin took a chance on Bennett. Both came out winners.

dpa

On September 7, 1994, the Stars and Stripes at the
U.S. headquarters are lowered for a final time.

NOTES

Introduction

1. General Frank Howley, *Berlin Command* (New York: G.P. Putnam's Sons, 1950), p. 5.
2. Deane and David Heller, *The Berlin Crisis: Prelude to World War III?* (Derby, Conn.: Monarch, 1961), p. 9.

Chapter 1

1. Walter Krumholz, *Berlin-ABC* (Berlin: Presse-und-Informationsamt des Landes Berlin, 1968), p. 104.
2. Tony Le Tissier, *Berlin Then and Now* (London: Battle of Britain Prints, 1992), p. 307.
3. General Frank Howley, Berlin Command (New York: G.P. Putnam's Sons, 1950), pp. 30–32.
4. Ibid, p. 43.
5. Rolf Gevelmann, *Wie aus Siegern Freunde Wurden: Die U.S. Army in Steglitz* (Berlin: Bezirksbuergermeister von Berlin-Steglitz, 1994), p. 20.
6. Howley, op. cit., p. 48.
7. *Welcome to the United States Army: Berlin and the Berlin Brigade* (Berlin: USAB / USMCA DPTM), p. 12.
8. Ibid., p. 16.
9. Ibid., p. 18.
10. Ibid., p. 20.
11. Le Tissier, op. cit., p. 306.
12. Howley, op. cit., p. 44.

13. Howley, op. cit., pp. 74–75.
14. Hubert G. Schmidt, *U.S. Military Government in Germany: Policy and Functioning in Industry, vol. I* (Karlsruhe, Germany: Historical Division, European Command, 1950), p. 9.
15. Howley, op. cit., p. 25.
16. D.G. White, *Historical Report of the Operations of the Office of Military Government Berlin District, APO 755, Berlin Germany, 1 July 1945–30 June 1946, vol.VI*, pp. 4–7.
17. Ibid., *vol. VI*, p. 14.
18. Ibid., *vol. IV,* p. 5.
19. White, op. cit., *vol. III*, p. 26.
20. White, op. cit., *vol. III*, p. 45.
21. Howley, op. cit., pp. 92–93.
22. White, op. cit., *vol. III*, p. 37.
23. White, op. cit., *vol III*, p. 32.

Chapter 2

1. Hubert G. Schmidt, *U.S. Military Government in Germany Policy and Functioning in Industry, vol. I* (Karlsruhe, Germany: Historical Division, European Command, 1950), p. 3.
2. Ibid., *vol. I,* p. 12.
3. Ibid., *vol. I,* p. 13.
4. Gerard H. Wilk, *Truman and Berlin: Decisive Years Between the Potsdam Conference and Marshall Plan* (Berlin: Berliner Forum, 1986), p. 15.
5. Ibid., p. 22.
6. Schmidt, op. cit., *vol. I*, p. 10.
7. Schmidt, op. cit., *vol. I*, p. 46.
8. Schmidt, op. cit., *vol. I*, p. 8.
9. Schmidt, op. cit., *vol. II*, p. 100.
10. Schmidt, op. cit., *vol. II*, p. 101.
11. General Frank Howley, *Berlin Command* (New York: G.P. Putnam's Sons, 1950), p. 11.
12. Earl F. Ziemke, *The U. S. Army in the Occupation of Germany 1944–1946* (Washington D.C.: U.S. Army Center of Military History, 1990), p. 374.
13. Erwin Leiser, *Nazi Cinema* (New York: Collier, 1975), pp. 127–129.
14. D.G. White, *Historical Report of the Operations of the Office of Military Government Berlin District, APO 755, Berlin Germany, 1 July 1945–30 June 1946, vol. II*, p. 10.
15. Ibid., *vol. II*, p. 26.
16. Ibid., *vol. II*, p. 44.
17. Ibid., *vol. II*, p. 54.
18. Ibid., *vol. II*, p. 106.

19. Ibid., *vol. V,* p. 3.
20. Ibid., *vol. V,* p. 1.
21. Ziemke, op. cit., p. 439.
22. White, op. cit., *vol. V,* p. 29.
23. Ziemke, op. cit., p. 388.
24. Ziemke, op. cit., p. 384.
25. Hans Habe, *Im Jahre Null* (Munich: Desch, 1966).
26. For Henry Alter's reports see Brewster Chamberlain, ed., *Kultur Auf Truemmern: Berliner Berichte der Amerikanischen Information Control Section. Juli–Dezember 1945* (Stuttgart: Deutsche Verlags-Anstalt, 1979).
27. Ziemke, op. cit., p. 388.
28. Alfred Grosser, *Germany in Our Time: A Political History* (New York: Praeger, 1970), pp. 42–44.
29. Will Tremper, *Meine wilden Jahre* (Berlin: Ullstein, 1993), pp. 18–19.
30. Howley, op. cit., p. 15.
31. White, op. cit., *vol. II,* p. 86.
32. Wilk, op. cit., p. 41.

Chapter 3

1. Hubert G. Schmidt, *U.S. Military Government in Germany: Policy and Functioning in Industry. Vol. I* (Karlsruhe, Germany: Historical Division, European Command, 1950), p. 39.
2. General Frank Howley, *Berlin Command* (New York: G.P. Putnam's Sons, 1950), p. 187.
3. Roger D. Launis and Coy F. Cross II, *MAC and the Legacy of the Berlin Airlift* (Scott Air Force Base, Illinois: Military Airlift Command, 1989), p. 6.
4. Lowell Bennett, *Berlin Bastion: The Epic of Post-War Berlin* (Frankfurt am Main: Fred Rudl, 1951), p. 48.
5. Robert Jackson, *The Berlin Airlift* (Wellingborough, England: Patrick Stephens, 1988), p. 71.
6. Launis, op. cit., p. 11.
7. Deane and David Heller, *The Berlin Crisis: Prelude to World War III?* (Derby, Conn.: Monarch, 1961), pp. 90–92.
8. Launis, op. cit., p. 7.
9. Launis, op. cit., p. 11.
10. Launis, op. cit., pp. 32–33.
11. For a complete description of "Operation Little Vittles," see Gail S. Halvorsen, *The Berlin Candy Bomber* (Bountiful, Utah: Horizon, 1990), pp. 113–151.
12. Bennett, op. cit., p. 218.
13. "Providing the Reins of Command,"(Airforce Communications Command), p. 54.

14. Gordon A. Craig, *The Germans* (New York: G.P. Putnam's Sons, 1982), p. 38.
15. Bennett, op. cit., p. 63.
16. Major General R. J. S. Corbett, *Berlin and the British Ally: 1945–1990* (Berlin: Zumm KG, 1991), p. 141.
17. Walter Krumholz, *Berlin-ABC* (Berlin: Presse-und-Informationsamt des Landes Berlin, 1968), p. 50.
18. Ruth Andreas-Friedrich, *Battleground Berlin: Diaries, 1945–48* (New York: Paragon House, 1990), p. 243.
19. Launis, op. cit., p. 50.
20. Launis, op. cit., pp. 5–9.

Chapter 4

1. David Childs, *Britain Since 1945: A Political History* (London: Methuen, 1979), pp. 23–24.
2. Freddie Laker, later to become Sir Freddie Laker, would go on to be famous as the owner and operator of Skytrain, the low price airline, which in the late 1970s promised to revolutionize transatlantic travel and challenged the International Air Transportation Association, which controlled every aspect of international aviation, including pricing. Skytrain operated from 1978 to 1982 when Laker was forced out of business through action by the big transatlantic carriers as was later revealed in a law suit. He now operates out of Miami. See: *The Independent,* February 1, 1992.
3. Major General R. J. S. Corbett, *Berlin and the British Ally: 1945–1990* (Berlin: Zumm KG, 1991), p. 30.

Chapter 5

1. Gerard H. Wilk, *Truman and Berlin: Decisive Years Between the Potsdam Conference and Marshall Plan* (Berlin: Berliner Forum, 1986), p. 46.
2. Will Tremper, *Meine wilden Jahre* (Berlin: Ullstein, 1993), pp. 402–405.
3. Tony Le Tissier, *Berlin Then and Now* (London: Battle of Britain Prints, 1992), p. 369.
4. Arnold Beichman, "East Berlin Thirty Years Ago—What Didn't Happen," *The Washington Times,* 20 June 1983, p. 2.
5. *Fragen an die deutsche Geschichte* (Bonn: German Bundestag Press and Information Centre, 1984), p. 388.
6. Le Tissier, op. cit., pp. 372–373.
7. Jean Edward Smith, *The Defense of Berlin* (Baltimore: Johns Hopkins, 1963), p. 184.
8. Honore M. Catudal, *Kennedy and the Berlin Wall Crisis* (Berlin: Berlin Verlag, 1980), p. 201.

9. For a detailed treatment of the relationship between Walter Ulbricht and Nikita Khrushchev, see Hope M. Harrison, "Ulbricht and the Concrete Rose: New Archival Evidence of the Dynamics of Soviet-East German Relations and the Berlin Crisis, 1958–1961," Cold War International History Project (Washington, D.C.: The Woodrow Wilson Center, 1993).
10. Deane and David Heller, *The Berlin Crisis: Prelude to World War III?* (Derby, Conn.: Monarch, 1961), pp. 177–178.
11. Ibid., p. 180.

Chapter 6

1. Peter Wyden, *Wall: The Inside Story of Divided Berlin* (New York: Simon & Schuster, 1989), p. 45.
2. *Die Mauer 13. August 1961–1988* (Berlin: Presse-und-Informationsamt des Landes Berlin, 1988), p. 13.
3. Ibid., p. 24.
4. Ibid., p. 22.
5. Jean Edward Smith, *The Defense of Berlin* (Baltimore: Johns Hopkins, 1963), pp. 267–277.
6. Ibid., pp. 292–297.
7. Ibid., p. 303.
8. Ibid., p. 203.
9. Ibid., p. 301.
10. Tony Le Tissier, *Berlin Then and Now.* (London: Battle of Britain Prints, 1992), p. 384.
11. Smith, op. cit., p. 323.
12. *Die Mauer 13. August 1961–1988*, p. 34.
13. *Die Mauer 13. August 1961–1988*, p. 27.
14. Le Tissier, op. cit., p. 398.

Chapter 7

1. General H. Norman Schwarzkopf, *It Doesn't Take a Hero* (New York: Bantam, 1992), p. 94.
2. Dick Rosse, "They Don't Make Walls Like Berlin's Anymore," *The Washington Post*, 19 August 1981, p. E2.

Chapter 8

1. Armed Forces Radio and Television Service, Broadcast of 15 August 1994.
2. For further information on AFN, see *Deutschland Magazin* 1993 (No. 9–10) pp. 27–31. And *History of AFRTS: The First 50 Years* (American Forces Information Service and Armed Forces Radio and Television Service, 1992).

Chapter 9

1. Willy Brandt, *My Life in Politics* (New York: Viking, 1992), p. 199.
2. Hope M. Harrison, *The Dynamics of Soviet-East German Relations and the Berlin Crisis, 1958–1961.* [Paper to the Annual Convention of the International Studies Association, Washington D.C., March 28–April 1, 1994.] Washington D.C.: International Studies Association, 1994: pp. 32–33.

Chapter 10

1. For a more extensive account of Spandau and its inmates, see Eugene K. Bird, *The Loneliest Man in the World* (New York: Viking, 1976).
2. Tony Le Tissier, *Farewell to Spandau* (Leatherhead, England: Ashford, Buchan & Enright, 1994), p. 14.
3. Ibid., p. 42.
4. Ibid., p. 72. For a precise description of the death of Rudolf Hess, see pp. 72–79.

Chapter 11

1. Elizabeth Pond, *Beyond the Wall* (Washington D.C.: The Brookings Institution, 1993), p. 4.
2. For Vernon Walters' view of German reunification, see Vernon Walters, *Die Vereinigung war voraussehbar: Hinter den Kulissen eines entscheidenden Jahres* (Berlin: Siedler Verlag, 1993).
3. Marc Fisher, "Soviet Bloc Had Detailed Plan to Invade West Germany," *The Washington Post,* 16 March 1993, p. A11.
4. Otto Wenzel, "Der Tag X: Wie West-Berlin erobert wurde," *Deutschland Archiv 12, Zeitschrift fuer das vereinigte Deutschland,* p. 1361.
5. Ibid., p. 1365.
6. Otto Wenzel, "Die Eroberung von West-Berlin: Wie die Stasi die Machtuebernahme plante," *Illustrierte Zitty Stadtzeitung Berlin,* p. 22.

BIBLIOGRAPHY

Ruth Andreas-Friedrich, *Battleground Berlin: Diaries 1945–48* (New York: Paragon House, 1990).

Jack O. Bennett, *10,000 Stunden am Himmel* (Berlin: Ullstein, 1985).

Lowell Bennett, *Berlin Bastion: The Epic of Post-War Berlin* (Frankfurt am Main: Fred Rudl Publisher, 1951).

Back issues of the *Berlin Observer*, back issues of *Stars and Stripes.*

Eugene K. Bird, *The Loneliest Man in the World* (New York: Viking, 1976).

Willy Brandt, *My Life in Politics* (New York: Viking, 1992).

Honore M. Catudal, *Kennedy and the Berlin Wall Crisis* (Berlin: Berlin Verlag, 1980).

Brewster Chamberlain, ed., *Kultur Auf Truemmern: Berliner Berichte der Amerikanischen Information Control Section. Juli–Dezember 1945* (Stuttgart: Deutsche Verlags-Anstalt, 1979).

R. J. S. Corbett, *Berlin and the British Ally 1945–1990* (Berlin: Zumm KG, 1991).

Rolf Gevelman, *Wie aus Siegern Freunde Wurden: Die U.S. Army in Steglitz* (Berlin: Bezirksbuegermeister von Berlin-Steglitz, 1994).

Alfred Grosser, *Germany in Our Time* (New York: Praeger, 1971).

Alfred Grosser, *The Western Alliance* (New York: Continuum, 1980).

Gail S. Halvorsen, *The Berlin Candy Bomber* (Bountiful, Utah: Horizon, 1990).

Hope Harrison, "Ulbricht and the Concrete Rose: New Archival Evidence on the Dynamics of Soviet–East German Relations and the Berlin Crisis, 1958–1961," Cold War International History Project (Washington, D.C.: The Woodrow Wilson Center, 1993).

Deane and David Heller, *The Berlin Crisis: Prelude to World War III?* (Derby, Conn.: Monarch, 1961).

Frank Howley, *Berlin Command* (New York: G.P. Putnam's Sons, 1950).

Josef Joffe, *The Limited Partnership* (Cambridge, Mass: Ballinger, 1987).

Roger D. Launis and Coy F. Cross II, *MAC and the Legacy of the Berlin Airlift* (Scott Airforce Base, Ill: Military Airlift Comand, 1989).

Tony Le Tissier, *Berlin Then and Now* (London: Battle of Britain Prints, 1992).

Tony Le Tissier, *Farewell to Spandau* (Leatherhead, England: Ashford, Buchan & Enright, 1994).

Erwin Leiser, *Nazi Cinema* (New York: Collier, 1975).

Herbert S. Parmet, *JFK: The Presidency of John F. Kennedy* (New York: Dial Press, 1983).

Elizabeth Pond, *Beyond the Wall: Germany's Road to Unification* (Washington, D.C.: The Brookings Institution, 1993).

Julius W. Pratt, Vincent P. DeSantis, and Joseph M. Siracusa, *A History of United States Foreign Policy* (Englewood Cliffs, N.J.: Prentice Hall, 1980).

Hubert G. Schmidt, *Policy and Functioning in Industry, Vols I, II,* and *III* (Karlsruhe, Germany: 1950).

Jean Edward Smith, *The Defense of Berlin* (Baltimore: Johns Hopkins Press, 1963).

The 1946th and the Berlin Airlift, Memorial Issue.

Will Tremper, *Meine wilden Jahre* (Berlin: Ullstein, 1993).

Bryan T. van Sweringen, *Kabarettist an der Front des Kalten Krieges* (Passau: Wissenschaft Verlag Richard Rothe, 1989).

Udo Wetzlaug, *Die Allierten in Berlin* (Berlin: Verlag Arno Spitz, 1988).

Gerald H. Wilk, *Truman and Berlin* (Berlin: Berliner Forum, 1986).

Peter Wyden, *Wall: Inside the Story of Divided Berlin* (New York: Simon and Schuster, 1989).

Earl F. Ziemke, *The U.S. Army in the Occupation of Germany 1944–46* (Washington D.C.: U.S. Army Center of Military History, 1990).

Among U.S. journalists, Henrik Bering is one of the most experienced foreign correspondents. He has covered Europe, the former Soviet Union, and the Middle East, and his byline has appeared in publications such as *The Wall Street Journal, Commentary, National Review,* and *The American Spectator.* A graduate of Oxford University (Pembroke College), he has been a Professional Journalism Fellow at Stanford University. He lives in Washington, D.C.

BERLIN
Journey of a City

A One-Hour Video Documentary that brings the history of Berlin from 1945 to 1994 to life

German Information Center

Witness the story of this "Island" city, the drama of its people, and the international forces that helped define the course of world relations for fifty turbulent years. Enter history through the voices and images of those who lived the drama.

In the summer of 1945 the Allies occupied Berlin, a city destroyed and torn apart by the conflicts and forces of World War II.

Over the next half century Berlin was center stage in the drama of the Cold War and the conflict between East and West.

With the building of the Berlin Wall in 1961 and its dismantling in 1989, the city came to symbolize a world divided and then reunited.

In September of 1994, after 49 years, the Allies left Berlin. Now the city and its citizens have embarked on a journey toward a new future and identity.

German Information Center

German Information Center

German Information Center

Berlin: Journey of a City

A one-hour documentary available on videocassette.
Call 1-800-655-1998 or send check or money order to:
Think Media, 515 Madison Avenue, New York, New York 10022

$19.98 plus $3.95 postage and handling charges